D0990281

From Revolution
to Revolution:
England 1688–1776

Development
of English Society

Series Editor:

Dorothy Marshall
Formerly Reader in History in the University of Wales

The series will sketch the ways in which English society, seen as an entity, has developed from the England of the Anglo-Saxons to the England of Elizabeth II. Each volume is a separate study of a period of significant change, as seen by a specialist on that period. Nevertheless it is hoped that, taken as a whole, the series will provide some answers to the question 'How did we get from there to here?'

Other titles include

Industrial England 1776–1851 *by Dorothy Marshall*
The Making of Modern English Society from 1850 *by Janet Roebuck*

From Revolution to Revolution: England 1688-1776

John Carswell

Charles Scribner's Sons

New York

1 3 5 7 9 11 13 15 17 19 I/C 20 18 16 14 12 10 8 6 4 2

Printed in Great Britain
Library of Congress Catalog Card Number 73-9340
SBN 684-13566-3 (cloth)

Series Editor's Preface

It is a truism that 'of the making of books there is no end' but, at least with regard to the study of history, there are two cogent reasons why this should be so. One is that each decade sees the examination of more and more source material as the increasing flood of research continues to rise. This in itself can necessitate the revision of older views and older certainties in the light of new knowledge. But even if no new material were available there would still be a need for new books because every generation asks its own questions and demands its own answers that make, or at least attempt to make, sense to contemporaries. The nineteenth-century student of history was concerned mainly with the world of politics, with the growth of the constitutional monarchy and of religious and personal freedom. Then with the turn of the century men began to ask different questions, questions concerned with the industrial society in which they lived, and Archdeacon Cunningham produced his pioneering work, *The Growth of English Industry and Commerce*. For the first decades of the twentieth century the emphasis was on economic rather than social developments, though to begin with there was no very clear distinction between them. As economic history became more technical there also emerged a growing interest on the part of the non-specialist public in the everyday life of their ancestors. The success of G. M. Trevelyan's *Social History* demonstrated how widespread the appetite for this kind of information was. Meanwhile the growth of the welfare state incited more and more people to ask questions about the history of the society in which they lived. How, for instance, had the relationships between the various layers which comprised it altered over the centuries? How far was social structure determined by economic factors? To what extent did the distribution of wealth within a society determine its form of government, both national and local? To what extent were ways of thought and attitudes towards religion, social problems, changing as the structure of society changed? The questions are endless.

It would be presumptuous to suggest that this series on 'The Development of English Society' can even begin to answer them. Its aim is the much more modest one of sketching out the major ways in which English society, seen as an entity, has developed from the England of the Anglo-Saxons to the England of Elizabeth II. Each volume is a separate study of a period of significant change, as seen by a specialist on that period. Because each period presents different problems there can be no uniform pattern of treatment. Each author must make his or her own selection of where to place the emphasis in each phase of development. Nevertheless it is hoped that, taken as a whole, the series will provide some answers to the question 'How did we get from there to here?' This series is not therefore intended for specialists or to add to the volume of existing research; it is designed primarily for students whose courses, one hopes, will be enriched by a greater understanding of the main trends and developments in English society. It is intended to be a background book, not a text book, and as such the series should appeal to that increasingly wide circle of readers who, while not wanting to be bombarded by too much detail and too many facts, are interested in tracing back to its roots English society as we know it today.

The period between the English Revolution of 1688 and the American Revolution of 1776 is of particular importance because it was during these years that the fundamental character of Britain as an industrial democracy and a great power in the world was formed. Before the Revolution of 1688 England was on the road to autocracy: by 1776 Britain, now a united island, was committed to the rule of Law and to a government by king and Parliament in which Parliament was the predominating partner.

For this reason any study of eighteenth-century society necessarily involves both what Parliament did, and how its work was organized, its factions and its leading figures. In every period there is some one element that makes society 'tick', and in the eighteenth century this was the landed classes—titled and untitled—and the leading business men, whose ambition it usually was to finish up as landed proprietors themselves. Parliament was the instrument of their power and the mirror of their society, so that the balance within it faithfully reflected the contemporary social balance of power. The questions on which they concentrated were those of how society was to be governed, and in no period are constitutional and legal questions more bound up with the development of society itself.

What was new, and what was to influence the thinking of future generations, similarly emanated from the ranks of the parliamentary classes, or those whom they patronized. The climate of opinion of the age—views on religion, on art, on architecture—was aristocratic. But from the very slowly changing face of the countryside and the small towns came ideas and efforts that were to transform the British way of living to dependence on power-driven industrialism. The aristocracy and the great men of finance had little to do with Boulton and Watt, Arkwright, the Darbys, or Dud Dudley.

Nor is it possible to concentrate purely on English issues in a period which not only saw the Union with Scotland and the dependence of Ireland but an expansion into America, India, and to some extent Africa which imparted lasting consequences to the development of the world. It is in a way natural that such a period should end with what was in essence a civil war between Britain and her rebellious American colonies.

War necessarily bulks large in any account of eighteenth-century society. Had William III not fought Louis XIV it is probable that the king, not the landed gentry, would have dominated British government, with all that would have implied for the future. It was war, too, that secured Britain her overseas trade and the wealth that it brought —wealth which provided the capital for industrial development.

For it was during these years that Britain was generating the economic expansion known as the Industrial Revolution which has since transformed the entire world. By the end of this period a new urbanism was evident, with London the largest urban area not only in Europe but in the world. The century had produced a prolific crop of poets, novelists, artists and architects, and a periodical press which in itself was one of the transforming agents of society.

Contents

Chronological Table

The method of this table follows that of G. M. Young in his *Victorian England: Portrait of an Age*. For the *Flourished* column I have taken the date on which the age thirty was reached. The superior figures after the names in the *Died* column indicate the date of birth. The items in the *Literature, Art, Architecture* column which are preceded by an author's name are literary works; where the name follows they are works of art, architecture, or music. Architectural works are given in the year in which they were begun. The last column is more miscellaneous than the heading caters for—for instance, it includes science and exploration, which underlie technology and commerce. A few items from outside Britain have been included for their influence on British life. All entries are as brief as possible (I have not, for instance, put in the composer of the *Messiah*) but almost all are at least touched upon in the text.

	Flourished	Died	Politics and War	Literature, Art, Architecture	Social Affairs, Technology, Industry and Commerce
1688	Purcell Paterson	Bunyan[28]	The Revolution	Chatsworth	Middleton and Campbell's Bank (later Coutts)
1689		Dundee[49] Jeffreys[48] Aphra Behn[40]	WILLIAM AND MARY Bill of Rights Killiecrankie Toleration Act	Kensington Palace (Wren)	
1690	George Lewis of Hanover Charles, Earl of Shrewsbury Hans Sloane Sarah Churchill	Schomberg[15]	General Election The Boyne	Locke's *Essay on Human Understanding*	English station established at Calcutta
1691	Harley Montagu Hawksmoor Defoe	Tyrconnel[30] George Fox[24]	Treaty of Limerick		'New' East India Company Petty's *Political Arithmetic*
1692	Bentley Mary II Atterbury	Ludlow[17]	La Hogue Steenkirk Glencoe		Lloyd's Coffee House
1693	Newcomen	Sancroft[17]	Neerwinden	Congreve's *Old Bachelor* and *The Double Dealer*	The Darien Company

	Flourished	Died	Politics and War	Literature, Art, Architecture	Social Affairs, Technology, Industry and Commerce
1700	Congreve Mandeville Toland	Dryden[31]	General Election Second Partition Treaty	Drelincourt On Death Farquhar's Constant Couple Congreve's Way of the World Sewall's Selling of Joseph	
1701	Colley Cibber	James II[33]	Act of Settlement General Election	Addison's Christian Hero	Yale Tull's Drill Society for Propagation of the Gospel
1702	Steele Addison	William III[51] Sunderland[40]	ANNE General Election War of Spanish Succession Godolphin Lord High Treasurer Marlborough Commander in Chief	Clarendon's History of the Great Rebellion	
1703	Stanhope George Graham Wade	Pepys[33]	Ashby v. White Methuen Treaty		Daily Courant
1704	Townshend Isaac Watts Jethro Tull	Locke[32]	Blenheim Gibraltar British		Newton's Opticks Ray's Historia Plantarum First Newcomen engine

	Flourished	Died	Politics and War	Literature, Art, Architecture	Social Affairs, Technology, Industry and Commerce
1705	Thornhill Mohun	Titus Oates[49] John Ray[27]	General Election		'Beau' Nash at Bath
1706	Walpole Hoadly	John Evelyn[20]	Ramillies	Farquhar's *Recruiting Officer* White Kennett's *Compleat History of England*	The Sun Fire Office Mill's carriage spring
1707	Abraham Darby	Farquhar[78]	Almanza Union with Scotland The Place Act	Farquhar's *Beaux' Stratagem*	
1708	St John Argyll		General Election Second Junto Minorca British General Naturalization Act	Handel's *Agrippina* Dome of St Paul's completed	Merger of East India Companies
1709	'George Psalmanazar'	Bentinck (Portland)[49]	Malplaquet	*Tatler* Marlborough House (Wren) End of Wren's work on St Paul's	Iron smelted with coke (Darby)
1710		Holt[42]	Sacheverell General Election Harley Lord Treasurer Property Qualification Act	Berkeley's *Principles* *Examiner*	

	Flourished	Died	Politics and War	Literature, Art, Architecture	Social Affairs, Technology, Industry and Commerce
1711	Henrietta Howard	Ken[37]	Occasional Conformity Act	*Spectator* Pope's *Essay on Criticism*	Ascot begins South Sea Company floated
1712	Jonathan Wild Gibbs	Danby (Leeds)[31] Godolphin[45] Richard Cromwell[26] Gregory King[48]		*The Rape of the Lock* St George's, Hanover Square (James)	Last execution for witchcraft
1713	George [II] Edward Young	Tompion[39] Shaftesbury[71]	General Election Treaty of Utrecht Asiento	*Guardian* Addison's *Cato*	
1714	Pulteney	Anne Radcliffe[50] Davenant[56] Sharp[45]	GEORGE I Schism Act	St Mary-le-Strand (Gibbs) Mandeville's *Fable of the Bees*	
1715	Handel Gay Berkeley	Montagu (Halifax)[61] Wharton[48] Burnet[43] Carstares[49] Louis XIV[42] Tenison[36]	Riot Act Sheriffmuir and Preston	Pope's *Iliad*, vol. 1 Campbell's *Vitruvius Britannicus* vol. 1	First Liverpool dock

	Flourished	Died	Politics and War	Literature, Art, Architecture	Social Affairs, Technology, Industry and Commerce
1716	William Law Allan Ramsay	Somers[51] Wycherley[40] Herbert (Torrington)[47]	Septennial Act	St Mary Woolnoth (Hawksmoor)	First union of Freemasons
1717			Triple Alliance	Hoadly's Bangor sermon	
1718	The Old Pretender Pope	Shrewsbury[60] Penn[44]	Sunderland/Stanhope Ministry Cape Passaro Quadruple Alliance	Echard's *History of the Revolution*	Inoculation The Society of Antiquaries
1719	Lady Mary Wortley Montagu Richardson	Addison[72] Flamsteed[46] Paterson[58]	Peerage Bill Transportation Act Vigo raid	*Robinson Crusoe*	Westminster Hospital
1720	Yorke (Hardwicke) Carteret	Grinling Gibbons[48]	Judicial Supremacy in Ireland Atterbury's Plot	Chiswick House (Burlington) Marble Hill	South Sea Bubble Greenwich Observatory
1721	Bubb Dodington	Stanhope[73] Prior[64]	Walpole minister		
1722	Caslon	Marlborough[50] Sunderland[74] Toland[70]	General Election Wood's Halfpence	St Martin-in-the-Fields (Gibbs)	

	Flourished	Died	Politics and War	Literature, Art, Architecture	Social Affairs, Technology, Industry and Commerce
1723	Duke of Newcastle Quin	Wren[32] Kneller[46]		Rapin's History of England Burnet's History of My Own Time	Knatchbull's Act
1724	Chesterfield Ralph Allen	Jack Sheppard[02] Harley[61]		Swift's Drapier's Letters Ramsay's Tea-Table Miscellany	
1725	Pelham Burlington	Jonathan Wild[82]			Guy's Hospital
1726	Hervey Oglethorpe	Vanbrugh[64] Collier[50]		Craftsman Gulliver's Travels	
1727	Hogarth Flitcroft Macklin	Newton[42] Edward Russell (Orford)[53] George I[60]	GEORGE II General Election		Voltaire's visit to England
1728	Warburton Maclaurin			The Beggar's Opera Law's Serious Call to a Devout and Holy Life The Dunciad	
1729		Congreve[70] Steele[72] Newcomen[63]		Oldmixon's History of England Queen Square, Bath	Oglethorpe's enquiry into debtors' prisons Brewster sessions begin

	Flourished	Died	Politics and War	Literature, Art, Architecture	Social Affairs, Technology, Industry and Commerce
1730	Thomson			The Seasons	English the language of the law
1731		Defoe[61]			Gentleman's Magazine
1732		Gay[85] Atterbury[62]			Vauxhall opens Georgia founded
1733	Wesley	Mandeville[70]	Molasses Act Excise Crisis	Essay on Man	St George's Hospital Kay's Flying Shuttle
1734	Soame Jenyns	Thornhill[75]	General Election	Reresby's Memoirs	Bentley victorious
1735	Murray (Mansfield) Wood of Bath Hartley Henry Fox	Arbuthnot[67]		Rake's Progress (Hogarth) Wood's Ruins of Palmyra	Society of Dilettanti
1736	Baskerville Franklin	Tonson[56]?	Porteous riots	Warburton's Alliance between Church and State Herculaneum discovered	White's club founded Gin Act Repeal of Witchcraft Acts John Harrison's chronometer

Flourished	Died	Politics and War	Literature, Art, Architecture	Social Affairs, Technology, Industry and Commerce
1737 Frederick Prince of Wales Fielding		Civil List crisis		Licensing Act for plays *Manchester Magazine*
1738 Pitt Dashwood	Townshend[74]		Bolingbroke's *Patriot King*	Wesley's mission begins *Scots Magazine*–London
1739 Johnson Beckford	Dick Turpin[06]	War with Spain	Hume's *Treatise of Human Nature*	Parliament fixes size of bricks
1740 Arne			North's *Examen* Richardson's *Pamela* Cibber's *Apology* 'Rule Britannia'	Huntsman produces crucible steel
1741 Earl Temple Hume	Jethro Tull[74]	General Election	Garrick's *Richard III*	
1742 Jonas Hanway Grenville	Bentley[62] Halley[56] Savage[96]	Fall of Walpole 'Broad Bottom'	*Messiah* Young's *Night Thoughts* *Dunciad*	Nash's Code posted at Bath
1743 Bute Sterne	Argyll[78]	Dettingen	Blair's *Grave* Fielding's *Jonathan Wild the Great*	

	Flourished	Died	Politics and War	Literature, Art, Architecture	Social Affairs, Technology, Industry and Commerce
1744	Shenstone Peg Woffington Whitefield Camden	Sarah Churchill[60] Pope[88]			First Methodist Conference Anson's voyage
1745	'Capability' Brown	Walpole[76] Swift[67]	The Forty-five Fontenoy		Foundling Hospital
1746	Gray Brindley	Maclaurin[98]	Pelham minister Culloden	'God Save the King' Canaletto in England (till 1755)	
1747	Horace Walpole Garrick			Warburton's Shakespeare Collins's Odes	
1748		Thomson[00] Wade[73]	Peace of Aix-la-Chapelle	Richardson's Clarissa Smollett's Roderick Random Pompeii discovered	Franklin's Battery
1749	Spranger Barry			Tom Jones Hartley's Observations on Man The Vanity of Human Wishes Westminster Bridge	Buffon's Histoire Naturelle The Belvoir

	Flourished	Died	Politics and War	Literature, Art, Architecture	Social Affairs, Technology, Industry and Commerce
1750	The Young Pretender Foote			*Rambler* Gray's *Elegy* The Horse Guards (Kent)	The Pytchley The Jockey Club
1751	Robertson Smollett Dowdeswell Collins	Bolingbroke[78] (St John) Frederick, Prince of Wales[07]	Capture of Arcot	Hume's *Enquiry into Human Understanding*	New Style Consols Linnaeus's *Philosophia Botanica* *Encyclopédie* begins
1752	Carlyle of Inveresk Burgoyne				The London Hospital Chippendale's *The Gentleman's and Cabinet Maker's Director*
1753	Reynolds Adam Smith Blackstone Price Adam Ferguson	Sloane[60] Berkeley[85]			Last woman burned at the stake The British Museum Elizabeth Canning The Marriage Act The Jew Bill
1754	Stubbs	Pelham[95] Fielding[07]	General Election Albany Congress Newcastle minister		The Select Society The Royal Society of Arts

	Flourished	Died	Politics and War	Literature, Art, Architecture	Social Affairs, Technology, Industry and Commerce
1755	Clive Charles Townshend	Braddock[95]	Paoli's rising in Corsica Pitt resigns	Johnson's Dictionary of the English Language	Lisbon earthquake Middlesex Hospital
1756	Howard Chambers Burney		'Black Hole' of Calcutta Seven Years War Pitt minister	Home's Douglas Burke On the Sublime and the Beautiful	
1757	Wilkes Gainsborough	Admiral Byng[04]	Plassey Pitt-Newcastle coalition Franklin in England	Smollett's History of England Soame Jenyns's Free Enquiry into the Nature and Origin of Evil	Warrington Academy founded
1758	Robert Adam Chevalier d'Eon Black Boulton Goldsmith Cook				Bridgewater canal
1759	Burke Percy	Handel[85] Wolfe[27] Collins[21] Allan Ramsay[86]	Minden Quiberon Bay Quebec Masulipatam	Johnson's Rasselas Chamber's Treatise of Civil Architecture	Annual Register

	Flourished	Died	Politics and War	Literature, Art, Architecture	Social Affairs, Technology, Industry and Commerce
1760	Rockingham Bruce Wedgwood Goldsmith	George II[83]	GEORGE III	Tristram Shandy Blackfriars Bridge	
1761	Cowper Cavendish George Anne Bellamy Charles Churchill Dunning	Hoadly[76] Law[86]	Bute minister General Election	Hume's History of England Churchill's Rosciad	
1762	North Hastings Flood Arkwright	Lady Mary Wortley Montagu[89] 'Beau' Nash[74] Bubb Dodington (Melcombe)[91]		Hurd's Chivalry and Romance Ossian's Poems Rousseau's Social Contract Stuart's Antiquities of Athens	The Cock Lane Ghost
1763	Priestley Zoffany	Shenstone[14] 'Psalmanazar'[79]? Granville[90] (Carteret)	Peace of Paris Settlement beyond the Alleghenies banned Grenville minister 'Number 45'	Boswell meets Johnson	

	Flourished	Died	Politics and War	Literature, Art, Architecture	Social Affairs, Technology, Industry and Commerce
1764		Hardwicke (Yorke)[90] Bath (Pulteney)[84] Hogarth[97] Allen[94] Churchill[31]	Wilkes expelled from Commons	The Literary Club Walpole's *Castle of Otranto* Winckelmann's *History of Ancient Art* Gibbon in Rome	Brooks's club founded The separate condenser (Watt) Beccaria's *Penology* Almack's resolves against vails
1765	Grafton Coutts Granville Sharp Jesse Ramsden	'Butcher' Cumberland[21] Edward Young[83]	Stamp Act Rockingham minister	Percy's *Reliques of Ancient English Poetry* Blackstone's *Commentaries on the Laws of England*	Granville Sharp meets Jonathan Strong Donn's one-inch map of Devonshire Hargreaves' Spinning Jenny
1766	Horne Tooke Macpherson Watt	Caslon[92] The Old Pretender[88] Quin[93]	Stamp Act repealed Declaratory Act Chatham minister General warrants illegal	Goldsmith's *Vicar of Wakefield* John Gwynn's *London and Westminster Improv'd*	Hydrogen discovered by Cavendish
1767	Shelburne Tom Paine Gibbon	Charles Townshend[25]	Townshend duties	Ferguson's *Essay on Civil Society*	

	Flourished	Died	Politics and War	Literature, Art, Architecture	Social Affairs, Technology, Industry and Commerce
1768	Cornwallis	Newcastle[93] Sterne[13]	General Election Almon's parliamentary debates Grafton minister	Junius Royal Academy Adelphi (Adam brothers) Sterne's *Sentimental Journey*	Cook sails in the *Endeavour*
1769			Wilkes elected and excluded Nullum Tempus	Robertson's *Charles V* The Shakespeare Jubilee	Wedgwood's Etruria Arkwright's first spinning mill The iron bridge over the Severn
1770	Francis Boswell Wyvill	Grenville[12] Chatterton[52] Whitefield[14]	North minister Burke's *Thoughts on the Present Discontents* The Boston Massacre	Goldsmith's *Deserted Village*	Bruce discovers source of the Blue Nile
1771	Arthur Young Fuseli		The Printers' Case		*Encyclopaedia Britannica*
1772	Dundas	Brindley[16]	Royal Marriage Act		Somersett's case Cook sails in the *Resolution* Rutherford's *Dissertation on Nitrogen* The Feathers Tavern Petition

	Flourished	Died	Politics and War	Literature, Art, Architecture	Social Affairs, Technology, Industry and Commerce
1773	Joseph Banks Paley		The Regulating Act The Boston Tea-Party	Robert and James Adam, *Works in Architecture* Herder, *Über Shakespeare* Goldsmith's *She Stoops to Conquer* Johnson's tour of Scotland	The Stock Exchange
1774		Henry Fox[05] (Holland) Goldsmith[30]	Quebec Act Philadelphia Congress	The Building Act	Priestley discovers oxygen Essex St Unitarian chapel Serfdom in Scotland ended
1775			Lexington Concord Bunkers Hill	Sheridan's *The Rivals*	
1776	Grattan	Hume[11]	Declaration of American Independence	*The Wealth of Nations* *The Decline and Fall of The Roman Empire vol. 1* Jenyns's *View of the Internal Evidence of the Christian Religion* Paine's *Common Sense* Somerset House (Chambers)	Trial of the Duchess of Kingston

Chapter 1

Post-Revolutionary England

The social development of a hundred years can sometimes be illustrated by three generations of a single family. Edward Gibbon of Leadenhall Street, linen draper, was born in the year the Great Fire destroyed wooden London and was twenty-three when the heralds proclaimed William and Mary in the February drizzle of 1689. Thirty years later Gibbon's prosperous career, which had climbed from drapery by way of bill-broking to international finance and carried him to a seat in Parliament, was wrecked in the South Sea disaster. But enough was left to provide for his son, a second Edward, to live as a country gentleman and sit also in Parliament. As member for the modest borough of Southampton the second Edward Gibbon had the satisfaction of joining in the pack that pulled down his father's old persecutor, Robert Walpole, in 1742, after twenty-one years of power.

The third, and great, Edward Gibbon had been born four years before this ending of the 'Robinocracy' (as Robert Walpole's twenty-one years of power were nicknamed) and survived until the last decade of the century, sitting like his father and grandfather on the back benches in Parliament, and leaving behind him the work which is in many ways the supreme literary product of English civilization between the English and American Revolutions. *The Decline and Fall of the Roman Empire* raised the interpretation of the past to a new level, and reflects in a peculiar degree the virtues and faults of the age that had formed its author: its stoicism, its rationality, its detachment, its carefully cultivated charm; and on the darker side its mistrust of emotion, its absence of striving into the speculative, its complacency and its artificiality.

The first Gibbon lived to seventy, the second to sixty-three, and the third to fifty-seven, so all three belonged to the robust and lucky 10 per cent or so who survived into later middle age. The linen draper's career covers the years in which it is still true to say that the foundations of modern Britain were established. His lifetime included the Revolution since which Parliament has never ceased to meet and to

1

form the centre of British political life, and the Union of 1707 by which Britain ceased to have a land frontier. The new journalists transformed the language to achieve a lucid yet dignified style which provided standard prose for the whole kingdom for more than a century. Newton explained the universe and Locke the workings of the human mind. The foundations of scientific economics were laid. There was a new spirit in the air, compounded of Dutch business methods, Atlantic opportunity, and a sense of Britain, for the first time, as a great power. 'This great British Empire,' exclaimed Defoe in 1724, 'the most flourishing and opulent country in the world.' He saw infinite possibilities ahead. 'No cloaths can be made to fit a growing child.'

The growing child had begun to run before it could walk. The third and fourth decades of the century appear in most respects calm, even stagnant. Though London grew, sucking into itself more and more migrants to make up for its hideous death-rate, the total population of the country was almost stationary. But everywhere change was at work though it moved quietly. Thousands of acres of old open fields and 'waste' were enclosed, and the familiar hedge pattern of England, punctuated by the long brick and stone walls of the parks of the prosperous, began to impose itself on the forests and plains. Year after year small groups trickled away across the Atlantic to build up the two millions that America contained when independence was declared. The mechanical and physical discoveries which were to enable power to be added to industry were silently being made, and the technology of precision which was necessary to make them effective was being perfected. At the same time the charm of stability and the steady development of what was known as 'interest' in every part of society from top to bottom forged bonds that were to last for generations.* The reign of Walpole lies like a huge flat stone at the bottom of English self-sufficiency. It was this that so impressed Voltaire on his visit of 1727. It seemed to him that it was the most powerful guarantee of the freedom of the individual.

These were the years in which hearts hardened and institutions narrowed. In disputes the tendency of the courts was to restrict rather than enlarge and to convert what was originally a privilege into a species of saleable property. The system of purchasing commissions in the army received official recognition in 1720. Open corporations became closed, and close ones closer still. Decisions on election peti-

---

* 'Interest' in the seventeenth and eighteenth centuries meant organized and recognized influence.

tions tended to contract the number of voters. The Peerage Bill of 1719 would have limited the number of the House of Lords if it had not been defeated by the country gentlemen of the Commons who had an eye to their own family aspirations.

Money was moving into England, above all in the shape of investments from Holland, and the Dutch rentier, seeking safety and 3½ per cent in funds guaranteed by the British Parliament, was now providing an important part of British financial strength. London, as a great international financial centre, was assuming a marked appearance of cosmopolitanism. Yet London never bred a race of merchant princes like her predecessors, Venice and Amsterdam, though in Queen Anne's time it had looked as if she might. The power that went with the possession of land was too great, the country was wider and more profitable than the marshes on which the Venetians and the Dutch had been compelled to make their livings by trade. Parliament and the substance of local government remained in the hands of the landowners, and the ambition of the successful city man was to escape from the dirt, disease, and risk of London, to secure his fortune and status in an estate. For twenty-one years Walpole, the politically gifted squire, munching apples on the Treasury bench and supported by a majority of landed men, ruled Britain; and near Walpole's Houghton is Heveningham Hall, which commemorates the business enterprise of Joshua Van Neck ennobled as Lord Huntingfield.

Underneath the gross materialism of the Robinocracy, there was the beginning of something deeply different, which had nothing to do with the possessors of land or the new commercial class. This was Methodism—a movement essentially urban in its inspiration and lower-middle class in its membership. Wesley's system of 'classes' for joint spiritual therapy could never have found roots in a rural society, and was devised to counter the social as well as the spiritual squalor, that Wesley found in the towns. Whether one regards Wesley as the heir of the non-jurors who left the established church rather than accept the Revolution, or as the precursor of Victorian evangelicalism, his enormous career, which virtually spans the century, is unique. It marks the humanitarianism and intensity which is no less characteristic of eighteenth-century Britain than its superficial complacency and elegance.

In the fifth decade, and with gathering force in the sixth, the life of the nation is infused with a new spirit. Pope and Swift, the last of the Augustans, have disappeared by 1750. Walpole has gone, and so has the Jacobitism he watched so sharply and used so skilfully. Pelham, the last representative of the Whigs who had once faced real Tories, was to die in 1754 and thereby create a political vacuum. George II and the Duke of Newcastle laboured on, apparently indestructible, but the new face of affairs was clearly visible well before 1760.

British society had moved from a period of accumulative calm into one of dynamic achievement, and the leaders of the high Georgian era are cast in an appropriate mould. These are the years of the meteor-like rise of Pitt, Johnson's majestic systematization of English in his *Dictionary*, Anson's circumnavigation, the beginnings of the English novel. Fanciful gothick and the spindly elegance of Adam are on the way to replacing the formality of Palladianism. In Scotland the influence of moderate clergy and improved agriculture begin to bear down Cameronian narrowness, celtic feudalism, and chronic rural poverty.

The high Georgian era that was now beginning was characterized by war on a scale the country had never known, even at the zenith of the struggle with Louis XIV. In 1762 the number of men under arms rose to over 200,000 for the first time in British history, involving well over 10 per cent of the adult male population; and the British began to have a sense of global power associated with their military and naval success. Yet the war was disliked by the possessing classes who had to pay for it. It seemed to many of them, and to the new king who had succeeded George II, that at last the time for British consolidation had come. The old self-seeking parties, the troublesome continental connexions, almost the very need for a machine at the centre of government, might perhaps at last be put aside.

It was far too late. The sixties and peace abroad brought new transforming developments on every hand. A succession of shortlived Prime Ministers struggled with the problems of a transatlantic possession which had silently assumed a life of its own. In his Glasgow laboratory the sleek and inoffensive Joseph Black established the principles of latent heat and the theoretical basis of steam power. In London and the other major towns the lower middle class was beginning to stir. The 1760s mark the beginning of radicalism, raucous and disrespectful. If one figure typifies the decade it is the ugly, shameless figure of Wilkes.

The struggle in America, to which events were now inevitably leading, was to be the first British overseas war that was opposed ideologically at home, and brought Britain itself to the verge of revolution. The later seventies, and early eighties, mark the crisis of the century. Revolution in the formal sense was avoided, but the climate of reform was set. The power of the land was to endure for many years to come but by 1776 the transition from an agricultural to an urban society was determined. That year saw not only American Independence and the finest flower of the old world—Gibbon's *Decline and Fall*—but the textbook for the new economics, produced by a Glasgow professor, in Adam Smith's *The Wealth of Nations*.

Properly considered, then, the period between the English and American Revolutions is far from being all of a piece, and generalizations about the mercantile and partisan effervescence of the true Augustan age (roughly 1689–1720) are by no means always applicable to the period of stability under the Robinocracy (1721–54), or the high Georgian era that succeeded it, when men on the edge of developments they could not imagine thought they had at last reached the platform from which it was possible to look comfortably back at the ages of barbarism and ignorance. But taken as a whole it is a period in which social and national confidence struck deep roots. It is not insignificant that the first seventy years of the eighteenth century saw the production of history on an impressive scale. Whatever else may be said about Whig history, the Whig era is the first in which social stability has sought to base itself not on tradition alone but on what professed at any rate to be an explanation of real events and a justification for the existing order of things.

This basis was the Revolution by which one king had been deposed and another substituted by Parliament. It is true that the Revolution made little immediate difference to the organization of the everyday life of most people. From King William's point of view his invasion of England had primarily been an armed move in European power politics. His chief supporters in Britain had been ambitious but frustrated politicians. There had in no sense been a spontaneous rising or a party programme. But to look at the Revolution in this way would be wholly to misunderstand its immense significance. For a few months, from December 1688 when James had fled, until February 1689 when William and Mary were proclaimed, the British people were formally in a state of nature, entitled to make a free choice of their form of government. The lasting magic of the Revolution was the feeling that under historic and recorded circumstances power had relapsed to society and the social contract between state and people had been visibly renewed.

The people had not made the Revolution, but they had seen it happen. In the year preceding it they had seen their usual magistrates replaced wholesale by comparatively unknown figures. Thousands had seen the sensational trial and acquittal of the seven bishops, for seditious libel against James II, and at the verdict raised a roar of triumph which could be heard from Westminster Hall to the Strand. Crowds on the Kentish coast had seen the invasion fleet, with its propagandist streamers flying, sail through the straits of Dover; and the slow passage of William's invading army from Torbay to London had been through England's most densely populated counties. There had been the rattle of musketry at Caversham where the invaders had crossed the Thames, the sudden occupation of York by the revolutionary leaders in the north, the flight of Princess Anne to hold court at Nottingham, and the flight of her father the king to be mobbed by fishermen at Faversham. Irish regiments had tramped through the midlands from Chester to London, and the panic rumour of an intended Irish massacre had swept across the country. Pamphlets and counter-pamphlets had been everywhere. Even remote villages had seen parties of foraging dragoons, armed gentlemen's servants, and fugitive deserters, and had grasped their significance. There had been a decisive change.

From the time of the Revolution one can write of the history of Great Britain and of British society. Although the question of the unity of the island was to agitate politics for twenty years after the Revolution, and was not finally determined until 1746, the prospects of economic and political singleness were immensely strengthened by the accession of William, and many of the traditional obstacles were swept away in the whirlwind of new ideas and changes which it released. William himself was an international statesman whose interest it was that the island should form one unit of power. He was called as a parliamentary monarch not only to the English throne, but to the Scottish. It was the Scots Parliament, not the English, that coined the phrase, in its resolution deposing James, declaring that the constitution was 'a limited monarchy'. Scots had played a great part in the Revolution itself and in its planning—both on behalf of their own country, and as William's closest advisers. One such adviser, Burnet, was to find his career as an Anglican bishop in the south, and another no less important, William Carstares, was to preside over the religious settlement north of the Border: and it was above all religious organization that had so bedevilled the relationship between the two countries.

Paradoxically enough, recognition and guarantee of the two different systems of religious organization each in its own country did more than anything else to pave the way for political union. The ancient battle which had begun fifty years earlier when Charles I took the road northwards to impose episcopacy on the Scots, ended with the acquiescence of the London government that Scotland should be officially Presbyterian. At the same time the comfort and support which dissent in England had drawn from Scotland during the years of struggle began to fade now that the Scots no longer had an interest in embarrassing a persecuting Anglican government in the south.* Presbytery, in the new more liberal form Carstares helped to give it, wore a much less grim appearance for Englishmen than in the days of the Covenant: for one thing, as the landed classes were glad to note, it was better disposed to the influence of local proprietors in appointments for livings. Although Cameronians and Sandemanians might secede in protest against such 'carnal Erastianism' (just as a good churchman in the south was to call one of the new Whig bishops 'a fanatic in lawn sleeves') the Scottish church, like the English, was launched on the path of moderation and latitudinarianism. Though progress was long and slow, in the next age such men as Carlyle of Inveresk and Principal Robertson were to lead Scotland towards her greatest age of the intellect.

During the seventeenth century Scotland had depended more on the continent for trade and education than England had done, and it was towards the continent that William's intervention opened new channels. Scotland was as deeply interested as England in the economic and political opportunities created by William's success in making Britain the stronghold for the Protestant and particularist contest against the France of Louis XIV—a contest which many were beginning to see already as one in which the mastery of the Atlantic and the trade routes to the East were at stake as well as the more obvious struggle against popery and arbitrary power. English economic selfishness still tried to exclude the northern kingdom from the prospects that were opening on the other side of the Atlantic, and the Scots, in pride and desperation, embarked on the experiment of autonomous colonization with the fatal Darien scheme of 1695. But it is an instructive irony that the Scottish mind of Paterson which conceived the spectacular failure in Darien, had only one year previously promoted the spectacularly successful Bank of England. The identity of economic interest between the two countries, which William Paterson personifies, was to take a few more years to be fully understood, but from

* Yet it remained significant. For the rest of the century the English dissenting academist looked to the Scottish universities for degrees. Price and Priestley both held doctorates from Scottish universities.

1689 onwards it can be said that there was in practice a political system covering the whole island.

It was otherwise with Ireland and the still thinly populated colonies on the other side of the Atlantic. To treat them as irrelevant to English or British history until the arrival of political upheaval in the seventies is a supreme mistake, and the evolution of Britain and British society throughout the century cannot be understood without following their progress and bearing in mind the fundamental attitude of the British towards their dependencies. The inhabitants of Britain, whether townsmen or squires, considered that the dependencies, including Ireland, were economically and politically subordinate to the metropolis. They were subsidiaries of a business, not additional counties of England.

Accordingly the British Parliament assumed the right to legislate for all territories owing allegiance to the Crown. This did not imply, of course, that the British Parliament was the only legislature of the colonies or of Ireland, as well as of Britain. On the contrary, the British legislative power over Ireland and America was conceived as being exercised exclusively in the interests of the British economy: to ensure that colonial and Irish goods were carried as far as possible in British ships; that colonial and Irish manufactures were not allowed to compete with those of Britain; that the trade of the dependencies should be conducted exclusively through Britain. Practices which are considered by contemporaries as part of the obvious order of things are the most important features of a society. For most of the eighteenth century the principle underlying the Navigation Acts was part of the natural order of things for most Englishmen. That principle was that the maximum profits of trade should accrue to the inhabitants of the island of Britain.

The counterpart of the protective system was smuggling on a vast scale. No picture of English society can be complete without the smuggler, and every section of society had its relations with him. A trip abroad was incomplete without commissions from lady friends and relations for silk. One of the advantages of a diplomatic post abroad was the opportunity it gave of obliging friends through the diplomatic bag. Walpole, whose ambition as Prime Minister was to make the Customs more efficient, had his own supplies of brandy smuggled. Even the law-abiding Parson Woodforde was not above contact with a gang of smugglers for his supply of tea.

The Revolution placed a Huguenot on the throne. William, so often called Dutch, was in truth an international being, the head of a great European interest,* the chief executive of six out of the seven Dutch provinces, and prince in his own right of a scattered medley of dominions in the Low Countries and Germany—not to mention Orange itself, in the heart of Louis XIV's dominions.† Asthmatic, stunted, almost insanely courageous, yet deeply reserved, he is the most interesting man among our modern kings. His whole career was devoted to the containment of France, and his invasion of England and his acceptance of its crown had been stations on that pilgrimage. He had not wanted to fight in Ireland, and would have been content with a tolerant settlement there until it became clear that Ireland was going to be used as a back door by his grand opponent. His main interest in his new kingdoms was that they should give no trouble as his base of operations, and to that end he exerted his very considerable talents as a politician.

William, and those he brought over with him from Holland, symbolized a competitor the English and Scots had long resented, but also a system they had long admired. The Dutch, it was widely and correctly believed, had discovered the secret of commercial success. Their celebrated bank, their paper credit, their business efficiency, and their highly profitable industries, such as type-founding and paper-making, made them rivals to be envied and imitated. France might be the most powerful political and military force in Europe, but the United Provinces was undoubtedly the economic leader. Even King James II had admitted as much when he quoted Dutch commercial success as the fruit of the version of religious toleration which he so eagerly offered his subjects.

William's accession marked the beginning of an economic and cultural association between Britain and Holland that was to last for nearly a century before it foundered in the catastrophe of the American war. The symbiosis reached also to the military sphere, and mixed forces of British, Dutch, and Germans such as those that had given muscle to the intervention of November 1688, were to fight on many European battlefields in the coming century, and appear for the last time in victory at Waterloo. More Dutchmen than Englishmen fought at Blenheim and fell at Malplaquet; and 6,000 Dutch regulars were sent to England in 1715 to support the Government forces against

* His four grandparents were, respectively, German, French, Scottish and Dutch.
† William never visited Orange, but it was near his heart because it gave him the one sovereignty to which he had clear hereditary right and had always been a Huguenot enclave in the heart of France. It even possessed a protestant university, of which the celebrated physician, Hans Sloane, was a graduate. William insisted that it should be returned to him by the Treaty of Rijswick in 1697.

the Jacobites, just as they had once been sent—in 1685—to support King James against the rebellion of Monmouth.

Dutch influence was everywhere, from the growing business empire of the Van Necks in the sober grandeur of their Putney palace, to the gin—for which Holland was the synonym—that was increasingly the refuge and curse of the urban poor. As Defoe noted, the evergreens began to sprout in the sandy Surrey gardens of the well-to-do, for the laurel was a favourite Dutch middle-class taste shared by William himself. Dutch, too, was the neatly proportioned, regular, red-brick style of domestic building, exemplified by the new palace of Kensington and the impressive development of Hampton Court.

The new regime not only brought the styles of Holland to Britain, but set the seal on the country as the city of refuge for the Huguenot craftsman and entrepreneur. England has always attracted immigrants and this particular immigration had been in progress for many years past, driven on by the tightening of discriminatory laws in France. British Huguenots of the second generation were already common by the time of the Revolution; but after 1685 and the Revocation of the Edict of Nantes the immigration had become intense. Now, in the whirlpool of innovation that followed on the Revolution, Huguenots began to emerge in leading roles in British business. Houblon and Letheullier, des Bouverie and Papillon soon came to rank as names of credit with Vyner, Heathcote, Hoare, and Child. Many of them brought with them international links with Huguenots dispersed elsewhere in Europe, notably in the Low Countries, the Rhineland, and Brandenburg. In the developing cosmopolis of London it was not only Dutch and Huguenots who were finding a place. There were Germans, such as Jacobsen the steelmaster with his Baltic connexions, and Sephardic Jews—da Costas, Medinas, and Mendeses from the free world of Amsterdam. It becomes a commonplace to find London stockbrokers' accounts kept in Portuguese, and Highgate was already a favourite quarter for these Mediterranean men.

About six million people lived in the island of Great Britain when, in the words of the Prayer Book, 'a new song was put into our mouths, by bringing his Majesty King William, for the deliverance of our Church and nation from Popish tyranny and arbitrary power'. The population of Ireland and the transatlantic colonies of the West Indies and the seaboard of the American continent* brought the subjects of William and Mary to perhaps seven and a half million

* In the West Indies, Jamaica and Barbados. On the mainland, Hudson's Bay, Newfoundland, Massachusetts, Pennsylvania, Connecticut, Rhode Island, New

altogether.* Even with these additions Great Britain with its dependencies, was in 1689 a small nation by the standards of our time, and not a very large one even by the standards of its own.

Europe at the end of the seventeenth century is estimated to have had about 100 million inhabitants, of whom one-fifth were ruled by 'the French King', as Englishmen, remembering their own monarch's retention of 'King of France' among his titles, liked to describe Louis XIV. France, with nearly twenty million people, then bulked as large in Europe as today the United States or the Soviet Union in the world, and this alone was a reason for the widespread European resistance to its encroachments. It was to be many years before the population of Great Britain exceeded that of France,† and for most of the eighteenth century the demographic ratio between the two countries was between 21: and 31:.

The population of the island was even less regularly distributed than it is today, though Scotland, as will have been noted, had almost one-sixth of it, as against its present one-eleventh. There were probably more people in some of the Highland counties than there are today, but the main body of the Scots was concentrated, then as now, in the narrow waist nipped by the firths of Forth and Clyde.‡ Over

---

* Six millions for Great Britain is a somewhat lower figure than that given by some standard authors (e.g. David Ogg, *England in the Reigns of James II and William III*, pp. 1, 31). It is based on Gregory King's estimate of 5·5 million for England and Wales as modified by D. V. Glass (see D. V. Glass and D. E. C. Eversley, *Population in History*, pp. 211f.). I have taken the population of Scotland as 0·75 million, on the assumption that the figure established by Webster's census of Scotland in 1755 and that found by the census of 1801 are points on an evenly rising line which can be taken as valid also for the late seventeenth century. I have taken the transatlantic population as a two hundred thousand, and the Irish as 1·2 million. This last figure is slightly higher than that given by Talbot Griffith for 1695 in *Population Problems of the Age of Malthus* (Frank Cass, 1967), p. 45, which is almost certainly on the low side. But the estimates of Irish population vary wildly. See Appendix 1.
† The population of France exceeded that of Great Britain until nearly the end of the nineteenth century.
‡ J. G. Kyd, 'Scottish Population Statistics', *Proceedings of the Scottish Historical Society*, 3rd Series, vol. 44 (1952), p. xviii. Webster, in 1755, found the population density of nine central counties was 110 to the square mile, as against 31 in the Highlands, and 36 in the outer Lowlands and Borders. Present comparative figures are 900, 47, and 61. E. C. K. Gonner, 'The Population of England in the Eighteenth Century', *Journal of the Royal Statistical Society*, vol. 76 (1913), calculates the density of population in various English counties in 1700. The figures range from 141 to the square mile in Worcestershire to 91 to the square mile in the West Riding of Yorkshire.

Jersey, New York, Virginia, and the Carolinas. Most of the mainland colonies had been formed by James II into a monolithic 'Dominion of New England'. The Revolution restored autonomy to the individual provinces, an act which was to have important consequences for the future of the world.

most of England the average was much the same as in Central Scotland—about 100 to the square mile—but in the lower Thames valley the inhabitants crowded densely on the ground, and in London* itself more than half a million were packed far closer than anything we know in contemporary urban society. London, with 527,000 inhabitants, was already the largest town in Europe, perhaps the largest in the world.

This metropolis—almost a city state—extended far beyond the old City, both eastwards and westwards. By the end of the seventeenth century the Strand, connecting commercial London and royal Westminster, was no longer a piece of palatial ribbon development but the southern boundary of a townscape extending as far north as Great Russell Street, where the windows looked out over the still agricultural Bedford estate towards the heights of Hampstead. Soho, St Giles's and the still newer development south of Piccadilly, were the centres of fashionable life. To the east of the City, in Wapping and the hamlets round the Tower, lay a growing area of shanties, huts, and workshops, the homes of migrant poor and riverside industry, almost outside the pale of regulation and government. The material for London's creation and extension was ready to hand in the troops of migrants who constantly arrived there and the viscous subsoil of clay from which its brown bricks were baked.

London and its neighbourhood contained the schools whose pupils were to dominate the intellectual world of the eighteenth century: Westminster above all, under the tremendous headmastership of Richard Busby which spanned almost sixty years (1638–95), produced Locke and Dryden, Jeffreys and Wren, Mordaunt and Montagu, Prior and Atterbury. Towards the end of Queen Anne's reign half the bench of bishops were Old Westminsters. But although Steele hardly exaggerated when he said Busby 'had as great an effect on the age he lived in, as that of any ancient philosopher', he had himself been schooled alongside Addison at Charterhouse, the school which was later to produce Wesley; whilst St Paul's, Merchant Taylors', Christ's Hospital and, not far from London, Eton, all contributed to the strength of education in the metropolitan region. Of the great educational institutions only Winchester, and the two universities, lay outside it. The necessity of attending a provincial centre for university education had a notable influence on English life in the eighteenth

---

* I use this term for the built-up area covering the City of London and its 'liberties' and the developed areas of Middlesex, Essex and Surrey bordering on it—already constituting a single agglomeration, though not governed as such.

century, and provided virtually the only counter-magnet to London until the dawn of industrialism.

England thus had the characteristics at the same time of a mercantile city state on the Thames and of a populous, rural, but not by any means entirely agricultural nation with its linguistic and geographical boundaries well defined, except at the northern extremity, by the sea. Gregory King, writing at the end of the century, distinguished only four towns outside London as deserving special distinction: York, Norwich, Bristol, and Exeter; and forty 'large towns', all with population of less than 20,000. No English town outside London came within striking distance of the size of Dublin, which, with its 60,000 inhabitants was the second largest town in the British Isles and remained so until the end of the eighteenth century, if not longer. The first four, and fourteen of the others* claimed independence of their surrounding counties, and it is interesting to note that no fewer than fourteen of these eighteen predecessors of the county boroughs lay to the south of the Trent. The same is true of the overwhelming majority of the parliamentary boroughs.

The provincial towns are not to be underestimated in their contribution to British society. They provided its markets and its centres of communication. In them the Quarter Sessions met, and the judges held their assizes. Most of them were small enough for all the citizens to be known to each other, yet to lead an intensely urban life. Much of the educational effort was provided by their grammar schools. Newton was educated at Grantham, Sterne at Halifax. It was from Lichfield that Johnson and Garrick set out to seek their fortunes in London.

Gregory King carried out a special survey of his native place—Lichfield—and found it had 2,861 inhabitants. Thirty years later, though it had not grown much in the meantime, Defoe counted Lichfield as one of the principal towns in the midlands. Yet from what we would consider to be hardly more than a large village, there came in the course of the century not only King but Addison and Smalridge, Garrick, Samuel Johnson, and Anna Seward.

Out in the counties the density of population was roughly that of present-day Cumberland. They took in three-fifths of the English population living in small towns, villages, scattered homesteads, huts and caves, under hedges in the open air, wandering from place to place, casual labourers, pedlars, beggars, prostitutes and thieves. Whole tracts were still desolate and unsettled. Defoe describes his struggle

* Canterbury, Carmarthen, Chester, Coventry, Gloucester, Haverfordwest, Hull, Lichfield, Lincoln, Newcastle, Nottingham, Poole, Southampton and Worcester.

across the mountains of North Wales thirty years after the Revolution in terms which might have been applied to a journey in the Andes; in the High Peak district he found 'the most desolate, wild, and abandoned country in all England'; and even within forty miles of the capital, riding from Petersfield to Bagshot, he traversed what was virtually a desert, and was nearly blinded with driving sand.

In this small, thinly populated England children were many, and the old very few. It was a rule of thumb among the pioneers of demography that in any population one-half would be under sixteen, and King's Lichfield survey comes near confirming this. He found that 1,071 of Lichfield's 2,861 inhabitants were under fifteen. Only 179 were over sixty, and only 30 were over seventy. Life was cheap, and death was familiar. From such a population structure, and from the scale on which man was related to his surroundings, much followed about the nature of eighteenth-century society.

One must think in small numbers. For instance, during the wars of William III and Anne, when British armies were for the first time conducting major campaigns on the continent, the nation contained only about one million men between sixteen and sixty on whom the armed forces (which ran to nearly 200,000 at the height of the war) could draw. Then again, if there had been manhood suffrage, the constituency of each of England's 513 Members of Parliament would have been only about 4,000: admittedly a great many more than in most of the actual constituencies, but a figure which puts into proportion some of the criticisms of the unreformed Parliament. Outside London 'masses' in the modern sense could not yet be said to exist.*

Though the old were so few, they were important, for they were the survivors of a stern process of selection, and on the whole were a tougher group, physically and intellectually, than they are today. It was well for them, because the concept of retirement was unknown. For the 'decayed' and 'impotent' with no other resources there was at best a place in an almshouse; to retire, except in the sense of using one's gains in a lower station to move into the leisured class, was out of the question. As a result, succession in office and advancement in a profession were slow affairs, unless a pass-key of patronage could be

---

* See W. A. Speck, *Tory and Whig, 1701–1715*, pp. 16–17, where the number of voters (all men of course) in 1715 is estimated at about 250,000, so that in the reign of Queen Anne something like 10 per cent of the adult male population had the vote. This average conceals wide variations between constituencies; and it is important to remember that since the franchise depended on property qualification it was perfectly in order to have a vote in more than one constituency. Many electors in Westminster, for instance, were also electors in Middlesex.

found, and men continued active as bishops, judges, officials, and business men until very advanced ages. 'Old Scrope', who had been out with Monmouth in the rebellion of 1685 died at eighty-four, in 1752, in his twenty-ninth year as Secretary to the Treasury. John Hough, hero of the Magdalen resistance in 1687, survived to the age of ninety-two, after twenty-three years, as Bishop of Worcester and more than fifty years in the episcopate.* Gilbert Heathcote, one of the founders of the Bank of England, and among the greatest financial figures of his generation, sat in Parliament until he died at the age of eighty-two, and the year before his death was appointed one of the commissioners to found the new colony of Georgia. Ligonier, who had fought as a major at Blenheim, commanded at Fontenoy forty-two years later, and remained Master-General of the Ordnance until he was eighty-two. John Aislabie entered Parliament for Ripon at the age of twenty in 1721, and died, still Member for Ripon, sixty years later: probably a record.

Land gave independence, land gave power. This was the true significance of the Whig slogan 'liberty and property'. So precious was land that it was hardly regarded as the possession of a single individual but as the perpetual territory of a family, and elaborate precautions were taken to ensure this by the increasingly popular process of 'strict settlement' by which a landowner could ensure that his estate remained intact until his eldest grandson came of age. The making of a settlement, renewed by each generation on the marriage of the eldest son to extend to his future children, was the great day in the life of a landed family, on which the three existing generations as it were took hands to provide for the future.†

Not to be a landed man was a point against a justice of the peace or a Member of Parliament. 'Very meane and slight persons . . . of neither reputation nor interest' Evelyn had written about the membership of the House of Commons of 1685, which contained an undue proportion of landless men. The same criticism had been made of the justices James had tried to substitute for the traditional masters of the countryside in his campaign to secure a sympathetic magistracy. From the

---

* Hough was exceptional, perhaps unique, in surviving a golden jubilee as an Anglican bishop, but very long episcopates are not hard to find. Mathias Mawson (1683–1770) and Edmund Gibson (1669–1748) were both bishops for thirty-two years, Jonathan Trelawny (1650–1721) for thirty-six years, Thomas Sherlock (1678–1761) for thirty-four, and the celebrated Benjamin Hoadly (1676–1761) for forty-six.

† On settlements see H. J. Habakkuk, 'Marriage Settlements in the Eighteenth Century', *Transactions of the Royal Historical Society,* vol. 32 (1950) p. 15.

Revolution onwards it was almost impossible, outside the corporate towns, for a man to become a justice unless he were a landowner, and of the 16,000 or so major landowners some 2,500, or one in six, were justices. The office, originally designed to carry out the orders of Tudor despotism, at this point in its history showed its flexibility by serving as the means by which the landed classes governed rural society with the minimum of direction from above. The justice was an administrator as well as a magistrate, and so intertwined were his functions that he passed from punishing a criminal to admonishing a parish road overseer about his duty without particularly noticing that the one was judicial, the other executive. Singly, in his parlour, the justice enforced the game laws, made orders for the maintenance of bastards, sentenced vagrants to whipping, and audited the parish accounts. United with his brethren in Quarter Sessions he dealt with serious crime, imposed county rates, reviewed the state of roads and bridges, and considered the nagging question of 'the poor'—that all-embracing expression which included not only paupers but all who lacked property or an approved trade, and were not servants. The landed men considered 'the poor' not as citizens but as a liability to the nation's and his own estate, just as he regarded the government in London as a remote nuisance, to one of whose hated 'placemen' he might some day have to apply to provide for a younger son in the navy.

The landed men had been reluctant to condemn James, cavalierly though he had treated them. The monarchy seemed to them the guarantee of their own estates against the return of the 'cruel and unreasonable men' whose terrible Committees on Compounding had bled landowners white in the middle of the seventeenth century. They liked to think of the Crown itself as a kind of entailed estate, passing like their own by indefeasible hereditary right, interference with which would strike at the whole basis of landed power and property. This notion of security was what lay at the heart of the cluster of ideas in which loyalty, non-resistance, passive obedience and *jure divino* had their place.

Yet on a poll conducted by the king himself the landowners had rejected his policy on religion* and not even a minority had been prepared to strike a blow against the foreign invaders in 1688. The staunchly Tory Earl of Abingdon had summed up the reason when the Revolution was over: 'There was a necessity either to part with our religion and properties or do it.' In the eyes of such men as Abing-

* See my analysis in *The Descent on England*, pp. 238–43.

don, James had been steering too uncertain a course, which might land the country either in republicanism again, with landed property no longer safe, or, more probably, in the state of affairs they saw on the other side of the Channel, where all the effective decisions were taken at Versailles and the landed man had to choose between being a courtier or a despised provincial.

Abingdon mentioned religion, and mentioned it first, where a Whig would have put 'liberty'. In doing so he was commenting on something that lay even deeper than property rights and the perpetuation of families—he was touching on a question of identity. Such men sincerely loved the Anglican Church, almost as part of their own being. It seemed to them pure and orderly, traditional and apostolic, and to belong especially to England. The thought of an alternative marred their happiness and undermined their self-confidence, for they could not envisage a country without an official religion, and they could not bear the idea of an official religion that was not Anglican.

Chapter 2

Commercial and Political Growth

Altogether the landowners made up about one-fifth of the families of England, and commanded about half of the national income.* But at the time of the Revolution only about 10 per cent of these were major landowners—either peers or great commoners such as Sir Edward Seymour, the great landowner in the West Country, or even proprietors substantial enough to be justices, like the Shropshire squires of Farquhar's or Congreve's comedies. There were still, therefore, a great many small proprietors, who might indeed rent some land in addition to what they owned, and were hardly distinguishable socially from 'the middling sort' of tenant farmers, craftsmen and traders, but for one vital difference: they had votes. Below them in the hierachy of rural society stretched the landless and the voteless population of labourers, outworkers—mainly weavers—who manned the rural textile industry, and servants.

The servants deserve more than a passing mention. They probably formed the largest single class of employee in English society, and must have numbered hundreds of thousands, though King does not even notice them separately. They were indispensable and ubiquitous. Even a moderate family of the 'middling sort' would have four or five servants: a nobleman would have fifty or more. Every kind of work was represented, for private service provided not only the scullery maids and the footmen, the coachmen and gardeners, the valets and cooks, that made genteel life possible in an age without labour-saving devices or mechanical transport; but the land stewards, secretaries, bailiffs, butlers and housekeepers, who in practice managed a great deal of property and exercised much patronage. Such upper servants, who often started in the lower ranks, sometimes ended by achieving independence. Service offered better rewards

* G. E. Mingay, *English Landed Society in the Eighteenth Century*, p. 4. I agree with Mr Mingay's view (p. 11) that 'it is an important truth that in the landowners' hey-day their virtual monopoly of government proved to be consistent with the maintenance and extension of national liberty.'

than manual labour, and a better chance of moving upwards in the social hierarchy. The wages of a footman, at £5 or £6 a year, were higher than those of a living-in farm hand, and the board and lodging was better. Nominal wages, too, could be more than doubled by perquisites, especially by the levies on visitors which were known as 'vails' and were extorted even from dinner-guests.* Service offered security, with the prospect of a legacy, a tenancy, or a modest sinecure as provision for old age. Above all it allowed contact with the educated, the fashionable, and the wealthy, thereby opening the way for social promotion. Dodsley, the publisher and friend of Pope, started as a footman; Capability Brown as a gardener's boy in Northumberland; while Mrs Elizabeth Raffald, who had been a housekeeper, founded a successful publishing business in Manchester which issued a newspaper, commercial directories, and a popular book on household management. Those who broke free in this way were, of course, comparatively few, but to attain even the status of an upper servant was to enjoy an income well above what was received by many clergymen, schoolmasters, shopkeepers and farmers. A career in service was one of the most powerful attractions exerted by London to recruit its population.

The dependence of the upper and middle classes upon domestic service, and the dependence of large numbers of the population on providing it, is one of the central facts about society in the eighteenth century. It accounts for many of that society's characteristics. If one remembers that much of the life of the upper classes was necessarily lived under the scrutiny of servants, it is much easier to understand the formality of their manners and their determination to keep up appearances. The invention (in the 1730s) of the 'dumb waiter' that allowed them briefly to talk to one another as they pleased was greeted with unmistakable relief. The master exploited the servant, but there was a very real sense in which the servants regarded a great household as an enterprise run primarily for their benefit, the royal

---

* This hated custom made dining out almost as expensive as eating in a restaurant. Among other recognized perquisites were 'card-money' (the servants sold the cards to the players); candle-ends sold off to tallow-chandlers; clothes (the servant was usually entitled to sell his old livery when a new one was supplied, which could bring in the equivalent of three years' wages); 'poundage' on provisions bought from tradesmen; and, of course, straightforward embezzlement. Some employers operated a pooling system for perquisites, and a few were even suspected of taking a share themselves. Much light on the servant class is shed by J. Jean Hecht, *The Domestic Servant Class in Eighteenth Century England,* (Routledge and Kegan Paul, 1956).

household being a conspicuous, but not the only, example.

For most people the substance of social organization was the parish. There were some 9,000 of them, rural and urban, large and small, similar to one another only in being the basic units of social organization, and completely covering the country with their network.* Some took in a whole area into which great towns such as Leeds and Liverpool were to develop and in due course provided the only government such towns possessed. Others, like the ninety-eight parishes into which the old City of London was divided, were very small, and yielded in local importance to other forms of organization, such as guilds and wards. On the whole the rural parishes, which formed the great majority of the total number, were small enough for every inhabitant to be known personally to all the others.

The parish was part of an organic system whose origins were lost in antiquity. It had always been there, so far as the English were concerned. No Act of Parliament said there should be a parish system or systematically laid down boundaries, though occasionally Parliament would create a new parish. Some parishes straddled county boundaries. Instances are recorded of contiguous parishes altering their boundaries by no more than agreement between themselves.

The parish was secular. While the souls it contained were committed to its incumbent (or his curate if, as often happened, he had more than one benefice and did not reside) and it had a pre-eminent duty to maintain its church, its officers—even the churchwardens— were mainly concerned with temporal matters. Different parishes gave different weights to the duties of their four principal officers, and had different constitutions. Two of these officers, the surveyor of the highways and the overseer of the poor, owed their existence to Acts of Parliament and were appointed by the justices, though often on the initiative of the parish. The other two, the constable and the churchwarden, arose from the organic character of the parish itself; and though the constable was in effect the justices' man, the churchwarden, one way or another, emerged from the will of the parish people. He normally kept the parish accounts, convened the vestry or parish assembly, and had care of the 'parish stock'. A rash archdeacon once tried to dispute the right of a parish to choose its

---

* Like all generalizations about English local government this is not quite correct. A few areas claimed not to be in any parish. Canvey Island in Essex was one such 'extra-parochial place'. See Sidney and Beatrice Webb, *History of English Local Government* (Frank Cass, 1963), vol. 1, p. 10, note 1. But all rested on tradition. There was no map of the parish structure.

churchwarden. 'The churchwarden,' said the court,* 'is a temporal officer; he has the property and custody of the parish goods; and as it is at the peril of the parishioners, so they may choose and trust whom they think fit.' The parish, said Lord Chief Justice Holt, on a church attendance case, is made for the people, not for the clergyman. Parliament never tired of heaping obligations on the parish system. In 1708 it was required to provide fire engines; in 1753 to license public houses; in 1738 to take steps for the suppression of alcoholism; but no machinery except the justices was ever called into existence to see that these provisions were carried out.

Below Parliament itself, the parish alone had a traditional right regularly to raise money for public purposes. Rating—and here the deeply distributive character of the eighteenth century betrays itself —was on whatever basis the parish thought best after discussion in the vestry, whether an open vestry, held in the church and open to all inhabitants, or a select vestry consisting of the principal inhabitants and adjourned from a formal meeting in church to a business meeting in the local tavern. Such a rate might be applied to almost any purpose —the relief of the poor, the prosecution of criminals, destroying mad dogs, rooting up deadly nightshade, suppressing dangerous games, repairing the church, killing caterpillars. The accounts of the church-wardens may be the annals of the poor, but they are neither short nor simple.

There were elements of democracy in the parish, haphazard and rooted in custom, but corresponding to the notion of civic equality and far removed from the hierarchical society that governed the county. Parish office, which was regarded as a burden as well as a privilege, went in some parishes by election, in others by rotation, often by turns to the holders of particular properties, so that a woman might find herself overseer of the poor, as happened in Ribchester, in Lancashire. Sir John Strange held that a woman could vote in a parish election, and no authority laid down precisely who might be present at an open vestry. In some of the larger parishes energetic incumbents or citizens were able as the century wore on to establish effective units of local government, complete with salaried officers and substantial budgets.

Every parish had its clergyman, and to this extent the secular and religious communities at the lowest level were coterminous; and besides his pre-eminence in parish society as an educated man, the

---

* *Morgan* v. *Archdeacon of Cardigan* (W. Salkeld, *Reports of Cases,* vol. 1, p. 165). See also S. and B. Webb, *op. cit.,* vol. 1, p. 23.

clergyman was its registrar, and very often its schoolmaster; for if a clergyman of the established church chose to keep a school, nobody else in his parish was allowed to do so. This right was especially important to the hundreds of curates who were expected to look after rural parishes for absentee pluralists in return for a tiny salary. Such men could expect little in the way of promotion, and were completely at the mercy of the incumbents they served; and from their unprivileged ranks were to emerge some of the most characteristic and interesting men of the century: Laurence Sterne, Gilbert White, John Wesley.

The Revolution touched little of the parish structure. In 1691 Parliament imposed new responsibilities on the parishes for the maintenance of highways—a system that could not conceivably be efficient —and almost annually it reiterated the local responsibility for the poor. Harsh the Poor Law undoubtedly was; but, apart from Holland, where social support for the poor had made great advances even by the middle of the seventeenth century, England was peculiar among European nations in having any regular recourse for those who lacked the means of subsistence. The able bodied, whether men, women or children, came off worst. But the old and the widowed, as the parish records testify, could usually look to their local community for support. Above all, therefore, it was essential to have a local settlement.

Though the law of 1662 which enforced settlement as the basis of the Poor Law was often breached, and at last broke utterly under the stress of the Industrial Revolution, it was the fundamental social law of England at the time of the Revolution and for many years afterwards. Its provisions were simple. Each person was conceived to have a settlement in one particular parish—where he had property, where he had been bound apprentice, or, failing all else, where he had been born; and that parish alone was collectively responsible for him if he fell on bad times. Technically anyone who settled in a parish and did not rent land to the value of at least £10 a year could be removed to his parish of origin unless he gave security against becoming chargeable. And in actual fact tens of thousands of people a year were removed in this way. Disputes between parishes over the responsibility for individual paupers provided much the largest flow of civil litigation throughout the century.

By the end of the seventeenth century it was already becoming clear that the parish base for the Poor Law was becoming inadequate, and that larger units were necessary for dealing with the problem. Larger units had been noticed in Holland, and the spirit of the age suggested that efficient methods might enable the poor not only to earn their keep, which had been the modest objective of Elizabethan legislators, but to show a profit for the community on which they depended. By 1696, with the establishment of the Bristol workhouse by Private Act, the long process of transferring the Poor Law away from the parish began, and two expressions came into use which were to echo down the centuries. The Bristol workhouse was operated by a 'union' of parishes; and in 1697, borrowing perhaps consciously from Plato, Locke coined the expression 'Guardians of the Poor' for the body organizing a union of parishes for the relief of the poor.

The law of settlement and the whole system of poor relief that went with it, was peculiar to England and Wales: it did not extend to either Scotland or Ireland. It increased the pull of London, for the parishes there, while trying to keep their relief for those possessing a genuine settlement, were comparatively easy-going about an arrival from elsewhere so long as he did not trouble the parish officers. The Irish immigrant, the north-country girl looking for a job as a servant, the runaway apprentice from Nottingham or Norwich, were soon spotted in a small rural community and sent on their way. But they were quickly absorbed into the morass of London.

At the very centre of national affairs Parliament had come into its own. It had shown that it could not only create a king, but could recreate itself without the summons of a king. The sequence of constitutional events in 1688–9, though carefully designed to look as if it followed the precedent of 1660, marks as clear a hiatus in the succession of Parliaments as it does in the monarchy. While the Revolution was still in the balance an assembly of peers, presided over by Halifax, had sat in London as the only vestige of Parliamentary government. With the establishment of the Prince of Orange as the dominant force in England, the peers gave way to a transient meeting of all the surviving members of Charles II's Houses of Commons who could be found, and it was they who asked William—not yet a king—to issue writs for the general election which produced the Convention Parliament.

The period immediately following of mainly triennial Parliaments, down to 1716, when the longer stroke of septennial Parliaments begins, is one of the most vigorous periods in British parliamentary history. The new engine was, as it were, tested at high pressure. There were twelve general elections in thirty years: another eighty years were to elapse before another twelve would be reckoned. The conditions were perfectly suited to the development of a party system.

The surest sign of the new predominance of Parliament is the flowering of the first great parliamentary generation since the outbreak of the Civil War. Parliament was the road to power for the individual, as it had not been for half a century. Somers, counsel for the Seven Bishops and draftsman of the Bill of Rights; Wharton, the rake who had turned to the business of political organization; Montagu, Newton's Cambridge friend with a talent for finance; and above all Robert Harley, who deliberately made himself a master of parliamentary procedure as the first step in his ascent to power: made up a generation of startling and variegated political talent, centred on achievement in the House of Commons.

By what seems at first sight a paradox, the counties, where most of the population lived, were represented by only about one-fifth of the members of the House of Commons. These representatives of the rural nation had, on the whole, the most democratic constituencies, for the forty shilling freehold franchise brought in voters who were well down the social scale. Even though the poorer freeholders were exposed to the influence of the bigger gentry, it was difficult for a single interest to dominate a county, and so nominate its representatives. Members were usually chosen after considerable consultation among the principal families, and enjoyed a weight and respect that was disproportionate to their numbers in the House. They were knights of the shire, not recipients of borough interest, and they rarely accepted office.

The other four-fifths of the seats in the Commons made up an extraordinary mosaic based on the rights of particular geographical places to representation. There were 214 of them, and to complete the House, two corporations—the Universities of Oxford and Cambridge —also returned Members. About one-quarter of the so-called 'boroughs' were not even incorporated as boroughs in the usual sense, and the right to vote in these cases was usually tied to the ownership of certain plots of land. The basis of parliamentary representation, like so much in eighteenth-century England was geographical privilege, and the rights of particular areas* to return Members were paralleled by innumerable other privileges and exemptions: to hold a market; to restrict shopkeeping to freemen; to hold a court; to collect tolls; to appoint certain functionaries. Where the franchise was widely distributed, as in a few boroughs such as Westminster or Preston, the democracy was purely a coincidence.

* Parliamentary boroughs such as Old Sarum, with its handful of voters, are the obvious examples. But even the counties were extremely diverse. Yorkshire returned two Members: so did Rutland.

This notion of privilege attaching to particular sites, which shows so sharply in the method of electing Parliament, had very important consequences. It was so engrained that it was easy for the Englishman to think of the whole country, in relation to the outside world, as an area of privilege, so that it seemed perfectly natural for its Parliament to legislate for places like Ireland and America, which did not contain the precious privileged acres on which English liberty was founded. Second, and perhaps of even more importance, corporate privilege discouraged economic growth. Entry into a trade, the right to start a business, in a privileged area were jealously guarded by existing interests. It is therefore not wholly an accident that the new industry, when it came into existence, tended to develop in towns which had no parliamentary representation. James Watt, expelled from Glasgow by the jealousy of the Corporation of Hammermen, settled for Birmingham.

Most of the non-corporate parliamentary boroughs, and many of the corporate towns, were as much under the influence of landed gentry as the counties. Some, notably in over-represented Cornwall with its forty-four seats, and in sea-ports where government officials and expenditure counted, were at the disposal of government agencies and sent officials to Parliament. A few sent business men, sometimes because a business man had acquired the 'interest', sometimes because trade dominated the electorate. London's four Members were usually merchants, and Southwark almost always returned two brewers.

It has sometimes been said that the Parliaments of the eighteenth century showed very little interest in social and economic legislation on a national scale. Much the greater part of their time was indeed spent on local measures, and from this has been inferred a Parliament whose Members thought fundamentally in terms of their own localities. While this is true, it was also true that the cumulative effect of local measures, for which a national authority was now available in regular session, was immense.

The gigantic series of river improvement acts, turnpike trust acts, workhouse acts, and acts constituting joint stock companies, all begin with the Revolution. Under the prerevolutionary order the monarchy had been the authority from whom entrepreneurs had sought the powers of a corporate body to dredge and drain, hold land, use a common seal, acquire property or raise capital. The engine had been the prerogative, and it had moved rustily. Parliament, with its long intervals between meetings and its dependence on the will of the king, had offered no satisfactory alternative. But from the Revolution onwards Parliament was as permanent as the Crown. The years 1697–1700 alone saw the passage of eight river improvement acts, and seven acts setting up workhouses; and what was set in motion in those years for the navigation of the Colne and the Trent, the Bristol Avon and the Aire and Calder; and for the poor of Bristol, Hull, Tiverton and Exeter, was to be repeated scores of times for different localities in the years to come.

In one sphere, finance, the new-found permanency of Parliament established by the Revolution was all-important. A permanent assembly with the power to tax could raise money on credit. Newton's brilliant friend, Charles Montagu, was quick to perceive the possibility in proposing the Act which, in January 1693, raised a loan and guaranteed the interest on the security of certain duties on beer and other commodities. In the following year another statute created the Bank of England for the specific purpose of advancing money to the government in return for a monopoly in handling future state loans.

The substitution of parliamentary credit for the tarnished credit of the Crown had far-reaching social and economic consequences. It sucked out resources for the war against Louis XIV which no king could ever have extracted from the people. It drew into England funds from abroad, chiefly from Holland and Switzerland, which would never have been entrusted to a Stuart government. But above all it made Parliament itself the source to which increasing numbers of people—widows, bankers, trustees, and orphans—looked for their security. It was no longer a purely legislative assembly which voted money to the Crown if the Crown could not find money elsewhere, but a national institution in itself.

Parliamentary finance came into its own alongside the beginnings of modern economics as a science. The late seventeenth century is the earliest period for which it is possible to quote contemporary authority on economics. Gregory King, genealogist, herald and statistician, made the first approaches to the scientific study of population, national income, and expenditure scales, and his most important work, *Natural and Political Observations and Conclusions upon the State and Condition of England,* was published in 1696.* Davenant's *Essay upon the Ways and Means of Supplying the War* had come out in the year before, and the year after came Locke's *Essay on the Coinage.* The temper of the age was practical

---

* For King, see D. V. Glass's paper in D. V. Glass and D. E. C. Eversley, *Population in History,* p. 159; and for the early economists W. R. Letwin, *The Origins of Scientific Economics* (Methuen, 1963).

and the new economics, though it was detached in the sense of not being imprisoned by preconceived opinions, fastened firmly on specific current problems in taxation, currency, banking and credit. Great theoreticians in other fields, such as Locke and Newton, became highly practical when they turned to economics. Locke's contribution to solution of the recoinage problem was rejected in favour of Lowndes's. But Newton, as Master of the Mint, permanently settled the puzzle of bimetallism by establishing the guinea as twenty-one shillings; and calculated the compensation which Scotland should receive for shouldering the service of her share of the thirteen-year-old English National Debt after the Union. It went largely towards making good the losses of the disastrous Darien Company.

That trade was the foundation of national strength was already a commonplace at all levels of society. Ownership of land might be the mark of power, but the current ethos was that of the city state, with its emphasis on accumulation and protection. The reigns of the last two Stuarts had seen considerable economic growth. An East India Company share bought in 1660 had increased ninefold in value by the time of the Revolution, and still yielded 10 per cent on the higher price. Alongside the new flow of trade a sophisticated apparatus of finance, banking, broking and insurance was beginning to take shape. Joint stock enterprise was increasingly used to develop new industries, such as paper; and new public utilities, such as town water supply, river improvements, drainage schemes, and street lighting. Barbon's fire insurance company had been launched in the reign of Charles II; and the beginnings of the Stock Exchange were already arousing hostility.

The Revolution acted on this developing situation as if by releasing a spring, or bursting a dyke, and made the next thirty years a great age of economic enterprise and financial innovation. The often muddy waters of the business world in the 1690s bore up multitudes of projects and promotions, and it was easier than it had ever been to find money for an idea. A most encouraging feature was that business, and the profits from it, were virtually untaxed. Almost equally encouraging was the steady demand for manufactured goods to carry on the war. Birmingham was already a centre for the arms trade, and a single contract there was producing 200 muskets a month.

It is one of the paradoxes of a trading country ruled by landowners that the main burden of taxation should have fallen on the land. The squires paid for the war, and they paid most towards the service of the debt which the war created. Nor were they unaware of the fact. Contemporaries saw clearly enough the distinction between the landed interest and the moneyed interest, which were supposed to be rivals, both economically and socially. There were indeed practical points of tension, as when schemes for improved communication, which would benefit manufacturers, were opposed by landed interests trying to maintain the price of their primary products. But on the whole the landowner was resigned to being a principal taxpayer. He was, after all, himself the recipient of much of the profit from trade and manufacture, and payment of an assessed tax on his land was a badge—if a tiresome one—of his power.

Manufacturing industry still worked close to its raw materials, which were mainly on the backs of the sheep in Wiltshire, the Cotswolds, and the West Riding. Long before the arrival of the factory and the mill England was an industrial country. In many districts the rural worker was quite as likely to be a weaver as a ploughman, and Defoe commented on the intense use of child labour in the cottage industries more than a century before nineteenth-century reformers began to deplore its presence in factories. Wool, not corn, was universally considered to be the most precious national product, because it provided employment and could be sold abroad in manufactured form. Its export unmanufactured was absolutely forbidden, and the 'lightowlers', or smugglers of wool were as active in the marshes of Kent and Essex in the export trade as their brethren of the south coast were in the business of forbidden imports. Merely to possess wool within five miles of the sea-coast without a licence was declared an offence by Parliament in the year of the Revolution.

People and goods, like ideas, moved slowly over the face of England, and in the first half of the century it was quicker as well as more convenient to travel by water than by land. In the ordinary way it would take the better part of a week to travel by road from London to Exeter or Newcastle,* whereas one could be in Amsterdam in thirty-six hours. Moving the huge timbers from the forests of Hampshire to the ship-building yards of Chatham could take a year or more, at the rate of a few miles a day in good weather and none at all in bad. Wherever possible movement by water was preferred: the Thames was

---

* Land transport could, however, put on a spurt if no expense was spared. Defoe (*A Tour Thro' the Whole Island of Great Britain* (1724 ed.), vol. 3, p. 190) reports that salmon could be got by special messenger from Workington reasonably fresh to the slab at Billingsgate. The difference in the price of the fish at the fishing towns and in London illustrates the high cost of rapid land transport.

London's principal thoroughfare; travellers from Kent ended their land journey at Gravesend and continued by wherry up the river; much of London's corn, and all its coal, came along the coast. Inland the mileage of navigable waterways based on the main river systems was being pushed ahead. In the year of the Restoration there had been fewer than 700 miles of it, mostly unimproved. By 1700 there were nearly 1,000 miles, and by 1720 only the Pennines and the Welsh mountains were more than fifteen miles from navigable water.* Towns many miles inland—Bawtry, Gainsborough, Nottingham, Exeter—were important ports. It was not international but internal trade that determined the growth points as the outlets of the major river systems, above all at London, Bristol, and Liverpool.

Ease of movement by water was also important for the exertion of military force in any part of the island where it was necessary, as it often was. The parliamentary navy had been a silent but important factor in the winning of the Civil War, and the defection of James's navy had been decisive in the Revolution. Fifty years later naval operations were to ensure that the Jacobite bid of 1745 could not succeed, and Charles Edward was to be crushed by an army which had been transported almost to Culloden itself by water.

Ships carried other things besides merchandise and soldiers. William's success in undermining James's forces had owed much to the thousands of pamphlets printed in Holland and shifted across the North Sea for free distribution to booksellers and subsequent resale by them for their own benefit. William had even included a printing press in the baggage of the army of intervention, and the bloodlessness of the Revolution owed much to the fact that Englishmen were becoming used to the idea of reading about their domestic politics, rather than fighting about them. As Johnston, William's principal agent in England before the Revolution had said, 'If you intend to keep the nation in humour, you must entertain it by papers.'

The first great age of papers was just opening, and without journalism the eighteenth century cannot be fully understood. Journalism, both periodical and occasional, soon became indispensable to civilized life. It was oral, as well as printed, for papers and pamphlets were regularly read aloud to circles in coffee houses. Each copy of the *Spectator* was said to reach ten people in this way, so that the print of between three and four thousand had an 'audience' of perhaps

* See T. S. Willan's two important contributions, *River Navigation in England, 1600–1750* (1936) with its interesting series of maps, and *The English Coasting Trade, 1600–1750* (1938).

35,000.* This was in the hey-day of Augustan journalism, when London had eighteen newspapers; but already by 1695 there were at least five triweekly papers in the capital, and the first daily—significantly borrowing the Dutch mast-head of *Courant*—began to appear in 1702.

The importance of journalism was as much commercial as it was political or literary. One of the first fields for the new periodical press was the publication of the movement of share prices, and every promotion had its accompanying flotilla of pamphlets, puffs, and advertisements. Defoe combined City journalism with political and religious polemics, and the Stock Exchange budding round Garraway's Coffee House owed both its fame and its notoriety to Grub Street.

The Stuart monarchy had kept the printed word under control with some success until the last year of James's reign; and the repeal of the Licensing Act in 1696 was undoubtedly one of those measures of the postrevolutionary period that broke down restraint on a development which was already pent-up and ready to go far. But governments continued to look on the press with suspicion, and the laws of libel and sedition were still energetically though sporadically used against the pamphleteers and newspaper men. For nearly eighty years after the Revolution, until the tornado of *North Briton* 'Number 45' hit the unsuspecting Lord Halifax in 1763, successive secretaries of state considered they had the right to close down periodicals they found especially offensive and to prosecute their authors.

The age of journalism coincided with an age of constitutional debate. The very use of the word 'constitution' to mean a body of fundamental law, which gathered so much emotional strength during the eighteenth century, is almost coterminous with the Revolution, when it was employed in the fundamental resolutions of Parliament in both England and Scotland, depriving James of the crown. The idea that there was a constitution, indeed, preceded clarification of what that constitution was. The political achievement of the next thirty

* See Donald F. Bond (ed.), Introduction to *The Spectator* (Oxford University Press, 1965), pp. xxvii, xxviii, where the method of producing large numbers of copies by the use of hand presses is discussed. Several presses, and an accumulation of 'standing copy' were the secrets. As an example of the multiplication of readership, see Scott's *Waverley*, chapter 2, where he describes the circulation of Sir Everard Waverley's copy of Dyer's *Weekly Letter*—'After it had gratified Sir Everard's curiosity, his sister's, and that of his aged butler [it] was regularly passed from the Hall to the rectory, from the rectory to Squire Stubbs's at the Grange, from the Squire to the Baronet's steward . . . from the steward to the bailiff, and from him to a huge circle . . .'

years was to arrive at a body of constitutional law which was not the less binding on account of being arrived at piecemeal.

John Somers, fresh from his triumph at the trial of the seven bishops, in which he had made his name,* had intended the Bill of Rights to be a far more comprehensive and elaborate document than was actually the case. The rapid progress of events in the early months of 1689 caused his work to be curtailed, and swept into an omnibus document which included the formal offer of the crown to William and Mary by Parliament, an entail on the succession, and a catalogue of James II's twelve offences against his subjects which had led to the Revolution and were in future to be unlawful.† These last represent what Somers had intended to expand into a separate code of rights, and some of them are no more than a recitation of particular acts (such as the prosecution of the bishops) which had led to the crisis.

There is, nevertheless, a great deal that is fundamental to any free society embodied in the Bill of Rights, and phrases in it have been echoed in many more formal constitutions since, including the American Bill of Rights: the right to petition, the freedom of elections, the need for parliamentary approval of taxation, freedom of speech in Parliament, and the ban on cruel and unusual punishments. Oddly enough, the authors of the Bill of Rights did not at first provide for anything about the meeting of Parliament except that it should be 'frequent'. It was not until 1694 that triennial elections were enacted in the teeth of royal opposition, and a term independent of the king's will was put to the duration of all Parliaments. In a way this was the most revolutionary innovation of all, for it was a derogation from what till then had been the unchallenged right of the government to keep a friendly Parliament in being as long as it liked.

The Toleration Act, the other pillar of the Revolution Settlement, was also the creation of circumstances, not doctrine. The hope had been for a scheme of 'Comprehension'—i.e. absorption of the Dis-

---

* Somers was the most junior of the counsel employed by the defence, but he was also the most effective. His fee (£32 18s.) was much the smallest.
† The text may be conveniently found in E. N. Williams, *The Eighteenth Century Constitution, 1688–1715*, pp. 26–33. The entailment of the succession out of the normal course was a most unusual exercise of parliamentary authority—and was paradoxically a concession to the Tories, who wanted it to return to the direct line of James II if that could safely be done. The arrangement therefore was that the crown should pass, after the deaths of William and Mary to the children of Mary (if any), then to her sister Anne, and only thereafter to any children William might have by a second marriage. All Catholics were to be passed over 'as if naturally dead'. The language used was borrowed exactly from the wording that would have been suitable for entailing landed property.

senters into the state church on a broader theological and organizational basis. The idea was reactionary, looking back as it did to the notion of an official church coterminous with society itself. In its rejection the great concession was made that the Anglican church would no longer be even in theory the church of all. This, rather than any general toleration, is the significance of the Toleration Act. Protestant Nonconformists were relieved of the Penal Laws, and their ministers of the restrictions of the so-called 'Clarendon Code', subject to oaths of political loyalty to the new regime and acceptance of what the Anglican authors of the Act considered the irreducible rudiments of Christianity.* Roman Catholics were of course completely excluded from any relief, though William would himself have been glad to see them given the same concessions as the Protestant Dissenters; so the Penal Laws of Elizabeth remained in force against Catholics for another century and a half: generally unenforced, perhaps, but a continuing source of tension.

Catholic and Dissenter alike remained subject to the Test and Corporation Acts, those great strokes of the Cavalier Parliament which effectively excluded those not taking the Anglican communion from any significant public office, from commissions in the armed forces, from Parliament, from the universities and from local government. Anglicanism was still at any rate to be the religion of those who wanted to exercise the full rights of citizenship. But the old, fervent generation of dissent was fading. Bunyan died in the year of Revolution, Muggleton was to follow him in 1698. The passion and vision had gone from dissent, and the Dissenters, though still a quarter of a million strong, and a majority in some parts of the country, were to survive in a different and quieter role, as pressure groups.

The position of the Dissenters had been one of the great issues on which the Revolution had turned, and it had been William's political triumph to woo them away at the critical moment from James's offer of general toleration by persuading them that it was a poisoned fruit. But he had always said he would maintain the Test, and the Dissenters were at any rate not cheated at the Revolution as they had been when they helped Charles II back. John Locke heartily approved of the solution embodied in the Toleration Act. To tolerate worship outside the state church, while limiting the political rights of those so toler-

* These were quite considerable. The Anglicans found themselves able to drop only three and a half articles of the thirty-nine, which was not enough to bring the Quakers within the Act. For the Quaker campaign to enlarge the Toleration Act—one of the earliest examples of pressure group politics—see N. C. Hunt, *Two Early Political Associations* (Clarendon, 1961).

ated, seemed to him very far from being an inconsistency, and forty years later Warburton was to make a reputation by advancing a brilliant and sophisticated explanation of the concordance between the Test and the Toleration; discovering in the process an important principle about men in society which still has force.

Retention of the Test Act did not allow the Church of England to emerge unchanged from the destruction of the magical monarchy that had called it into existence. Led by five bishops—five of the very seven who had led the defiance to James—a substantial body of the clergy refused to accept the new order. The departure of these nonjurors marks the end of the Church of England as an integral part of the fabric of government. 'the glue', as Hooker had put it in a homely metaphor, 'and soder of the publick weal, the ligament which tieth and connecteth the limbs of this body politick to each other'. The average man, whether Dissenter or Anglican, still did not see how civilized life could be organized unless there was general religious belief, but the claims of the Church of England to a monopoly in the organization of that belief, though they were to be pressed with an eagerness tinged with desperation, were permanently damaged.

In metropolitan life—the life of the city state of London and the most active members of the governing class—a wholly new attitude to religion was beginning to show itself. The first ripples of rationalism were lapping against revelation as the basis for belief about the universe and the nature of man. Men had succeeded—as the work of Locke among others exemplifies—in detaching the process of reasoning about observed phenomena from preconceived beliefs about what ought to be. A fuller understanding of nature did not necessarily lead them to discard or even modify those beliefs. Their faith was not affected by an understanding of the mechanism of the universe or the discovery of the unknown world of the micro-organism; but equally their scientific operations were not influenced by their faith. It seemed to them possible, indeed, that a deeper understanding of science would confirm religious truths which earlier generations had been obliged to take on trust, and that the great reconciliation between faith and reason might be the ultimate prize of science.

The Revolution brought new and younger men to prominence on the national scene as well as new ideas. William himself was thirty-eight when he was crowned, and only Sunderland, Danby, and Halifax, among established senior politicians, managed effectively to cross the divide and continue their careers in the new reign. In the year of the Revolution, Marlborough and his rival Talmash were the same age as the king they helped to make, and Godolphin was forty-three. Somers, Wharton, Harley, and Shrewsbury were all under forty. Charles Montagu, perhaps the ablest of all the postrevolution Whigs, was only twenty-seven. And promotion was lavish. Few kings have had more opportunities for generosity than William, and few have taken them more enthusiastically. His reign saw sixteen new promotions to the episcopal bench (and there were only twenty-six sees); an almost complete renewal of the judiciary; seven dukedoms, and numerous other promotions in the peerage; and far-reaching changes in the higher ranks of the army and navy, mainly for the benefit of those who had led the invading forces. Many of the generals in the great campaigns of Marlborough had been field officers in the Anglo-Dutch regiments that had landed at Torbay. In many ways this renewal of the national leadership—for William did not promote the incompetent—was as important a consequence of the Revolution as the institutional changes for which it is famous.

Nevertheless, the demographic picture in which some 10 per cent who had survived to old age held far more than 10 per cent of property and senior offices remains valid for the period as a whole. The survivor was also an accumulator of inherited wealth by sheer force of longevity. In such a world, where much was in the hands of comparatively few, and none were willing to surrender management until the last possible moment; where there were few recognized qualifications for advancement, and fewer opportunities of getting known even to a comparatively small public: there was only one way of getting on the road to success, unless a man was willing to take up business. That way was patronage. It had been so for generations, and there was nothing new about it. It was one of William's great qualifications as a king that he thoroughly understood patronage, having learned the art in the political world of the United Netherlands. 'Slow rises worth, by poverty depress'd', wrote Johnson, some forty years after the Revolution, and he had every reason for knowing its truth. But it would be wrong to suppose that patronage, though its rewards were slow and capricious, excluded those who were born in obscurity. It meant that the able, if they wanted to get on, had to attract the favourable notice of an individual already established, and to retain a sense of obligation to him once the desired promotion was achieved. This held good not only in politics but in every walk of life from the highest to the lowest. The minor posts in towns were as much in the gift of councillors and vestrymen as the great officers of state were in the gift of the king. The form of liaison between client and patron was thoroughly understood and accepted; and was quite distinct from personal friendship. Warburton, who had himself risen by patronage from being the obscure son of a town clerk to a literary eminence which in its day towered above even Johnson's, drew the distinction clearly when he wrote to his friend Hurd that 'nothing but the obligations of gratitude could engage me in such a thing, or the stronger obligations of what one owes to a true friend.'* In the eighteenth century the obligation of loyalty was not so much to one's employer as to the person who arranged for the employment.

It is often thought that patronage, because it often involved the rejection of the best qualified if he lacked 'interest', implied the promotion of the incompetent. This was not altogether the case. One of the most notable features of the system as it operated in England was that it was worked in conjunction with the concept of qualification. Over a large area—the Customs service and the armed forces are leading examples—qualifications were always insisted upon, and patrons were driven to distraction by the applications of unsuitable people. 'I have so many solicitations that I have no credit left', wrote Colonel Liddel, M.P. 'He should get up a case where and how long he has served, and in what regiments.' Or again, 'It is not practicable at this time to get your brother Robertson as a surgeon as he has not been in the Navy before'; or 'I really have done all in my power, and have had very high words with the Commissioners for refusing to give me a promise to make him a Supervisor, alleging that he is not qualified for it. But if not . . . I cannot pretend to get him it.' Tom Paine had to devote several months to study before he could qualify as an Excise Officer. Captain Cook, when still on the lower deck, was refused a commission, despite the application of influential friends, because he had not served the requisite six years.

During the thirty years that followed the Revolution four great issues dominated the life of this city state set in its rural framework: the achievement of political stability at the centre; the place of commerce

* *Letters from a Late Eminent Prelate* (1809), p. 37. Promotion in the church provides many interesting examples of advancement through patronage from humble origins. Two of the most notable prelates of the century—John Robinson, Bishop of London and the last bishop to reach cabinet rank, and Edmund Gibson, also Bishop of London and supreme master of ecclesiastical affairs under Walpole—were too poor to go to Oxford except as 'servitors' working their way through college. John Thomas (1691–1766)—one of the three eighteenth-century bishops of that name—who rose to be Bishop of Salisbury, was the son of a drayman. Archbishop Potter's father was a draper, Archbishop Sharp's a salter.

in a society dominated by landowners; the future of the national church; and the handling of Britain's new situation as a major European power. These constitute the ground on which the British party system took its first shape, and on each of them Whig and Tory confronted one another with different solutions. Each great crisis in the reigns of William and of Anne can be related to these four issues; and each was seen in a different light by those who lived in London, and by those who lived in 'The Country'.

Chapter 3   War, Science
                                 and Party Politics

The first nine years that William reigned were years of war with France, the first of Britain's great continental contests in which the military and economic strength of the country were exerted as they had never been before. The campaigns were not especially glorious, and there is a darkness, suffering, and futility of detail about William's battles that foreshadow later and even more terrible struggles in Flanders. In the lost battles of Steenkirk and Neerwinden and the almost endless siege of Namur (where Uncle Toby, in Sterne's *Tristram Shandy,* got his celebrated wound 'just between the hornwork and the covered way'), the British fighting army of the eighteenth century was hammered into shape under commanders which the Revolution had carried to high rank. Steenkirk saw the deaths of two of these stalwarts —old General Mackay who had led the Anglo-Dutch Brigade in the revolutionary invasion and faced out Bonnie Dundee at Killiekrankie, and Count Solms who had been the first Williamite officer ashore at Torbay. The trenches before Namur produced what was in some ways the most significant casualty of the whole war: Michael Godfrey, Governor of the newly founded Bank of England on a visit to the war he was doing so much to finance, was felled by a cannon shot when standing only a few feet from the king himself.

At sea, the older element for British warfare, the men of the Revolution did better, though again only after initial disaster. Herbert, who had commanded William's invasion armada, lost nearly a quarter of his fleet and the mastery of the Channel in the great action off Beachy Head in June 1691. Yet the following summer an even stronger Anglo-Dutch fleet of over ninety ships was mustered under another tried revolutionary, Edward Russell, who had carried the famous 'message of the seven' to William three years earlier. The battle that followed was one of the biggest naval encounters the world had so far known. More than 200 ships, mounting nearly 10,000 guns, and manned by about 100,000 men met off Barfleur and in two days, 19 and 20 May

37

1692, the naval power of Louis XIV was crippled. The effect of the so-called battle of la Hogue bears comparison with that of Trafalgar in the development of Britain as a maritime power.

In the background to the European war was the consciousness of Atlantic and transatlantic rivalry. Already there were some 200,000 British settlers on the far side of the Atlantic and Boston was on the way to becoming the first great British town outside the home islands. By contrast the French settlers, though more enterprising in exploration, were weaker in number. All through the nineties raids flickered between the two great colonizing powers with the Indian nations drawn more and more into the conflict. The protectionist system by which colonial goods could be carried only in British ships was finally secured by the Navigation Act of 1696, and the Westminster-controlled Customs service was established on both sides of the ocean.

The Customs was the only centrally controlled and locally available administrative service that the British Crown possessed. This unique network, by which much of the Crown's revenue was collected and through which alone attempts could be made to regulate the economy, lay under the ultimate control of the Treasury, and of the Treasury alone—a fact which goes a long way towards explaining the ultimate predominance of the Treasury among government departments as the eighteenth century advanced. Already in control of the Customs and the Excise before the Revolution, in the 1690s the Treasury added control over a whole series of further agencies which were brought into existence to finance the war—the commissioners of stamps, of hackney coaches, of hawkers and pedlars, and of salt—making it 'the largest departmental empire yet seen in English government'.*

The cost of William's war and Britain's arrival on the scene of world power was massive by any previous standard. Under James II the income and expenditure of the government had been in each case about £2 million a year. In the twelve and a half years between the Revolution and the death of William nearly £60 million was raised in taxation—an average of double the annual yield before the Revolution —and it was far from being enough. Expenditure over the same period, at £72 million, was at an annual rate two and a half times what it had been under James, creating a 'borrowing requirement' for the reign as a whole of nearly £13·5 million.

The fact that such a sum could now be borrowed and the methods employed in borrowing it dominate the political life of the time, and

* H. Roseveare, *The Treasury* (Allen Lane, 1969), p. 71.

add a financial and commercial flavour to Parliament and the growing partisanship of political society.* There was as yet no Cabinet system, though there were parliamentary managers, notably the so-called 'Junto' of Whig power-seekers who had helped to make the Revolution —Shrewsbury, Somers, Wharton, Russell and Montagu. But William was always disinclined to lean on any close-knit group of politicians, and took great care, throughout his reign, to keep most of the important departments, especially the Treasury, under groups of commissioners. Nevertheless it was through partisanship that the great strokes of war finance were achieved. The politician who most effectively grasped the connexion between the needs of government, the management of Parliament, and the bubbling energy of the City, was Charles Montagu.

Montagu, one of the first English ministers who can claim to be an intellectual, did not enter Parliament until 1689, when he was twenty-eight, and in the following ten years his name is associated with a long series of achievements in public finance: the inception of the National Debt in 1693; the foundation of the Bank of England in 1694; the recoinage of 1696; the first circulation of paper money (Exchequer Bills) in the same year; and the opening of the monopoly of the East India trade to a rival company in 1698. Almost all these operations were characterized by a gain to the Exchequer, competition between financial groups, and partisan action in Parliament. The growth of parliamentary finance and the development of party go hand in hand.

One cannot, however, satisfactorily identify parties with the interests of particular social classes. Party, which seems so precise a concept, is among the most elusive that historians employ. It is not enough to define it as organized opinion, or to speak merely of a struggle for power between 'ins' and 'outs'. Certainly the party struggle is not like the *Tales of Hoffman*, a series of scenes in which the same characters struggle under different labels in a perpetual contest between 'right' and 'left', between a force generally progressive and a force generally reactionary. Temperament and hereditary prejudice influence individuals in their choice of a political party quite as much as interest or opinion. The God-fearing, modest Newton was a Whig: his close friend and collaborator, the ebullient, sceptical Edmond Halley, was a Tory. Edward Harley began his political career as an ardent supporter of the Revolution and ended it as a Tory chieftain. It could be said

* See P. G. M. Dickson, *The Financial Revolution in England*, p. 10, for the figures which show that during all periods of war between 1688 and 1815 approximately one-third of war expenditure was met by loan. Also appendix 2.

that from 1689 onwards both Whigs and Tories were conservatives, but they differed in what they thought it most important to defend.

Party emerges when a society faces a new range of issues. The confrontation that follows need not reflect the application of any set of principles adopted initially and then worked out in relation to the issues. The only requirement is that when an issue is presented to the partisan he can be relied upon to react to one side or the other in a foreseeable way. If there are enough such issues it becomes possible, as it were, to join each set of partisan attitudes into a kind of profile, and by profiles of this kind it is possible to recognize a Whig or a Tory during the years following the Revolution.

The two words Whig and Tory both came from the peripheral kingdoms and originally described extremists. Whig was a fanatical Scottish robber, Tory fanatical Irish bandit. Until well into the eighteenth century they remained terms of abuse by which a party identified its opponents rather than rallying cries of self-identification. The terms are found before the Revolution—Burnet noticed them in 1679—but the Revolution and the attitudes taken during it are the decisive points in the two profiles. For the Whig the Revolution meant pluralism and a limited monarchy; for the Tory it had been a painful necessity which had hazarded the due and proper relationships of society. When the Whig spoke of the Revolution he tended to speak of 'honesty', meaning the frank recognition of the fact that Parliament had altered the succession to the Crown; and of 'liberty and property', meaning that the sanctity of private property was the only effective guarantee of individual liberty. The Tory attitude was summed up in the slightly different phrase, 'religion and property'. The property factor, it will be noticed, is common to both; but the emphasis is very different. For the Whig the relevance of property is to connect self-interest and the stability of society; for the Tory it is to symbolize habit and tradition as the guarantees of order.

It is an oversimplification to see the Whigs as the party of business and the Tories of seigneurial power. Some of the greatest aristocrats were resolute Whigs, and some of the keenest battles in the City of London were fought between rival groups of business men with Whig and Tory backing. But one can safely contrast emphasis on commerce as a point in the Whig profile, and emphasis on agriculture as a point in the Tory one. So, too, the Whigs tended to internationalism—to 'Dutch finance' under William, and 'no peace without Spain' under Anne; while the Tory was inward-looking and protectionist. The Tory was insular, the Whig European; the Whig favoured immigration, especially of refugee Protestants, the Tory deplored the admission of 'useless and necessitous foreigners'; the Tory tended to peace, the Whig to war.

In the new 'mixed constitution' of King, Lords and Commons, the Whig dwelt on the supremacy of Parliament and the Tory on the continuity symbolized by the monarchy. The Tory still hoped to ignore or repair the breaches in the Church of England's monopoly that had been made by the Toleration Act, and therefore had much to say about the privileges and incomes of the established clergy. The Whig was not averse to the penetration of the church by bishops who were prepared to take a broad view of the church's role in society, and derided its claims to be a separate estate of the realm or the peculiar repository of Christian truth in the southern half of the island. But it was to be some years yet before the decisive blow on this front was to be struck by Hoadly's Bangor sermon.

In the postrevolutionary House of Commons, representing as it did the acres rather than the bank balances of England, Tories constituted a natural majority. In a sense they were not a party but a body of opinion which could be marshalled, as Harley marshalled it in the nineties for purposes of opposition. The Whigs were more tightly organized. But while there were the rudiments of a party system, the concept of party government, where it was considered at all, was rejected with horror by most people. They considered that for the government to depend on a party majority was to remove power from the place where it rightly belonged—the Crown and Parliament—and allow it to be exercised by people who were responsible only to themselves. To the man of the late seventeenth century, and for his sons and grandsons late into the eighteenth, the Houses of Parliament could be divided in two different ways: into those who supported the Government—'The Court'; and those who were independent of it—'The Country'; and into those who were Tory in outlook and those who were Whig in outlook. The two kinds of division almost invariably cut across one another, and it was considered a serious mischance if, as happened in 1708, there was a close correspondence between the two, with 'The Court' relying principally on one body of opinion. Thus, to call such men as Marlborough or Godolphin Whigs or Tories is to read the politics of the nineteenth and twentieth centuries into the reigns of William and Anne. The purpose of such leaders in parliamentary management was to secure a majority for the one measure on which the life of government depended—the voting of money: the composition of that majority in terms of political opinion was of secondary importance. Hence the bitterness, which had important consequences, that Godolphin felt against the extreme Tories who tried to tack their party measure—the Occasional Conformity Bill—to the voting of money for the war.

Party feeling entered as strongly into questions connected with British commercial development overseas as it did into domestic issues. On no subject, perhaps, did it show itself more vigorously than over Britain's toe-hold in India, where the Dutch and Portuguese had so long been the leading European mercantile powers. In India, as in so many other British affairs, the Revolution coincides with decisive development, for in May 1687 Bombay had become the British headquarters on the western coast, and Governor Child wrote of his intention 'to establish such a politie of civill and military power, and create and secure such a large revenue to maintain both . . . as may bee the foundation of a large, well-grounded, sure English dominion in India for all time to come.' In 1690 the Mogul Emperor Aurangzebe confirmed the East India Company's rights in their main base on the eastern coast, Madras; and in 1696 Fort William was established on the site that was to grow into Calcutta, the port from which the Company exported, among other commodities, Bengal saltpetre for Marlborough's batteries and Admiral Russell's broadsides.

It was not to be expected that in the postrevolutionary world the profits of the India trade could be reserved for a group of monopolists who had been chartered by the Stuart monarchy. Parliament claimed a voice, and competitive business men a share. At Westminster and in India (where the rivalry at times verged on civil war), the struggle was fought for nearly twenty years, leading at different crises to the final downfall of the veteran Stuart politican Danby (elevated since the Revolution to the Dukedom of Leeds), and the expulsion of Speaker Trevor from the House of Commons. It is true that in the end the Old (Tory) and New (Whig) East India Companies were united by the supremely non-partisan Godolphin, and monopoly renewed its sway. But this time it was a parliamentary monopoly, not a royal one, and it was subject to parliamentary renewal from time to time. Parliament —and therefore English society as a whole—took the first step towards responsibility for India with the resolution of 1693 declaring that it alone had power to decide what Englishmen could trade there.

On the edges of the party conflict, and contributing to its bitterness by their existence, lay the two extremes that King James II had once tried to unite against the centre with his policy of Indulgence. Beyond the Tories lay the Jacobites, who refused to accept the new state of affairs and looked to the exiled king, now a client of Louis XIV. But the Jacobites were a shifting group. There were conscience-stricken men among them, but for many others devotion to the 'king over the water' was no more than the symptom of particular discontents: the nationalism of Celtic Ireland and Highland Scotland, and the resentment of the English Catholic minority at their continued exclusion from political life. The Jacobite cry could be no more than the passing indignation of a mob against high prices; and a carefully drafted letter to the court of the Old Pretender (of which even Marlborough was not guiltless) no more than a politician's reinsurance policy. Just the same, the Jacobite threat was enough to produce a true whiff of seventeenth-century politics in England. In 1696 Sir John Fenwick was sent to his death by Act of Attainder because a trial would have been too risky. It was the last time Parliament was to be used for such a purpose.

Dissent was a far more powerful and problematical interest than Catholicism, partly because of its economic strength, partly because it had once, within living memory, dominated British society, and partly because of the skill and determination of its propagandists. Until well after the beginning of the eighteenth century it was far from clear that the old Nonconformist spirit that had split the country for so long was in fact a declining force. Its dynamism showed chiefly in education. Dissenting education seemed to gather strength after the Toleration Act, with new academies coming into flourishing existence Some of the major municipal corporations were dominated by Dissenters, and Dissenters made up an important block vote in many parliamentary constituencies. Politicians with a dissenting background—men who even now rarely went to church—such as Robert Harley, Jack Howe, Paul Foley, Tom Wharton, made rapid progress in the Parliament of the nineties. In 1697 the Lord Mayor of London demonstrated his Nonconformity by ostentatiously going to a dissenting meeting house with the City mace carried before him. Within the same year the young high-church champion, Francis Atterbury, launched his *Letter to a Convocation Man* claiming the restoration of the church's rightful autonomy within the state.

But it was in 1696 also that an enemy of the church appeared who was far more dangerous to the religious basis of society than any Dissenter: an enemy that in the end was to damage Dissent even more than Anglicanism. A young Irishman named Thomas Toland published a work entitled *Christianity not Mysterious*, in which the whole notion of revealed religion came under attack. It was impossible said

Toland, for the mind to tolerate a logical inconsistency as a religious truth. The Deity must be supposed to preside over a rational religion. Toland was careful to say that his view did not involve him in rejecting a single word of the Bible. Many things might be outside normal experience, or even contrary to the observed laws of nature, without being against reason. It was logically conceivable that the sun should stand still, as recorded in the Book of Joshua. What was not conceivable was that it should stand still and move simultaneously. Toland was aiming chiefly against Roman Catholic doctrine, but the attack bit far deeper, into the whole fabric of an organized church from which 'revealed' truth should be accepted. Toland's book was never re-printed, and he spent the rest of his life as a second-rate Whig journalist under grave suspicion of atheism. But he had opened up the great controversy between natural and revealed religion which transformed the intellectual climate over the next twenty years.

The advance of rationalism went hand in hand with the advance of science. Newton might be a devout Anglican who maintained that his work only reinforced the religious view of the universe as the product of a single gigantic intellect. The young Bentley made his name by expounding this argument. But surely, said the rationalist, this meant that it was possible to discard the help of the Fathers and the traditions of the church, and found religion instead on a rational understanding of God's works? Few were yet so bold as to suggest there could be works without an author, yet because the necessity of the church seemed to be diminished, so did its authority.

Rationalism affected only a few. The importance of the new science to society in general was the new precision it gave to classification and to measurement. During the last thirty years of the seventeenth century the technology of measurement and observation—clocks, telescopes, microscopes and charts—had improved beyond all recognition, and had been put to potent use. Edmond Halley, having helped to see Newton's *Principia* through the press and taken his share with other scientists in the great enterprise of the recoinage, carried out the first English voyage ever to be devoted entirely to scientific research. Between 1698 and 1700, as master of the *Paramour,* he established the magnetic variation of the compass—an advance for navigators only to be compared with the introduction of the compass itself. The voyage took him far to the south of the Cape of Good Hope, recently colonized by the Dutch, to the island of St Helena. Within a few years of his return the *Paramour* was at sea again with Halley in command, establishing the first accurate charts of the currents in the English

Channel and the Irish Sea. At much the same time Flamsteed was producing the most accurate celestial map so far made. The names of both men are connected with Nathaniel Hooke's in the development of the barometer as a navigational aid. The design of ships might not change much, but in providing improved charts, tables, methods of calculation, and weather forecasting, the first great generation of British scientists transformed the safety and accuracy of sea-traffic.

The work that went into description and classification of what grew and moved on the earth's surface provided another base for economic advance. John Ray's immense labours produced the first effective botanical classification, carried to still greater perfection thirty years later by Linnaeus. Ray also laid the foundations for the taxonomy of insects, and Nehemiah Grew established the fact of sex in plants, with incalculable consequences for agriculture. Method, classification, reliably observed and recorded facts, were replacing speculation and tradition along a broad front, and it was not a coincidence that towards the end of the century there was a growing acceptance in Western Europe that the world itself should be measured by reference to Flamsteed's royal observatory at Greenwich.

Theory hurried into practice, often faster than technology would give support, and the scene of the nineties is crowded with inventors and projectors. In the three years from 1691 to 1693 some sixty patents were taken out—three times as many as the half-dozen or so a year that were granted before the Revolution. Salvage schemes with patent diving apparatus were a favourite, and some of these were notably successful. Savery's steam engine was to bear fruit in Newcomen's steam pump within a decade. Yarranton's tin-plate process helped to establish the industry in South Wales. But Tyzack's burglar alarm, Puckle's plastic wood and machine gun, East's pianola, Neale's pin-table, Austin's 'musket-proof chariot', Sutton's waterproof overcoat rested on ideas which it was to take much longer to realize.

The Peace of Rijswick in 1697 saw both the end of King William's war and his recognition by France as king of a Britain that was rapidly developing, both economically and socially. For the postrevolutionary system of government it was an end and a beginning. The settlement that contained France broadly within her frontiers of seventeen years previously was negotiated on William's behalf by the same man that had smoothed William's way to England as his emissary in the eighties, the Dutchman Dijkvelt. But when the European war was resumed four years later over the great question of the future of Spain's worldwide dominions, the leadership of the coalition against France had passed to English hands, and Britain had become the senior partner in the Protestant alliance. There is a sense in which Marlborough, and not Queen Anne, is the successor to William of Orange's political heritage.

In that same year, 1697, another career began which was to make as great an impression on the British consciousness as many of her own kings and heroes have done. Charles XII of Sweden, later projected by Voltaire's brilliant biographical study, was to be the ideal of the European man of action—and not least the Englishman's—for the next half century or more. Charles Edward, the Young Pretender, almost certainly modelled his behaviour on the Swedish king's burning simplicity and almost crazy lust for adventure, and he was not the only one. It is not difficult to see in Clive and Wolfe the same elevation in the face of the apparently impossible that was shown by the northern hero celebrated in one of Samuel Johnson's most famous poems.

By the end of the seventeenth century a thrusting and successful England was reaching out to the world, but there was one realm of failure, yet one that also made an indispensable contribution to British civilization in the eighteenth century. King William had never wanted to go to Ireland, but had been forced to by the English Anglicans and French intervention. The victory of the Anglo-Dutch forces on the Boyne in 1690, the slaughter of Aughrim, the campaigns of Ginkel in the west ending with the siege and surrender of Limerick, had all been part of the struggle against Louis, but they gave the Protestant third of the population the ascendancy that was to last for two centuries. The Irish Parliament became their instrument, and the patronage of the Irish church and administration accrued largely to a governing class based in England.

Thus a dangerous time-fuse was laid. Yet evil as was the growing oppression enforced by the ascendancy, there was also a cultural sharing throughout the two islands that led to permanent gains, with Dublin the second metropolis of the British Isles and Trinity College contributing as much to British civilization as Oxford, Cambridge, or the four universities of Scotland. Not only Swift—working in the nineties as Sir William Temple's literary secretary and forming the style that cuts us loose from the seventeenth century—but Congreve also began his career at Trinity. Later in the century they were to be followed by Goldsmith, Burke, and Sheridan. Berkeley and Percy, two of the most distinguished intellects among the Anglican bishops of the century, both occupied Irish dioceses. Dublin was the birthplace of Steele, and its Georgian architecture was the setting for the first performance of the greatest British musical work of the century, Handel's *Messiah*. The oppressive political character of British Ireland must not be allowed to conceal its intellectual glory.

Congreve, Swift's schoolfellow at Kilkenny,* was still under thirty when the seventeenth century ended, and by then had written everything for which he is remembered: *The Double Dealer, The Old Bachelor, Love for Love, The Mourning Bride* (with its famous opening line 'Music has charms to sooth a savage breast') and his most brilliant drama of all, *The Way of the World*. In the interstices of this prodigious achievement he dealt with a strange and eloquent voice from the past, in Jeremy Collier's swingeing attack on the theatre, *A Short View of the Stage*. It was impossible, indeed, even for a preacher so eloquent as Collier, to check the drama. Congreve was only one star among many, who included two other notable expatriates, Vanbrugh and Farquhar, one the son of an immigrant Flemish book-keeper, the other an Irishman like Congreve himself. Collier was the last of his kind, a non-juror almost to the point of Jacobitism who caused scandal by absolving on the scaffold the two condemned for plotting against King William's life. To him the brazen drama of Congreve and Vanbrugh was a symbol of the general rottenness and materialism of his time. But he was also, on a different plane, making a foray alongside Atterbury and the claim that the church had the right to be heard on all human affairs.

Collier's anachronistic stand nevertheless belongs also to a deeper and more lasting movement, of which more was to be heard under a different name. As far back as the 1670s spontaneous groups, assembling mainly in London, had set modestly about the work of reinvigorating the Christian life of laymen. These 'religious societies' seem to have owed their beginning to a clergyman of German origin, Anthony Horneck, and after surviving the initial suspicion of the authorities they grew in number to about forty by the end of the century. Social improvement as well as piety were among the objectives of these lower-middle-class men; and in 1694 the most celebrated group of all, the Society for the Propagation of Christian Knowledge, broke for the first time into the field of missionary activity overseas. Like other movements of revival the society movement waned with time, and had lost most of its vigour before the death of Queen Anne: but not

* Kilkenny Grammar School can claim to be next after Westminster in its record for producing great Augustans. Among its pupils were Swift, Congreve and Berkeley.

before it had attracted an enthusiastic admirer in the rector of the obscure Lincolnshire parish of Epworth, the Reverend Samuel Wesley.

Before the century was out one great visible landmark of the old order vanished. Whitehall Palace, where William had always refused to live because the smoke of London aggravated his asthma, was burned down. It had been a huge, rambling establishment, half royal residence, half Kremlin, where the old monarchy had had its centre and almost anyone was admitted. It was never rebuilt, though from time to time grandiose plans were proposed, and for most of the succeeding century, as if to emphasize the more modest role now allotted to the monarchy, the unpretentious Tudor palace of St James's was the only visible seat of government in London. It was nevertheless important to decide, as the century drew to a close, who was to be its tenant after William died.

This was not a merely dynastic question, and the Act of Settlement, which decided it in 1701, had far-reaching consequences for the inhabitants of the three kingdoms and the development of the constitution under which they lived. In the course of settling the Crown, after the deaths of William and of Anne, on the Princess Sophia of Hanover and her heirs, Parliament laid down with considerable precision how they expected the new monarch and his government to behave. Of all English Acts of Parliament, the Act of Settlement comes nearest to providing a written constitution. The monarch should be a practising Anglican; he should not leave England without the consent of Parliament; if he had foreign dominions (as William had, and as Princess Sophia of Hanover's heirs had) England should not be obliged automatically to defend them; and all ministerial decisions should be taken in the Privy Council and properly minuted. Parliament should be closed to foreigners, and to office-holders; and no office-holder should be a foreigner. Finally the judges, except with the consent of both Houses of Parliament, should be irremovable except on the demise of the Crown. So Tory sentiment registered its version of what the Revolution should have achieved: if the squires were not to have a king in their own image, at least they would have one who was dependent on a Parliament dominated by them.

English squires, assuredly: the Act of Settlement did not apply to Scotland, and therein lay much of the sting of Louis XIV's recognition of the exiled King James's son as rightful king of both England and Scotland when King James died in 1701. The power to dispose of the

Crown of Scotland when the lives of William and Anne were over belonged to the Parliament of Scotland, and it is not surprising that one of William's last recorded conversations, before he was killed in the riding accident he had risked all his life, was about the need to resume serious discussion about a full union of the two kingdoms.

Chapter 4 Church, Queen and
the Union with Scotland

Although the makings of the Augustan Age, which we think of as corresponding to the early decades of the eighteenth century, go back to the Revolution and before it, the accession of Anne in 1702 seems to mark a change of weather, of sunshine after thunder, morning after twilight, confidence after stress. Yet William was only just over fifty when he died, and Marlborough, whom he had just made commander-in-chief of his armies on the continent—and, significantly, at the same time, ambassador to Holland—was only a few months younger; and Marlborough, at any rate, had the greatest moments of his life before him. Anne, for her part, could not have been in greater contrast to her predecessor, the dynamic, devoted, dwarfish Protestant hero. Large, blousy, unhealthy, unsure of herself and neurotically dependent on others, Anne was almost ashamed of her crown, which she uneasily felt belonged to her half-brother.

One makes no excuse for dwelling on the monarch in an account of eighteenth-century society. The monarch was a social, even a magical, figure of an importance we find it hard to imagine, and possessed great political power even when someone as ineffective as Anne exercised it. But quite apart from all this, and from his headship of the government and the armed forces, the monarch was in respect of his household alone, the largest employer in England. The court of the English monarch in the early eighteenth century employed well over a thousand people, and the cost absorbed something like one-third of the whole cost of civil government, into which it imperceptibly shaded. The purchasing power, the patronage, and the influence of this already anachronistic organization were very extensive. Chaplaincies (there were forty-two chaplains) led to bishoprics and deaneries; the Groom of the Stole (an office held by Sarah Churchill during Anne's reign and abolished in Victoria's, when the queen discovered that Stole meant Close Stool) received £5,000 a year and upwards. To control such patronage, to be able to use it for the reward of political
50

or official services, whether in Parliament or out of it, gave any monarch immense power.*

But this was by no means all. The monarch was a great property owner in his own right, with large estates in the neighbourhood of London, in Lancashire, and when there was no Prince of Wales, as was the case under Anne, in Cornwall. He was the patron of hundreds of livings, and nominated most of the cathedral clergy. He personally appointed all the officers of the armed forces, and exercised a particular control over his household troops, who were paid at much higher rates than ordinary soldiers. In certain towns, such as Windsor, his mere value as a customer made him a force in elections. His private resources made him the richest as well as the most ceremonially dignified person in the country.

Anne resumed one important area of social power which the busy William had been content to leave to others. Under William the royal patronage of the church had been left to a committee which Anne promptly brought to an end, and for the next twelve years the most effective voice in all church matters was her adviser John Sharp, Archbishop of York. Sharp was a safe man, a moderate Tory who had accepted the Revolution settlement, in which after all he had had his part—for it was his suspension by James II for an anti-Catholic sermon from his pulpit in St Giles in the Fields, that had led to the storm by which Compton and the whole body of London clergy had become involved in the Revolutionary conspiracy. On the face of things, Sharp's sway over the church achieved much for the institution that had been so badly shaken in 1688-9. St Paul's was completed and Parliament was persuaded, in 1710, to vote funds for the first major building programme ever undertaken by an English House of Commons: fifty new churches for the crowded capital. The salaries of the clergy were improved by the conversion of the so-called 'first fruits and tenths' into 'Queen Anne's Bounty', a fund for the augmentation of the poorer livings.

But these benefits to the church betrayed the fact that it was on the defensive, or at any rate was pressing hard to recover lost ground. The open Dissenters, tolerated but excluded from power, might no longer be the threat which Anglican pulpits had always proclaimed. The menace against which the church and its backers in Parliament struggled most violently was the Dissenter who masqueraded as an Anglican, the man who managed, by a purely token conformity, to

* For a most readable account of the intricacies of the English court in the early eighteenth century, see J. M. Beattie, *The English Court in the Reign of George I.*

exercise full political rights. If one substitutes the expression 'fellow traveller' for 'occasional conformist' it is possible to catch something of the passion with which the squires of Anne's first Parliament brought forward the Occasional Conformity Bill. It was not to pass then, but it was to provide at least two of the great crises of the decade —the struggle over 'The Tack', and the hysteria over Sacheverell.

The Anglican reaction was not confined to English society. It was far more severe in the ravaged society of Ireland, where William's anxiety to keep on good terms with his Catholic allies on the continent had made him hold the Anglo-Irish in check. Under Anne repression had a free rein: non-Anglicans, whether Catholics or Presbyterians, were not only excluded from the Irish Parliament and from all public offices, but they were deprived of the vote. One disability was heaped on another, much as Louis XIV had heaped disabilities on the Huguenots. The right to buy or inherit land, the right to own a horse of more than a certain value, the right to enter most trades, were all denied to non-Anglicans in a series of penal statutes that were not the less oppressive because they were hard to enforce, and were often enforced only sporadically. It is significant that except in time of war the greater part of the British army was stationed in Ireland throughout the eighteenth century.

If the hand of Anglicanism fell heavily in Ireland, it was felt very little in the social structure of Britain's possessions on other continents. No missionary effort was launched in India—a negative decision which was to have permanent consequences on the development of the British presence there. The East India Company even avoided the expense of ships' chaplains required by law, by keeping the tonnage of East Indiamen below the level at which a chaplain was compulsory. In America the Society for the Propagation of the Gospel (which had been split off from the Society for the Propagation of Christian Knowledge in 1701 to work in the mission field) was the only substantial Anglican agency, and it depended entirely on voluntary contributions. The Anglican organization of parishes, beneficed clergy, and bishops was never effectively exported. Instead the Bishop of London, throughout the eighteenth century, struggled with a vague responsibility for the church in America, and the fields of education and preaching on the other side of the Atlantic were largely left to Nonconformists, or, later, to the followers of Wesley and Whitefield. Berkeley's idea of an Anglican university in Bermuda, carrying civilization and religion to the American Indians, remained a dream. Yale College, founded in the same year as the Society for the Propagation of the Gospel was, like Harvard, a Non-conformist institution. Dissenting education might not have a future in Britain, but in America it was to provide the basis for a system which rejected clerical authority.

The eyes of Englishmen were not at that moment on America but on Europe, where the prophecy Marvell had once made about Cromwell seemed to be coming true in Marlborough:

As Caesar, he, ere long, to Gaul,
To Italy an Hannibal

Certainly the scene of action seemed to be moving away from the line of the Channel and the Low Countries, where so much of William's war had been fought. In 1702 came the first British victory of the war in the destruction of the Franco-Spanish treasure fleet in Vigo Bay. So opened the land campaign in the Peninsula which had almost as much impact on British politics and social life as the more spectacular operations in central Europe and the Low Countries. Vigo led directly to the Methuen Treaties which secured Portugal as an ally of Britain for the next two centuries, and with it a permanent naval footing for the South Atlantic and the Mediterranean. It also transformed the drinking habits of the English upper classes by giving port a preferential advantage over claret and brandy. Port gained not only a market but a special status among wines, as if to commemorate the years in which Britain exploded onto the world stage.

On 13 July 1704 the foothold in Portugal was used to make a second British lodgement in southern Europe. Admirals Rooke and Byng, supported by a land force under the German princeling George of Hesse, occupied the rock of Gibraltar, almost without firing a shot. It would be possible, from now on, for a British fleet to operate in the Mediterranean without returning regularly to its home bases.

Exactly a month later came the victory that registered Britain as a major European power. The scene, almost precisely in the middle of the continent, could hardly have been better chosen. Marlborough, now a duke, had in three months marched his polyglot army clean across the front of the French armies on the Rhine, through the Black Forest, to a point on the Danube about twenty miles north of Augsburg. There, in combination with the emperor's forces under Prince Eugene, he destroyed the most powerful of the French armies, under Marshal Tallard. Never before had one of Louis XIV's armies been defeated in a direct encounter. By general consent the battle of Blenheim was regarded as a British victory, though only a quarter of the troops taking part in it were actually British. Vienna was saved from the French, and the long-enduring alliance between the Austrian Empire and the new island power, which stabilized European diplomacy until the middle of the century, was firmly established. The news, carried by an officer who took eight days to reach London travelling day and night, was embodied not in a formal despatch but in a letter from Marlborough to his wife. 'I have not time to say more, but to beg you will give my duty to the Queen, and let her know that Her Army has had a Glorious Victory.'

The moral effect of Blenheim was electric, but it exemplified more than a new military power. Its location, the nature of the forces taking part, and the source of their pay, neatly demonstrate a lasting economic development. The track followed by Marlborough's army from the Low Countries to the Danube was to be the path along which British goods flowed into central Europe for the next eighty years; and the pay of that army was provided by foreign exchange arising from investment through Amsterdam in British government funds. Among the things that made the British eighteenth century what it was almost none is more important than the financial partnership of Britain and Holland which had replaced the old commercial rivalry.

Amsterdam remained the major financial centre of Europe for many years after the Dutch had ceased to be the greatest of the trading nations; but the proceeds of the invisible trade from which Holland prospered so well were invested on an increasing scale in the funds of the country where stability seemed best assured—namely Britain. Dutch banks, Dutch widows and retired sea-captains, Dutch insurers and ship owners, found it easy and safe to put their capital into the securities backed by the British Parliament. His own former countrymen cannot have been far from King William's mind when, in his last speech from the throne, he urged that 'They shall never be losers who trust to Parliamentary security.' So, for nearly a century Holland helped her old economic rival by building up a stake which identified her political interest with British stability, and indirectly furnished British enterprise with a steady flow of funds. Britain prospered, though apparently loaded with public debt: a poor Exchequer but a wealthy community. Holland's Exchequer flourished while her industry, and eventually her visible overseas trade and her political influence, declined through starvation of investment.

Although the picture of politics under Anne is far from stable it was undergoing what Professor Plumb has called in his *The Growth of*

Political Stability in England 'a process of definition'—a definition of the influence of particular families and interests to correspond with their importance in society, a definition of how office was held and changed, and a definition of how Parliament itself, now placed socially as well as politically at the centre of affairs, should operate in relation to an executive government which had more resources in terms of men, money, and patronage, than ever before. Round this process of defining the role and nature of Parliament the party warfare of Anne's reign took place. The government dominated by Marlborough and Godolphin (who was Lord High Treasurer from 1702 to 1710) tried to follow the style of William III and ride on the backs of the disputing factions. But below them two unresolved views were in conflict. One, associated with the Whigs of the Junto, stood for the penetration of the legislature by party politicians, and for a spoils system in which jobs would be the reward of loyalty to the party leaders. The other view saw executive and Parliament—or at any rate executive and House of Commons—as distinct. According to these politicians—the Tories—the House of Commons should be purged of all those who might pollute it by their obligations to the executive—ministers, government officials, the younger sons of peers. The Whig view was increasingly favoured by the most powerful members of the aristocracy, the Tory by the generality of the landed gentry. It was the Tory view that underlay the Act of Settlement and the pressure to carry it further was regular and constant. Again and again 'Place Bills' were brought forward trying to exclude office-holders from Parliament; in 1696 the first of the Land Qualification Bills, requiring every M.P. to have substantial landed property as a condition of taking his seat, was pushed through the Commons but failed through Whig opposition in the Lords. The typical Tory Member of Parliament under Anne dreamed of the day when the House would consist exclusively of men like himself, each equipped with a certificate guaranteeing the possession of a minimum rent roll of £500 a year and regular attendance at Anglican communion.

The majority of the House of Commons was Tory in every one of Queen Anne's Parliaments except that of 1708, though the majority in 1705 was too small to be a guarantee of Tory predominance in default of effective whipping. The Tories could always depend on more safe seats than the Whigs—one recent estimate puts the constituencies which regularly returned Tories at 104 as against 74 which regularly returned Whigs. Significantly thirty of these Tory seats were in county constituencies, as against only four from counties that regularly voted Whig. Safe Tory seats were especially plentiful in Wales. Too much cannot be built on party affiliations, since the parties were groupings of opinion and family interest rather than organizations, but taking the reign as a whole it is not unreasonable to say that about five-twelfths of all those returned to Parliament were Tory in outlook, four-twelfths were Whig, and the remaining three-twelfths were non-party either because they were officials and therefore always voted for the government, or did not vote consistently for one outlook or the other.

The Tory inclination of the Commons was counterbalanced by Whig power in the House of Lords. All the members of the Whig Junto of Anne's reign were peers. Many of the bishops appointed in the wake of the Revolution were Whigs. But the Whiggish outlook of the Lords needs more explanation than this. A good many peers—Marlborough and Godolphin themselves were among them—had risen to the peerage through government service, and so were naturally disposed to the view that Parliament could not stand aside from the executive, but should collaborate with it. Some of the most powerful noblemen of all, men who owned whole counties and themselves nominated members for boroughs in the Lower House, also preferred the Whig view. The Revolution had delivered them from the fate of the French nobility and the gaudy ignominy of depending on an all-powerful central monarchy; and they had no intention of becoming dependent on a Parliament of squires instead. The great noblemen's seats of France date from the sixteenth century or earlier: those of England belong for the most part to the seventeenth century onwards, and especially to the eighteenth. Chatsworth, the greatest of them all, was completed in 1707, a monument to the Cavendish duke who had helped to make the Revolution. Their owners' interest in the social and business life of the London city state was at least as great as the value they put on even the largest of rent rolls. They might in some ways be the supreme representatives of the countryside, but they preferred letting their land to farming it themselves. They were proud to be lords lieutenant in their counties, but they also wanted the cash and influence that went with government office.

One significant cultural feature may illustrate the immense difference between the feudal nobility of Germany or the court nobility of France, and the English political peerage. No instance is recorded of an English nobleman maintaining that characteristic symbol of rule, an orchestra, and rarely was a nobleman patron of a composer. Whereas on the continent music was nourished by the small courts, in England the audience was far more widely diffused. Even the great Duke of Chandos, who maintained a small choir at his grand house at Edgware, was no true nobleman, having made his fortune by handling the army pay account in Marlborough's wars. By contrast the first public concert the world ever knew was staged in London in 1672; the Three Choirs Festival dates from 1724. By the early eighteenth century London was responding to the popular demand for music by rivalling Amsterdam as the major centre for music publishing in western Europe. Both Ranelagh and Vauxhall, the Londoner's favourite resorts for an evening out, always offered concerts. But the pleasure of music was not confined to London, any more than to a leisured class: it was widely diffused, often with the parish church as its focus, but not always. There was a celebrated song school based on the church of Newark; 'a band of two viols and a bass, playing trios of Kamell and Lampugnani, went to the wake every year at Ratby'; 'at Christmas the choir of Shepshed with voices and instruments took circuit round the town.' These were tiny Nottinghamshire villages. Domestic and municipal music flourished in eighteenth-century England at the humblest levels of society. Even so modest a town as Ashby de la Zouch was equal to a production of *Acis and Galatea*; many corporations maintained 'waits'. Defoe rhapsodized about the charms of Epsom, the lower middle-class resort corresponding to more fashionable Bath and Tunbridge Wells—where as evening falls 'the bowling green begins to fill, the music strikes up in the great room, and the company draws together apace'.*

Most peers were landowners, but many of them were not of particularly ancient race, and they were by no means a military cast. Not very far back in the ancestry of many of the English peers was a business man; and for years the monarchy had used seats in the House of Lords as a reward for political and military services. Even so, the temporal peerage at the time of the Revolution had numbered less than one hundred. William was generous with new peerages—mainly for politicians—and towards the end of Anne's reign Robert Harley conclusively politicized the House of Lords by creating twelve peers at a stroke to crack the Whig majority. To show how far lordship was from gentility it needed only George I's remark—significant as coming from a man who well understood the difference between feudal and political nobility—that though he could not make Bateman, the city merchant's son, a gentleman, he supposed he could make him a peer. By the middle of the century there were more than 150 peers.

* *A Tour Thro' the Whole Island of Great Britain* (1724 ed.), vol. 1, part 2, p. 112.

In the Lords, the city state and the countryside were fused. The object of a man who made his fortune in the city was to turn it into land, and move into the gentry in the next generation. And not only that. An object of many noblemen was to acquire urban building land in and around London, with the result that the street names of London today read like a roll-call of the aristocracy: Grosvenor and Bedford, Northampton and Portland, Cavendish and Grafton, represent estates on the map of London which yielded rents and influence no less important than those which these ducal families controlled in their counties. Few historical stereotypes are less accurate than that of the English peer as a feudal aristocrat.

As Britain's power grew, society became less insular. The British scientists were beginning to loom as large in Europe as the British parliamentary experiment or Marlborough's military presence. Newton's immense range, comprehending mathematics, physics, chemistry, astronomy and zoology; and the fact that in all the sciences he sought explanation rather than system, made him an international exemplar. Algarotti, for whom Lady Mary Wortley Montagu broke her heart, was to make his name from translating and popularizing Newton on the continent, but the fame of the English scientist long preceded his translation. Now president of the Royal Society, he envisaged it as the instrument through which the gigantic task of bringing the sciences to perfection would gradually be completed; and was to write towards the end of his life in his 'Scheme for Establishing the Royal Society', under which it was to be endowed as a research institution: 'Natural Philosophy consists in discovering the frame and operations of Nature, and reducing them, as far as may be, to general Rules or Laws,—establishing these rules by observations and experiments, and thence deducing the causes and effects of things.' The pious Newton laid the axe at the root of theism. It was to be wielded with deadly effect against the organized support of theism by the great European propagandist who was perhaps the most notable of Newton's admirers—Voltaire.

By the time Newton published his last major work, the *Opticks,* in 1704, the generation that had made the scientific revolution was dropping away. The work on light published in the *Opticks* had itself been done twenty years earlier. John Ray, having issued the last of his *Historia Plantarum* in the year of Blenheim, died in 1705. Locke died in 1704, and so did Pepys, who had given so much of his organizing capacity to the Royal Society. Evelyn followed them in 1706. Newton, it is true, was to survive another score of years, and Halley another forty, as secretary of the Royal Society and Astronomer Royal, but there were to be no new giants to replace them. Newton's scheme for a state-endowed Royal Society remained no more than a draft found among his papers after his death. Science, after passing through a theoretical stage of unprecedented brilliance was to become a field on the one hand for outstanding craftsmen, and on the other for noble amateurs.

An event of great importance to the development of British society—strictly indeed, its creation—was now becoming possible. The confidence bred by the victory on the Danube pointed the way psychologically to the abolition of the Tweed as a frontier. In the year before Blenheim the union of England and Scotland had suddenly seemed further off than ever. Negotiations had broken down over English selfishness (the precious colonial trade was to remain closed to the Scots, as it was to the Irish), and over Scottish suspicion about the financial burdens they would be asked to assume in helping to service the English National Debt. In 1704 the breach of negotiations had developed into open hostility, with the Parliaments of Edinburgh and Westminster engaging in a legislative duel, in the course of which Scotland enacted that succession to the Scottish Crown should not follow the English succession unless there was a full economic union, and England set a time limit after which all Scots would be treated as aliens. The first of these measures—the so-called Act of Security—which virtually threatened republicanism and a revival of the 'auld alliance' between Scotland and France, had received a reluctant royal assent from Queen Anne during the interval between the victory of Blenheim and the arrival of the news in London.

Yet by the spring of 1706 the two nations had appointed commissioners to negotiate a union, and within three months the terms were agreed. What had happened to change an embittered atmosphere in which, only a year previously, English sailors had been judicially murdered in an ugly outbreak of national passion in Edinburgh?

Part of the answer is to be found in a turn of English domestic politics by which the forces of the city state and the court obtained a temporary ascendancy over the squirearchy at Westminster. The general election of 1705 had followed on a desperate Tory plan to carry their favourite legislation against occasional conformity by 'tacking' it to the voting of money for the war—a manoeuvre which Godolphin, the Lord Treasurer, considered so disruptive as to make government impossible.

In the ensuing election, therefore, the whole influence of the government was thrown against those Tories who were 'tackers'. There were, it is true, many Tories who had not voted heroically for the 'tack'—the so-called 'sneakers'—but the highly organized Junto Whigs saw to it that Toryism thus divided was hammered without distinction when it came to the election and the machinery of party came into play. The result was a House of Commons from which fifty-four of the most inveterate Tories had been ousted, and the Court could command a majority only if it depended on the Whigs.

Union, the achievement of the Parliament of 1705, was not an issue in the campaign by which it was elected. But the attitudes of the two parties to Union were clearly differentiated. The Tories disliked it as a breach in the restrictive system they believed in and as likely to strengthen the dissenters whom they hated and feared; while the Whig political chiefs calculated (rightly) that adding a contingent of Scottish members to an enlarged Westminster Parliament offered the one chance of changing a natural balance in the House of Commons that would always favour the Tories. In terms of politics Scotland was to be called into a British Parliament to redress the balance between London and the shires. For the sake of this political prize the victorious Whigs were willing to offer generous terms to Scotland.

Then, in May 1706, the greatest of Marlborough's victories, Ramillies, gave a final boost to the confidence and magnetism of England. The French threat to the Low Countries was finally destroyed. The young Duke of Argyll, who had personally led the storming of the village of Ramillies, returned to Scotland that summer to head a Whiggish ministry in Edinburgh. He was at the same time the greatest of the clan chieftains and inheritor of a tradition of collaboration with the Lowlands. He was soon to be followed by Daniel Defoe, the agent of the English Secretary of State, Robert Harley, with the plainest instructions. 'You must show them,' wrote Harley, 'this is such an opportunity as once lost or neglected is not again to be recovered. England never was before in so good a disposition to make such large concessions.'

The opportunity was seized, and an ancient problem was peacefully solved—a thing rare in history. Scotland was admitted to the colonial trade and the potentialities of empire, from which she was to make so much. The Kirk, at the moment when rationalism had made its first inroads on theism, was guaranteed for all time continuing. The losses of the Darien Company were paid off by 'the Equivalent' from the English Exchequer, representing the burden assumed by the

Scottish taxpayer in relation to the English National Debt. The Scottish legal system remained intact, except that (after some subsequent dispute) the ultimate appellate jurisdiction of the House of Lords now applied to the whole kingdom. But the Scottish legislature and executive were dismantled, and the representation of Scotland at Westminster fixed at sixteen peers and forty-five commoners. The terms were generous in relation to the wealth Scotland brought to the Union, but mean in relation to the size of her population.

The importance of the Union went far beyond adding something short of a million people to the kingdom: it eliminated one of the fundamental instabilities of the island, and although there were to be troubles still in both England and Scotland, and between them, the century was to show the advantages of the Union to both countries, but more especially to the northern one. By the time Adam Smith wrote, seventy years after the Union, it would no longer be possible to sneer, as an English visitor put it in 1705, that the Scots had only eight commandments, because they had nothing to covet, and nothing to steal; or to feel, on crossing the Border that one was entering 'the most barbarous country in the world'.

However, the Scots were not rapidly assimilated into the main stream of British life. Equal in citizenship they might be, but their relative poverty, their very different speech (Carlyle and Hume spent years learning to speak southern English), and their tendency to clannishness, made them objects of dislike and suspicion in the south for two generations. Hostility to Scotsmen was one of the few characteristics shared by the Tory Dr Johnson and the radical Jack Wilkes. Yet the Scots made their way in the south, and above all in London, where in the next generation William Murray took up the law to become the greatest of eighteenth-century judges, David Malloch changed his name to Mallet and established himself as a literary entrepreneur, and James Thomson, after producing *The Seasons* (dedicated to a succession of four promising English politicians) was to crown the patriotism of the Union by writing 'Rule Britannia'.*

The Union represents the highest achievement of Whig statesmanship—bold, decisive, imaginative, and above all enduring. Even greater power was to come into the Junto's hands when the first Parliament of Great Britain assembled in 1708, but after that, for a time at least,

* One further field of Scottish distinction was architecture. Of the major architects in the eighteenth century no fewer than four were Scots—James Gibbs (1682–1754), Surveyor to the New Churches Commissioners and designer of, among other buildings, St Martin-in-the-Fields; Robert Mylne (1734–1811), who built Blackfriars Bridge; Robert Adam; and William Chambers.

the glimpse of the Whig Promised Land was to vanish. The reasons for the sudden reversal of fortune must be sought in the surprisingly resilient power of the church and all it stood for, and in a disaster abroad of which little is heard in traditional English history. On 25 August 1707, less than four months after the inauguration of the new state of Great Britain on 1 May, the British army in Spain, under its Dutch general Ginkel, was defeated and for the most part made prisoner by the French under the command of James II's illegitimate son, the Duke of Berwick. This humiliation of Almanza, and its aftermath in British politics, was to show how thin was the skin of confidence in the new kingdom.

Chapter 5   The Augustan World

The social contrast between London and the rest of the country grew sharper in the reign of Anne. Addison, in the *Spectator*, No. 112, thought weekly church a very good thing for country people. They would soon, he said, 'degenerate into a kind of savages and barbarians, were there not such frequent returns of a stated time, in which the whole village meet together . . . to . . . hear their duties explained to them.' The very lightness of Addison's touch shows how acceptable the idea was, and when he goes on to say that 'a country fellow distinguishes himself as much in the church-yard as a citizen does upon the Change', the detachment of London urbanism becomes obvious: and not only detachment but superiority.

London, in the middle years of Anne's reign, rejoiced in much that was completely new, and much of what then seemed so new has demonstrated its extraordinary vigour by surviving, even today, as old and faded. The periodical essays, of which the first great series was launched with Addison's *Tatler* in 1709, exemplify the freshness of metropolitan society, contempt for the 'reverend vegetables' outside it, and a general desire to raise standards of breeding to something more urbane. By September 1710 Addison was writing the first piece of journalism ever to appear in English on the subject of advertisements. 'The great art in writing advertisements,' observed *Tatler* 224, 'is the finding out a proper method to catch the reader's eye'; and, more pointedly still, 'a man that is by no means big enough for the gazette, may easily creep into the advertisements'.

What was new was not only the advertisement itself shyly making its appearance, but the evidence it provided of a market for small luxuries such as blacking, patent medicines, cosmetics, and textbooks. Much else was new also. The highest strut of the lantern of St Paul's was placed in position, completing the outline of a triumphant building which in size and style proclaimed London a European capital—a national temple, rather than a city cathedral. New schemes for piped water based on the Hampstead ponds and the New River

Head at Islington were in progress; a modicum of street lighting was being provided. Tea, coffee, and chocolate, though still expensive, were beginning to be within the reach of middle-class purses. Notable foreign musicians—Handel among them—were beginning to find their way to London in the confidence that they would find audiences.

The open coffee house was characteristic of this urban civilization, and had been multiplying as an amenity for the past forty years. By the early years of the eighteenth century there were some hundreds of these establishments, serving social purposes far more important than coffee. In many respects they served as offices. Dealers in different commodities, captains of ships on certain routes, stockbrokers, insurance men, journalists, systematically attended particular coffee houses during set hours, to receive visitors and collect correspondence. Some papers, such as Swift's *Guardian*, were virtually edited in coffee houses. Although, as in Macaulay's celebrated catalogue of the principal houses, many had particular clienteles, their openness is one of their most striking features. 'Here you will see,' wrote Macky in 1714, 'blue and green ribbons,* sitting familiarly and talking with the same freedom as if they had left their quality and degrees of distance at home, and a stranger tastes with pleasure the universal liberty of speech of the English nation.' But the habit and openness were not confined to the possessors of stars and garters. 'Workmen,' wrote the Swiss tourist de Saussure in 1727, 'habitually begin the day by going to coffee-rooms in order to read the daily news. Nothing is more entertaining than hearing men of this class discussing politics and topics of interest concerning royalty.' By 'workmen', of course, de Saussure meant tradesmen and craftsmen, not labourers, but the range between the quotations is great nevertheless.

It was the fate of the coffee house not to develop on the same lines as the continental café to which it originally corresponded. As the social arteries of the eighteenth century hardened the differentiation of the coffee houses grew into exclusiveness. Some became clubs, as White's coffee house did in 1730. Garraways' for long the haunt of the nascent profession of stockbroking, became the nucleus of the Stock Exchange, and Lloyd's of Lloyd's. By the middle of the century the coffee house had given way to the club, where the expression 'coffee room' for the dining room still commemorates the origins.

But of all the novelties multiplied by urban life, the most significant was the reformation of the written language, and through it (for what was written was in large measure intended to be read aloud) of a

* I.e. the ribbons of the Garter and St Patrick respectively.

standard upper-class English.* The journalism of Addison, Steele, and Swift, which seems stilted to the modern ear, was the creation of a very recent period, and an admirable vehicle for the spread of ideas. It was easy to read, its cadences were uniform, its sentences moved in accordance with expectation instead of rambling and curling back on themselves to fetch a conceit or explore a byway. The gulf that separates the sonorous and literary diction of Milton from the workmanlike clarity of, say, Defoe, is far wider than the gap between Defoe's style and that of journalists writing more than a hundred years after him, such as Leigh Hunt or Cobbett; yet Defoe was already a schoolboy when Milton died.

As late as the 1720s Defoe was finding the Somerset people almost impossible to understand. The young Alexander Carlyle, a clergyman's son in the comparatively civilized Lothian parish of Prestonpans, was taught by a widowed aunt from London 'to read English with a just pronunciation and a very tolerable accent—an accomplishment which in those days was very rare.' Welsh was still the main language throughout Wales, and even on the fringes of England. In Cornwall, there were still pockets of Gaelic speakers at the beginning of the century. It would not be an unreasonable claim to say that the eighteenth century witnessed the virtual conquest of the island by standard English.

Whereas German, Italian, and even French national identity rests in large measure on the fellowship of those who speak those languages, it was never the case that England as a nation was thought of as coterminous with those who spoke English, though standard English was to become the general language of the British. British national feeling was above all geographical and political, with the older nuggets of English, Welsh, and Scottish national identity still embedded in it. Such a nation, drawing its patriotic sense from so many sources, and distinguishing its citizens by the non-linguistic criterion of birth within geographical limits, possessed special advantages as a colonizing power.

The year 1708, in which the Whigs reaped the political harvest of the Union, and were for the first and only time returned to power with a clear partisan majority, richly demonstrates the growing internationalism of this curiously provincial state. In July Marlborough won the third of his great victories at Oudenarde, near Ghent, as a

---

* Today we shrink from sermons: in the eighteenth century they were the favourite form of reading. They were also the basic form of composition, and were designed for cadence. The tradition of the sermon has much to do with the fact that eighteenth-century English prose can always be read aloud.

result of which he found himself in command of a combined force of nearly 80,000 men, and without any serious opposing army between him and Paris. In September another pace was taken into the Mediterranean by the capture of Minorca—ostensibly in support of the Hapsburg candidate to the throne of Spain, but actually to serve as a major British base in the Mediterranean. It was made clear to the Hapsburg claimant, Charles III, that continued British support for his cause would depend on his willingness to make the island over to his allies.

Nor, with the advent of the Whigs to effective power, was internationalism solely a question of expansion abroad. Britain, according to the Whig view that there was an international Protestant interest, should be open to foreign Protestants, whether from France or the Rhineland, who had been driven to leave their homes by the persecution of Louis XIV. The proposal for a 'general naturalization' to confer British citizenship on such refugees, was to cost the Whigs the next election; but the cosmopolitan idea would remain a specifically Whig aim even in the shallows of Pelhamite Whiggery almost fifty years later.

Who were they, these founding fathers of Whig politics, whose principles were powerful enough, in an idealized form, to provide a background to the American constitution and fuel for British reform a hundred years after Queen Anne's death? There was Russell, the victor of La Hogue, now Earl of Orford, the professional sailor who had risen in James II's navy and quarrelled with his master: he had taken in commemoration of his victory, the title of Viscount Barfleur —the first Englishman to make such a capture; Montagu, the intellectual turned to finance, who had patronized Steele, Addison, Halley and Newton, and sailed so near the wind that even in the great days following 1708 it was not possible to give him office; Somers, the quiet, ruthless lawyer, whose passion for the written word caused him to accumulate almost every pamphlet published in that pamphleteering age; and the uproarious Wharton, son of a Puritan nobleman, author of at any rate the words of the Whig marching song 'Lilliburlero', a tireless political campaigner, and one of the first systematizers of constituency 'interest'. They were, on the whole, self-made men, and very far from the high aristocratic Whigs whom Burke was to venerate as the 'forest trees' of English politics. Each in his own way had carved out his own career, and was known to have done so. In the Kit-Cat Club at Barn Elms, where they took their ease, they recruited aspiring politicians who would form the next Whig generation: Robert Walpole, Stanhope, the younger Sutherland. These three were gentry, but some of the rising young Whigs were of very obscure origin—James Craggs, for instance. And characteristically the Kit-Cat met under the patronage of the greatest publisher of his time, Jacob Tonson, whose fortune was founded on his possession of the copyright of Milton.

Naturalization, weariness with the war, and the bottled-up anxieties of the Church of England, were fatal to the Whig ascendancy. In September 1709, in a gap in the woods not far from Mons, Marlborough won the last of his victories, the bloody battle of Malplaquet. There were bitter cries about 'the butcher's bill' with hardly a thought that the chief sufferers on the allied side had been the Dutch. Their losses were four times as great as the British, and their land forces were never to recover from that terrible blow. 'The Dutch', wrote the devout Colonel Blackadder after the battle, 'have suffered most in the battle of any. Their infantry is quite shattered . . . It is a wonder to me the British escape so cheap, who are the most heaven-daring sinners in this army. But God's judgments are a great depth.'

Worse was to follow. The great Whig cry of 'no peace without Spain' foundered in Stanhope's disastrous Spanish campaign of 1710, which ended with the surrender of Stanhope at Brihuega with 4,000 British troops—more than twice Marlborough's British losses at Malplaquet. The plan of excluding the Bourbons from Spain, for which the war had been begun, could no longer be sustained. Almost simultaneously the shires and the rectories exploded in the great movement of protest associated with the name of Henry Sacheverell.

The convulsion produced by Sacheverell was not religious, and it was not merely political: it was social. His text—'In peril among false brethren'—was designed to play on atavistic fears, and the occasion for his sermon—5 November—was intended as a provocation. The power of the pulpit and the press had never been more effectively demonstrated, 40,000 copies of the sermon being printed. The fatal decision to prosecute him, the excitement of his trial, and the triviality of his punishment (his conviction was only arrived at by a margin of seventeen in a packed House of Lords) allowed a countrywide demonstration of Toryism. Sacheverell, after a sentence of three years' suspension from preaching, made a progress from London to Oxford (where he was solemnly received by the Vice-Chancellor) and thence proceeded triumphantly to Shropshire, the bells being rung in almost every church along the route as he passed through. The effect was felt as far afield as the North Riding of Yorkshire, and in 1710 the House of Commons resumed its natural, shire-oriented complexion. Robert

Harley, the first man to be spoken of as 'Prime Minister', entered on his four years of office with the resolution to end the war and consolidate its political and commercial gains with the support of the squires.

The squires expected their price. At long last the Act against occasional conformity was passed, to be reinforced, four years later by the even more aggressive Schism Act, which aimed at the total suppression of Nonconformist education. No one was to keep a school or teach in one without proving his membership of the Church of England. Yet in this bitter denominational legislation there was a curious and significant exception, conceded by the Anglican countryside to the protests of the Londoners. Non-Anglicans were still to be allowed to teach reading, writing, arithmetic and navigation. The training of clerks and seamen transcended even the need to safeguard the church.

But this was by no means the whole of the legislative programme insisted upon by the Tory majority now that they were firmly entrenched. Never again should Parliament be exposed to the possibility of a majority of nominees who lacked the resources to speak independently. The Property Qualification Act of 1710 required that membership should be confined to persons possessed of landed property worth £600 a year (for county Members) or £300 a year (for borough Members). The university seats and Scotland escaped this legislation, which could be (and was) evaded by endowing a favoured candidate with the requisite paper qualification. But the emphasis it placed on land as a source of political power was none the less real, and remained part of the constitution until the middle of the nineteenth century.

Robert Harley, now carried to the rank of Lord High Treasurer, might let his Tory majority have their heads but he knew as well as anyone that there could be no government now without the support of business. It was his aim, pursued not without success, to build up an adequate financial counterforce to that represented by the great Whig corporations, notably the Bank of England. Just as he had not hesitated to employ the dissenter Defoe for intelligence and public relations, he now employed the Baptist scrivener, John Blunt, to design lottery loans and the flotation of the South Sea Company, which was to reap the commercial harvest from the peace settlement that Harley was now planning. In the meantime the squires in Parliament might grumble as much as they liked but the land tax stayed at four shillings in the pound.

The surging interest in trade had bitten so deep as to affect the most conservative profession of all, the law. The change in twenty years was startling. As recently as the reign of James II Chief Justice Jeffreys, in upholding the absolute right of the Crown to confer trading privileges, had declared that England was 'a country satisfied with her own wealth, and in no need of trade'. 'This island,' he had said, 'supported its inhabitants in many ages without any foreign trade at all, having in it all things necessary for the life of man.' Such a nostalgia for autarchy would have been inconceivable in Lord Chief Justice Holt, who presided over the Court of Queen's Bench for most of Queen Anne's reign. Holt laid the foundations of commercial law on which Mansfield was later to build. Through his judgments promissory notes became a negotiable currency, and order was brought to the situation in which means of production were owned by one man but used by another.

The costume of a judge became fixed in the reign of Queen Anne. The consciousness that the judge is not merely a 'lion under the throne' of Tudor and Stuart tradition but a law-giver who need not wait for legislature, and must react to the social situation as it develops in the cases coming before him for decision, emerges almost for the first time in the work of Holt. If we complain of the absence of social and economic legislation in the annals of eighteenth-century Parliaments, it is often because we are looking in the wrong place for such decisions. It is in the law reports, rather than the statute book, that we should search. While the criminal law remained, with some modifications of procedure, the savage and brutal code it had always been, the civil and constitutional law of the new city state is one of the remarkable achievements of the century.

Holt was a Whig whose views, like those of most of the judges raised to the bench in the clean sweep that followed the Revolution, had been formed under the Commonwealth. For twenty-two years, confirmed in office for life by the Act of Settlement, he was the senior judge in the country, and his contribution to its constitution was at least as great as Locke's. In the great electoral case of *Ashby* v. *White* he said:*

I find that I must begin to prove that the plaintiff had a *right* to vote. It is not to be doubted that the Commons of England form part of the Government, and have a share in the legislature, without whom no law passes; but, because of their numbers, this power is not exercisable by them in their proper persons, and

* Lord Campbell, *Lives of the Chief Justices of England* (Murray, 1849), vol. 2, p. 158.

therefore by the constitution of England it is to be exercised by representatives, chosen by and out of themselves.

This right to vote, he went on, was a right each voter possessed almost as if it was a piece of private property—'a right that a man hath to give his vote at the election of a person to represent him in Parliament, there to concur in the making of laws which are to bind his liberty and his property, is of a transcendant nature.' Ashby, the voter of Wycombe, whatever the House of Commons might say, was entitled to damages from White, the returning officer, for refusing to let him exercise his right.

Holt, however, retained some of the characteristics of a 'lion under the throne'. Like his successors for many years afterwards, he had little patience with the press when it attacked the government. He relied on the simple principle that 'if writers should not be called to account for possessing the people with an ill opinion of the government, no government can subsist.' But he established, once and for all, the unassailable status of the English judge with his defiant, 'I am not to be arraigned', in the teeth of a House of Lords who demanded to know the reasons for one of his decisions. It was Holt who laid down the rule that a prisoner charged with one offence could not be questioned about another, and declared (though in this he was later overthrown) that although slavery might be permissible in America, 'as soon as a negro comes to England he is free.' And he showed that Whiggery had discarded all traces of puritan ancestry. Eleven successive witchcraft cases were brought before him, and he directed an acquittal in every one.

The judge was a terrible figure in eighteenth-century England—and very often the only figure representing central authority that a citizen set eyes on throughout his life. The law was theatrical* and savage, but the fact that it was not at the call of the government and could not be manipulated, gave it the prestige of independence. There were only twelve High Court judges, sitting in their curtained recesses in Westminster Hall or trundling round the kingdom in semi-regal progress, unchallengeable umpires of Hogarthian England, 'trusted,' in Holt's words, 'with the law', and the guardians of the freedom which the English regarded as peculiarly their own.

* It is significant that in England the affinity between the Law and the Stage is strong. Garrick passionately admired Lord Mansfield. Trial scenes guarantee theatrical success. At least two distinguished twentieth-century judges have been brothers of distinguished actors.

Society had been profoundly stimulated by the war, but now it was overstretched and the landed classes longed for an end of the great continental adventure. Fortified by an even greater majority in the election of 1713 the Tories cantered steadily through the making of peace. Marlborough had been displaced, Godolphin was dead, the Junto had been vanquished even in the House of Lords, Swift's *Examiner* had beaten the Whig journalists out of the field. At Addison's *Cato* the defeated Whigs cheered every night when the play reached the line:

The post of honour is a private station.

It was clear that in whatever direction politics might move, the next generation of literary talent was not going to be Whiggish. The new star of poetry was the strange little Catholic dwarf, Pope, whose *Rape of the Lock* showed, in 1712, that the English language was capable of classical perfection. Dutch phlegm and dissenting politics seemed to have been banished.

Nothing could have more clearly shown the truthfulness of fashion than the political and military exhaustion of the Dutch. They had to accept the terms Harley and Bolingbroke negotiated, which were designed primarily, and ruthlessly, to consolidate the British position in Europe. By the Treaty of Utrecht Gibraltar and Minorca became British; Spain—the great issue over which the war had been fought—received its Bourbon monarch at last; but the Spanish Netherlands, which had so long been the shield between France and Holland, were assigned to Britain's most powerful European ally, the Hapsburg emperor. Most important of all—and here the interests of Britain and Holland coincided—the whole coast of the Netherlands from the mouth of the Scheldt to Calais was effectively demilitarized. The sterilization of Antwerp and the exclusion of France from the North Sea are the supreme data of English power between the end of Marlborough's war and the outbreak of the French Revolution.

The Peace was a triumph of expediency in a cynical age. While it brought an end to a war which was increasingly irrational, it left the Catalan separatists to the mercy of the Bourbons; the Dutch weaker, despite their sacrifices to Marlborough's victories; and the Hapsburgs abandoned to a solitary continuance of the struggle against King Louis. For the last time in English history a churchman, Robinson, Bishop of Bristol, put his hand to an international treaty, and for the first time Britain appeared as the decisive influence over its contents. But the signature of Bishop Robinson had hardly been affixed before the man whose pen had done so much to make the peace possible, and deserved the bishopric he longed for much more than Robinson, was consigned to exile in Ireland. The indifference of Harley, and the abiding hatred felt by Archbishop Sharp for the author of *The Tale of the Tub* decided that Swift should spend the rest of his life as Dean of St Patrick's, Dublin.

Queen Anne had sixteen months still to live when the Peace was signed. Within that span the Tory majority in the House of Commons was strengthened, the official heir to her throne, Sophia of Hanover, died and was replaced by her gloomy, businesslike son, George, and the ministry was split by the rivalry between the veteran Harley and the aspiring Bolingbroke. But at the centre of all this turbulence, and prominent in the elections all over England, was the contest over the commercial treaties with France and Spain which were to follow the Peace and register the gains of the war. The treaty with France was to introduce a measure of free trade which terrified the cloth industry and was defeated in Parliament. The proposition of free trade with Britain's nearest and largest neighbour was not to be renewed until Pitt, under the influence of Adam Smith, began to dismantle the protectionist system that made smuggling a national industry throughout the eighteenth century. More was hoped for from the treaty with Spain, which was intended to open up the South American eldorado to British commerce by the acquisition of the right—conceded by the Treaty of Utrecht—to supply slaves to the Spanish possessions. This trade which it was proposed to let to the newly created South Sea Company would, it was hoped, lead to trade on a broader basis.

There is a vaunting cupidity about these last Tory months which occurs again from time to time, like a vein of false gold in eighteenth-century commercial history. For a few years the new opportunities, real and imaginary, and the new theories of finance, only half understood, were to dazzle the country and expose possibilities of corruption in politics and public life on a scale that has never been known before or since. The newly found political stability, which permitted an almost noiseless change of dynasty in the critical summer of 1714, was to be a period of groping to discover the limitations of the greater world Britain had now entered.

Chapter 6　　　　The Advent of the Georges

The change of dynasty and the change in the centre of political gravity from Tory to Whig tend to conceal the fact that in many ways the first few years of George I's reign show a marked social and political continuity with the preceding one. The new king was provided with a careful list showing exactly which of his faithful Commons were Whigs, and which Tories, and the old virulence of party spirit showed little sign of weakening, even though the senior Whigs who had done so much to keep it alive seemed to feel their work was done now that the Hanoverian was on the throne. Somers, Wharton, and Montagu were all dead within two years of George's accession, but their spirit lived on in Stanhope and Walpole. The spoils system showed its claws in the sacking of the greatest architect England has produced in the year he completed his greatest work. At the age of eighty-four Christopher Wren reported that St Paul's was completed and was dismissed to make room for a Whig Surveyor of Public Works. There is a shamelessness about the politicians of the middling rank at this particular time—such men as Aislabie, the two Craggs's, and Parker —which even the Dodingtons and Rigbys later in the century were to find hard to match. The opportunities for self-enrichment seemed unlimited.

Yet one of the greatest Whigs of the new generations was to sacrifice his fortune to Whig politics. The flowing together of huge wealth in the hands of the young Thomas Pelham-Holles, soon to be Duke of Newcastle, was a dynastic event almost as significant for the future course of England as the accession of George I. The combination of marriages and settlements over more than a century, which made Newcastle the richest subject England had ever known, recall those which led to the empire of Charles V. His huge estates, notably in Sussex and Nottinghamshire, his lieutenancies in five counties, his descent from one of the celebrated 'five members', and his connexion with the great Whig family of the Sidneys, all helped to qualify him for his inordinate political career, in the course of which he held high

73

office for longer than any English politician except Gladstone. Yet Newcastle had only one genuine reason for devoting himself to political life—he loved the business of politics. Ideas, leadership, big decisions, he was willing, indeed anxious, to leave to others. He was content to embody the state of affairs as settled at the Revolution, and devote himself and his fortune to the detailed manipulations needed to keep matters so from year to year. He was not merely a party manager, but a party fund. When, in his old age, he was finally dismissed by the great grandson of the king he had first served he had spent almost his whole colossal fortune on his hobby of keeping the Whigs in office. He started worth £40,000 a year, and ended with £6,000.

The activities of such a man as Newcastle impinged directly on hundreds of thousands of daily lives—on the ironworkers of Sussex, the weavers and stocking-makers of Nottingham, the tradesmen and wool-merchants of Boroughbridge. These were the people who, for one reason or another, but in surprising numbers, had voted in 1715 for a House of Commons with the biggest Whig majority ever returned. In the town of Nottingham, for instance, nearly 1,300 people voted out of a total population of about 7,000. What was the condition of these people when the grumpy, elderly, German king, with his Huguenot advisers and his Turkish servants, took his place on the throne?

England was still a turbulent country—and not the less turbulent on account of its growing prosperity. In the past twenty years the production of spirits, mostly gin, had doubled so as to provide an annual gallon between every three members of the population. In another twenty years it was to be enough for a gallon per head per year. Beer, the first commodity in this country to be subjected to mass production methods, was already running at the rate of a barrel per head per year—sweet, pale, weak, and unstable in the country; dark, bitter and coarse in London. The cheap kinds could be had for as little as 1½d. a gallon, and the most expensive for round about 4d.

Again one must dwell on the difference between London and the rest of the country. Defoe, on the travels which eventually made up his *Tour Thro' the Whole Island of Great Britain,* was never able to forget the contrast and the interdependence. He watched the turkeys, 1,000 in a flock, crossing the Stour on their way to the London market, and reflected, eating a lobster in Totnes which cost him 8d., how it would have cost him 3s. in London. At Portland he noted the inroads on the quarries that had been made by the needs of St Paul's, and at Marlow he commented on the prosperity of the paper-mills being due to the requirements of the London newspapers.

In the country a careful farmer could compute that keeping a labourer cost a little more than twice the keep of a horse. The farm-hand who lived in the farm-stead with his master's family, waiting till a separate household should be dictated to him by a pregnancy, received a shilling or two a week apart from his keep. Such men rarely left their native districts throughout their lives. The overwhelming rule was marriage in the same parish or a contiguous one, and settlement was the poor man's insurance against old age.

In London wages were higher, and the struggle more bitter. The penny cover charge in a coffee house would not, perhaps, exclude the harness-maker or the coach-builder with a wage of ten shillings a week, but it kept out the poor. A penny was the price of a pint of beer, but of one two hundred and fortieth of a pound of tea. It would carry a letter weighing up to sixteen ounces anywhere in the London area, or a barrel from Gravesend to London Bridge by water. Service was cheap. For two pence a waterman would row a passenger across the Thames. But a hackney coach cost a shilling an hour, which was more than the daily allowance made by the army for an officer's servant.

The money economy, of course, was far from complete, and much income was still in kind: common rights, the keep of servants and apprentices, customary gifts and benefactions, dwellings enjoyed free of charge by custom or as a perquisite of office. But immense economic distinctions separated the better-off from the rest of the community. They alone paid direct taxes, and they alone consumed imports; and even indirect taxation, falling as it did on what were regarded as luxuries (except for salt) fell lightly on the poor. If the better-off controlled the apparatus of the state, they also paid most towards it; and they alone could afford the relatively enormous prices of such imports as silk and brandy, tea and coffee.

For the poorer man the more durable necessities had a lasting quality which they were gradually to lose with the Industrial Revolution. Clothes, furniture, household goods, such as they were, lasted a life-time, perhaps several. This slow rate of depreciation is one of the most significant differences between the eighteenth century and our own time, and it extended not only to household possessions but—with even more lasting effect—to capital goods. Farm implements, looms, wagons, ships, would have a life of fifty or sixty years, or more. The very notion of depreciation, let alone fashion, over a great part of the nation's fixed stock was hardly realized. It is this, rather than any conservatism of temperament, that accounts for the sameness of the scene over so much of the eighteenth century: a sameness that conceals a great measure of social and political change.

In many parts of the country the relics of the old regulated society of the Tudors and Stuarts still survived. The right to a market, which the law still held to be a special privilege, was limited to certain places and days, whereas in London it was recognized that every day except Sunday was lawfully market day. At some provincial Quarter Sessions the magistrates still tried with some success to regulate wages and prices. Above all the apprenticeship system still made for the subordination of youth to masters whose powers were almost unbounded. Nor was child labour the creation of the Industrial Revolution. To the industrial villager a child was an asset to the family, and Defoe rejoiced over the prosperous wool district of Taunton, where 'there is not a child in the town . . . of above five years old but if it was not neglected by its parents and untaught, could earn its bread' at the loom.

What then of education? At first sight it seems to belong to the same category as the imported luxuries, something to which the wealthy and a few of their protégés alone had access. Three major schools—Westminster where the Duke of Newcastle never forgot he had been educated; Eton, which by the middle of the century had ousted Westminster and reached the unprecedented number of 399 boys; and Winchester—provided such organized education as most members of the wealthier class acquired. Of 519 men who sat in the Commons between 1715 and 1754, 360 went to one of these three schools. But a closer look shows that the schools in the smaller towns were not without their glories. The grammar school at Lichfield (a more important town then, it is true, than it is today) produced not only Johnson, the son of a local stationer, but Garrick and seven judges who sat at Westminster at the same time. The huge deposit of town and parish records, compiled by humble constables and overseers chosen in rotation to serve unpaid, attest, though at a lower level, that some degree of literacy, and the power to keep accurate accounts, was surprisingly widespread.

University education was for the very few, but not necessarily the well-off. As the dissenting academics decayed—and the first wave of them hardly survived 1720—Oxford and Cambridge resumed their monopoly. Each contained about 1,000 students. Although the sons of gentlemen were sent there in increasing numbers to acquire the facility in the classics which was still considered the mark of civilization, the great majority of the undergraduates were destined for the church. The cost of the three-year course—the bills of one young man, called Francis Lynn came to £142 10s.—was outside the reach of many families; but some paid far less, either because they were provided with a scholarship, or because they worked as college servants. Samuel Johnson, for instance, was one of these 'sizars', receiving free tuition and earning his keep by waiting at table. In Scotland, which boasted four universities, though smaller ones, the costs were far lower. The Mackenzie boys at St Andrews in 1711–16 cost Sir Kenneth Mackenzie of Coul only about £70 each for the four-year course—including the expenses of golf, on which all three of them spent a good deal. They also received a much broader education than would have been offered them at Oxford or Cambridge, extending to the mathematics of Newton, astronomy, and surveying, besides Latin and Greek.

Education, however, was not, as it was to become, an escape from drudgery for large numbers. Often the short cut out of the subordinated labour for a living wage which was the lot of the majority, lay in crime. The accumulated wealth of London, and still more the movement of wealth to and from it, made crime profitable; and the virtual absence of administration made it easy. The early years of the eighteenth century saw the appearance of organized crime on an unusually large scale. Jonathan Wild, as his contemporaries were quick to see, was very much the man of his time—the organizer of protection rackets and bogus detective agencies operating against the criminals he himself employed. Wild, whose career began under Queen Anne and ended in 1725, was surprisingly modern in his methods, using the newspapers to advertise his services and the law to discipline his gangsters. He bridged the upper classes and the underworld, and his menacing presence was seen as far afield as the great fairs of the Midlands, such as Sturbridge, where 'the wholesale men from London ... transact their business wholly in their pocket books'. His organization bade fair to install a Mafia in London, and whatever else may be criticized about the law of the eighteenth century it succeeded in eradicating this particular criminal empire, which was later turned to such effective use by Gay in the *Beggar's Opera* to attack the political methods of Walpole.

The law-giver of the eighteenth century favoured a single answer to crime: physical punishment, usually death. As time passed the list of capital offences steadily grew, and the number of executions after each Sessions mounted to produce the dreadful carnival of Tyburn which defaces the mid-century. Nevertheless in 1719 an alternative punishment was suggested by Britain's growing consciousness of her overseas possessions, and Parliament passed the first Transportation Act. Although many of the transported felons returned, the numbers punished in this way were large, and the addition made to the population in America and the West Indies was not insignificant.

British crime was itself worldwide for this was also, *par excellence*, the age of the pirate. In 1722 fifty-two pirates from one pirate squadron were hanged at Cape Corso Castle on the Guinea Coast of West Africa —among them the Israel Hands whose name Stevenson has immortalized. It happens that their native places were noted in most cases. Twenty-six came from the west of England and thirteen from the riverside parishes of London. Five were Welsh, five Scots, and the rest came from scattered counties, including the Channel Islands and the Isle of Man. Plymouth, Bristol, and London were the home ports for most of them, just as they were for the thousands who served in the merchantmen or fell victims to the naval press-gangs.

The pirates are a not insignificant social group, for they illustrate the behaviour of ordinary men of the time, when freed from the traditional constraints of their society and committed to opposing it. They produced, if their surviving documents are anything to go by, surprisingly cohesive communities—almost floating parishes—which, though lawless, had their own officers and procedures, and their own, often elaborate, rules for dividing the booty by rank and trade. 'Every man,' ran the articles of Captain Bartholomew Roberts's crew, 'to be called fairly in turn, by list, on board of prizes . . . the Captain and Quartermaster to receive two shares of a prize, the master, boatswain, and gunner one share and a half, and other officers one share and a quarter.'* Captain Roberts's crew had a band, which was expected to play six days a week, the articles carefully specifying a rest day on the seventh. Here again the pirates resembled their law-abiding countrymen at home.

The idea of England as a deferential country, even after the achievement of political stability, must be at once dismissed. On the contrary, there was perpetual popular disturbance, and few years passed without major riots, which might or might not have an ostensible economic or political motive. At Peterborough, for instance, in 1740, a football match took place with an estimated five hundred players on each side. Often the riots were concerned with prices, and stocks were seized by the mob to be 'sold' at what were considered fair prices,

---

* For a history of pirates, see Captain Charles Johnson, *A General History of the Robberies and Murders of the Pirates*, Arthur L. Hayward (ed.) (Routledge , 1926). The work is sometimes attributed to Defoe.

the meagre yield often being handed to the unfortunate owners. As the century progressed the occasion for riot was often an enclosure or the routing of a turnpike road (which would interfere with traditional transport) or a new industrial process. The wearing of calico, imported from India and printed in Lancashire, caused serious disturbances in the early 1720s; and the collapse of the South Sea Bubble was accompanied by riots in London which spilt over into the House of Commons itself.

If there was a political cause on which these discontents could focus in the early Hanoverian years, it was Jacobitism, representing as it did the negation of the existing regime. Leaving aside the political aspirations of the Jacobite leaders, which were often the purest opportunism, and the nationalisms of outlying Scotland and Ireland, one finds in the ordinary followers of the White Cockade until the debacle of 1746 the same social pattern as in the Wilkite mob of the sixties. The Manchester men taken prisoner after the battle of Preston in 1746 were colliers and weavers, drapers, barbers and apothecaries. One was an organist, another a 'laevigator' or stone-polisher.

The mob, in fact, was a continuing force to be reckoned with. Its members might not have votes, but they had a considerable measure of collective power. The politicians had a term of art for the appeal to this force: 'popularity'—which meant reliance on popular support rather than the quality of being liked, just as 'patriotism' (a word which does not make its appearance in the language until the 1720s) meant the appeal to popular emotion rather than love of one's country. It was in this atmosphere of continuing turbulence, always liable to boil over into local upheaval, that the Riot Act of 1715 was passed to help magistrates to administer what was often the only available remedy—military force. Even so, it was a bold magistrate who was willing to use troops, even after reading the order to disperse that the act required. The mob not only had its powers but its rights, as Captain Porteous was to find in Scotland, and the London magistrates were to find during the Wilkite disturbance of 1768. In both cases murder charges were pressed.

The structure of society was certainly not so rigid as to prevent advancement to wealth and power from very humble beginnings. Nevertheless there was an immense gulf between the possessors and the poor, of a kind which we find it hard even to imagine. It was marked in two ways. First, even the tiniest income on the respectable side of the divide—say a curacy of thirty pounds a year—was several times larger than the income of an agricultural labourer, while the incomes of the better-off were ten or even a hundred times greater. Second, the fiscal system created a situation in which the possessors bore the main visible burden of sustaining the state. The poor could at least say that they contributed little or nothing. The sting the Excise agitation was to be the threat of a more far-reaching system of indirect taxation.

How could a man hoist himself across this divide—as so many did? The church offered one way, and one man in every hundred was a clergyman. In the first half of the century even the highest ranks of the church tended to be more open to men of humble origin than in the second half. Another way forward was through government service. A third was through trade. And a fourth, of which we know little, was through the hierarchies of great households (including the king's court) to positions of great practical influence, on which more than one family fortune was founded.

After the struggles, and what seemed to have been the victory, of Anne's reign, the church was forced to settle for far less than its claims. One by one the advanced positions it had established had to be evacuated: both the Schism Act and the Occasional Conformity Act were repealed in 1719. The Stanhope ministry muttered about an enquiry into the universities, and dragoons were quartered on Oxford. As legislative protection for the established church only the Tudor statutes and the Test Act remained; and the studies of the clergy were directed with peculiar intensity on the Henrician Act that laid down the conditions on which pluralities might be held, and the number of chaplains a nobleman might have as a nursery for promotion. The retreat of the church, though not its eclipse, was marked by the sermon preached by Benjamin Hoadly, the Whig Bishop of Bangor, to the text, 'My Kingdom is not of this world.'

Although the hubbub following Hoadly's sermon in 1717 is known as the Bangorian controversy, Hoadly in fact never visited his Welsh diocese in his life. The storm he aroused was due to his argument that the church was a society of men, and that there was no reason why such a society should be able to act with the exclusive authority of God in the world. It was a terrible doctrine, which once and for all shivered the claims of the Anglican church to a co-equal authority in the state, and with historic logic led to the final discontinuance of Convocation as an estate of the realm. The church remained an interest, a source of livelihood and of culture, but its magic had vanished. It is not of a magical institution that one speaks, as Bishop

Warburton was to speak some twenty years later, with the affection of familiarity, when he compared the Church of England to Noah's Ark.

If the church was still one way forward to a better income and a more respectable place in the world, government service was another, but the great prizes were fewer. The church offered 26 bishoprics, nearly 1,000 cathedral dignities, and some 9,000 benefices, apart from curacies and chaplaincies. Government service, outside the armed forces, consisted overwhelmingly of posts in the Customs and Excise, which provided a large number of relatively well-paid jobs, many of them performed through deputies. The patronage of the revenue, though not so important as the patronage of the church, was never far from the Duke of Newcastle's preoccupations, and revenue officers, like clergymen, were disqualified from voting, as likely to be dependent on the government of the day.

But further up the ladder of government service there were very few openings for the ambitious but obscure man. Some huge fortunes were made. Henry Guy, who had been James II's Secretary to the Treasury, returned to office after the Revolution and died in his Wren house at Tring leaving £100,000, which founded the fortunes of the Pulteney family. William Blathwayte, also one of James's administrators, doubled the posts of Secretary at War and Commissioner of Trade under William III and built his palace at Dyrham, in Gloucestershire. Richard Jones, who had started as a farmer of the Irish revenue, secured an Irish peerage and, in 1691, the Paymastership of the Forces, which he lost in 1702 after being expelled from the House of Commons for defalcations totalling £72,000. He was nevertheless made a governor of 'Queen Anne's Bounty' a year or two later. But the biggest fortune from government service was undoubtedly that of James Brydges, who was Paymaster during the last five years of Marlborough's war, and crowned his immense riches with a Dukedom (of Chandos) in 1719. His country house at Edgware—Canons—was the most gorgeous in the neighbourhood of London.

Government and business coalesced in the careers of such men as Chandos, and the connection between Whitehall and the Stock Exchange was never closer than in the years between the Hanoverian succession and the South Sea Bubble. That spectacular promotion, by which the debts of past wars were to be turned into an equity which would steadily appreciate in capital value, had its origins in Harley's desire to create a counterforce to the Bank of England in government finance. But its significance goes far beyond either Tory politics or monetary mania. The grotesque rise in the stock market of 1720 shows England as participating for the first time in a financial movement that affected the whole of western Europe. Foreign specu- lation in South Sea stock was counterbalanced by British operations in Law's parallel Mississippi Bubble in Paris. The techniques of trans- ferring funds, of buying and selling by remote control, of daily or weekly quotations, had developed with astonishing speed, and were available not just to a few financiers but to many thousands.

With the tortuous details of the South Sea affair we cannot here be concerned, and even its financial and political importance can receive no more than mentions. Its social impact, however, must be marked because it was the first secular, non-political, man-made event of modern times which could be said to affect the whole country. There was almost no family throughout Britain that was unaffected by the rise and fall of Sir John Blunt's financial dream: country clergymen, fashionable ladies, Scottish peers, importers of dried fruit, dealers in timber, coachmakers, brewers, booksellers (such as Thomas Guy, the stationer who founded a hospital with his winnings), the sophisticated Lady Mary Wortley Montagu (who was involved by a persuasive French speculator) and the veteran Isaac Newton, who declared that he could calculate the motions of the heavenly bodies but not the madness of the people.

The crash of autumn 1720, and the period of depression and chaos during the winter of 1720-1, bring an end to what might be called the prelude to the Robinocracy—the five years of manoeuvre between victorious Whig factions, groping for mastery of Britain's new-found power. But it also marks the end of the period of growth which began before the Revolution, but can take its epoch from the arrival of William of Orange. The smacks carrying financial news between Harwich and Amsterdam in the summer of 1720 belong to the same world as the flat-bottomed boats that brought William's troops on the perilous journey in the autumn of 1688. The links with Europe, the emphasis on trade, the amalgam of politics and business at the highest levels of affairs, are all reproduced again and again in those thirty-two formative years.

Though the years down to 1720 have a coherent character they were years of profound and lasting change, not only in the position of Britain in the world, but in the nature of British society. There was a new literary language and a habitual periodical press. Rationalism had made good its place in intellectual life, and the universe had been explained to the satisfaction of most people. The principle of public credit on the basis of the guarantee of an elected assembly had become part of everyday life. The gleam of empire had entered into the eyes of many Englishmen. Above all, the church, from being a power, had become an interest—widespread and influential it is true, but still primarily an interest which the true masters of Britain—the owners of land—had to take into account, and not a force over whose doctrines and organization the state itself took second place.

Yet these great changes—in their way as considerable as the technological changes of a hundred years later—left the face of Britain surprisingly unaltered. London had grown, it is true, and had already attained the full size it was to be for another half-century. Here and there, even in southern Scotland, progressive landlords were beginning to plant trees and enclose land, but on the whole hedges were still of the future. There was a new elegance in the country homes of the wealthy, particularly in the Thames valley, where Defoe noted the villas of the prosperous spreading handsomely. But the relative absence of technological change made for apparent sameness in the landscape and the lives of the people. When Robert Walpole emerged from the chaos caused by the South Sea affair as First Lord of the Treasury and Chancellor of the Exchequer, it was to govern a country which still had the reputation of turbulence, and did not appreciate that it was susceptible to anaesthesia after its exertions.

Chapter 7

'All those men have their price'

The Robinocracy—which lasted in spirit well beyond the fall of Sir Robert Walpole after twenty-one years of government—owed much of its durability to Walpole's profound insight into the structure of his society. He was a landowner with a talent, indeed a passion, for finance, who was as much at home with his banker Jacombe or in the labyrinths of insurance company promotions, as in the House of Commons or his gorgeous country seat at Houghton in Norfolk. While he was Prime Minister he never left England and he never sought a peerage. He understood, as Harley had understood before him, that the indispensable prop of government was the landed gentry in the House of Commons; and that the 'moneyed interest' of the City of London, properly handled and with its own ambitions to landed gentility, could develop financial strength on a scale that was probably unparalleled in history. In institutional terms Walpole's political system was based on the twin pillars of the House of Commons and the Treasury. This recipe for power, and its success, has been felt in English history ever since.

Harley had taken the Treasury less seriously. He had preferred the Secretary of State's responsibility for internal security and foreign policy as the dominant ingredient of supreme power. But of the two machines the Treasury was by far the most highly developed as an instrument for influencing society. In the Customs it controlled the only nation-wide network which was at the disposal of the central government. In the secret service fund it dealt with an important source of direct electoral power. Both were important sources of patronage. Through it ran the life-line to the Bank of England which, from the South Sea scandal onwards, had the exclusive right of hand-ling the government's borrowings. As Lord Chancellor Hardwicke put it to King George II, 'the Head of his Treasury was indeed an employment of great Business; very extensive, which allways went beyond the bare management of the Revenue. That is extended thro' both Houses of Parliamt., the Members of which were naturally to look thither.' From 1721 to 1754, with only the briefest of intervals, the offices of First Lord of the Treasury and Chancellor of the Exchequer were combined in the person of the man who led the House of Commons.

The only major administrative building erected under the Robinocracy was Kent's Treasury, built in 1734 and still standing in Whitehall as a background to Kent's military headquarters, the Horse Guards, which was constructed to gratify George II's love of military parades. No monument of a political arrangement could be more apt. There the long-serving Treasury officials wound out their long careers in the elaborate 'course of the Exchequer', which in the words of the contemporary handbook 'hath been found to be absolutely the best Way that ever was invented'. Their longevity, and their loyalty to successive governments were remarkable. Lowndes, who entered the Treasury in 1679, and became Secretary in 1695, was still there to tidy up the South Sea affair in the early 1720s. Christopher Tilson, who joined the Treasury in 1685, spent nearly fifty-eight years there. 'Old Scrope' succeeded Lowndes as Secretary in 1724 and died, still in office, nearly thirty years later at the age of ninety. Of such stuff is stability made.

During the short period between the death of the Queen and 1721 —that curious ante-chamber to Georgian England—a number of constitutional developments had taken place which notably strengthened a minister basing himself on the House of Commons and especially the squires in it. In 1719 an attempt to buttress the power of the House of Lords by limiting its numbers had been defeated, and with it the possibility of a hereditary, co-opting senate as the most powerful institution in the country. The move was designed to perpetuate an upper chamber in which Whigs had always commanded a majority. The failure of the Peerage Bill meant that a political leader who commanded the confidence of both Crown and Commons could be sure of the ultimate acquiescence of the Lords, for the power to create additional peers was in the hands of the Crown: and this was no theoretical power, as Harley had shown by creating a dozen peers at a blow to pass the Occasional Conformity Bill.

The Septennial Act of 1716 had already immensely strengthened the Commons and increased the attractiveness of a seat there, for it more than doubled each member's lease of power. The expense of acquiring a seat rose almost in proportion. If one is looking for a tranquillizing influence on eighteenth-century politics it can be found in the Act which enabled members of the House of Commons to put the prospect of election out of mind for many years together, and ministers to settle, and then live with, a relatively unchanged House.

The slower pace of political life, not to mention the easier availability of peerages, undoubtedly helped the systematic development of patronage as a political and social force. There was ample time now between elections for politicians and patrons to make sure the votes in small constituencies were in the right hands and to arrange for a compliant returning officer to be in position on the predictable day. It also allowed scope for deciding disputed elections with increasing effectiveness in favour of members who supported the ministry.*

Two other, more recognizable buttresses supported Walpole's Whig supremacy. In the House of Lords virtually all the twenty-six episcopal votes were at the disposal of the government. Many of the bishops (unlike the majority of the clergy) were Whigs by conviction as well as interest, and all except the most prosperous depended on the government for promotion through the wide span of episcopal incomes, ranging from the humble Welsh sees where a career on the bench usually began, to the great wealth of London, Durham, York and Canterbury.† In the Commons the forty-five Scottish Members showed the value of the political bargain the Junto had made for the Whig party in promoting the Union of 1707. They were returned for tiny electorates, and were Whigs almost to a man. Scotland as a whole, after the Union as before it, was susceptible to a far greater degree of central management than England, and under the Robinocracy this was exercised by the House of Argyll. In return for their mastery of Scotland the Campbells guaranteed Sir Robert Walpole about a twelfth of the House of Commons, a fair proportion of whom were bearers of the name of Campbell.

A seat in the Commons was worth possessing. Members did not, indeed, have salaries, but they had many other advantages. Their postage, for instance, was free, which was worth £1,000 a year to a business man who used it for all his firm's correspondence, and was a

---

* Between 1715 and 1734 there were no fewer than 316 disputed elections. Only 30 per cent of these were ever settled—on the whole those in which an Opposition member had been returned and the petitioner was a supporter of the ministry. The rest, in which a ministerialist had been returned, and the petitioner belonged to the Opposition, were adjourned. This process was described by Walpole as 'weeding the House'.

† Episcopal incomes climbed steadily throughout the eighteenth century. In 1688 Canterbury was worth £4,000, and the rest ranged down to the modest £380 of Bristol. By the reign of George III Canterbury was £7,000, Durham £6,000, London £4,000, although Bristol was still only £450. By 1831 Canterbury was worth nearly £20,000 a year, as was Durham, and London £14,000. Several others were into five figures.

useful perquisite to all those who gave franked envelopes to their friends, or even sold them. Membership carried immunity from the severe law for enforcement of debt, and Lady Mary Wortley Montagu's worthless son was put in for a pocket borough because his parents reckoned it was cheaper than paying off the creditors. Members were expected to be grateful. In the words of Burke a government supporter:*

> can do an infinite number of acts of generosity and kindness, and even of public spirit. He can procure indemnity from all quarters. He can procure advantages in trade. He can get pardons for offences. He can obtain a thousand favours, and avert a thousand evils. He may, while he betrays every valuable interest in the kingdom, be a benefactor, a patron, a father, a guardian angel to his borough.

The parliamentary boroughs of eighteenth-century England can be recognized today by the market halls, the corporation plate, the libraries and the almshouses conferred on them by their grateful representatives.

The electors were not unaware of the advantages which the parliamentary system brought them, and local interest shows sharply in the business Parliament itself transacted. Of the 2,779 acts passed between 1715 and 1754 the great majority—more than two-thirds—were concerned either with individuals on such topics as naturalization or divorce (each of which required a private act) or the enclosure of an estate; with local improvements enabling roads, canals, or harbours to be built, or were in some way concerned with the needs of a particular locality. On average only about twenty measures a year applied to the nation as a whole, and even these did not usually originate with the government but were the work of pressure groups operating through private members. Government measures were virtually confined to public finance and defence. To the early Georgian politician the idea of a legislative programme would have been meaningless, since the objects of government were to preserve the existing system and to remain in power.†

---

* *Thoughts on the Causes of the Present Discontents* (1770).
† More significant, perhaps, even than the subject matter of legislation is the extent to which Parliament was kept informed. A careful review of the surviving parliamentary papers in the first half of the eighteenth century, carried out by Sheila Lambert (*List of House of Commons Sessional Papers, 1701–1750*, List and Index Society Special Series, vol. 1 (1968)), shows that Parliament was given much more information during the years 1702–20 than in the next twenty years.

Twenty-one years' government by a realistic philistine had lasting consequences—and not in politics alone. Walpole disliked and distrusted the press. Even devoted Whig journalists, such as Steele, seemed to him impracticable and troublesome, asking more by way of recognition than their services were worth. He spent comparatively little, either in time or money, on a government press, and he did not hesitate to persecute, by general warrant or through the law of libel, the journalists who attacked him. The same applied to authors higher in the scale. His lowbrow, but penetrating intelligence told him that the literary world was likely to reject his style of government even while it profited by the stability which was his principal object of policy.

The rift between the intelligentsia and public life, which has been a feature of British life for more than two hundred years, dates from the Robinocracy. Milton and Marvell, Locke and Swift, Dryden and Prior, Addison and Steele, had all shared in the world of government in their day, and moved easily among statesmen. It was not so under Walpole, nor, for various causes, has it been so since his time.* There are exceptions, but on the whole England, unlike France, has had very few intellectuals among her politicians since Walpole's time, and the doors between the literary and political salons have usually remained closed, or at best slightly ajar.

Pope, the greatest poet of the Augustan age, was the reverse of a courtier. A Catholic, a critic of mediocrity, a lover of form rather than substance, this diminutive invalid was the extreme contrast to the hearty Prime Minister. Swift, the age's greatest prose writer, was hardly less of a contrast with the prevailing spirit of politics: an embittered Irish genius degenerating into misanthropy. The correspondence between the two great authors, though not primarily political, provides the obverse to the coarse realism of the Robinocracy. Within the strictly political arena the struggle of Whig factions for power and influence replaced the fundamental party battles of Anne's reign; while criticism of the system as a whole came from an intellectually detached world that was basically Tory in its sympathies. *The Drapier's Letters*, in which Ireland's wrongs were vented by Swift; the *Beggar's Opera*, in which Gay compared Walpole's regime with gangsterism; and *Jonathan Wild*, in which Fielding did the same; were more

* Alienation between the two worlds—cultural and political—persisted for a series of reasons. Under Walpole the opposition is between intellectuality and philistinism; later in the century it is between romantic liberalism and defence of the *status quo*. In the next century it develops into a socialist and humanitarian contrast with capitalism and imperialism.

effective in undermining Walpole than the speeches and intrigues of dissident Whigs or crypto-Jacobite Tories in Parliament. It is to Walpole that Britain owed the Licensing Act of 1737, subjecting the stage to the censorship of the Lord Chamberlain for more than two centuries. The motives of the Act were not moral but political.

There was another, more sensitive reaction to the grossness of the Robinocracy and the materialism that had come temporarily to grief in the Bubble. Pope and Swift possessed glittering, tough minds. Another Anglo-Irishman, who had also been to the remarkable school at Kilkenny was the brilliant George Berkeley, to whom the England of 1721 seemed already decadent, and European civilization itself to be on the decline. For Berkeley the new world across the Atlantic held out the only promise for a better, purer life.

'Westward the course of empire holds her way'.

He was thinking, not of a British empire but of the fifth and greatest monarchy. Berkeley was perhaps the first Englishman to love America. His feeling that in America it would be possible for humanity to make a fresh start lay fallow for the time.

But if imaginative literature and speculative thought went into almost permanent opposition to prevailing power, there was one major, lasting exception in the literary world. The writing of history became, and remained, a Whig preserve, handing down the Whig account of the Revolution and the party struggles that followed it. The histories of White Kennett (1706), Echard (1707), Boyer (1711–29), Rapin (1723), Oldmixon (1729–36), and above all of Burnet, in his *History of My Own Time,* posthumously published between 1723 and 1734, built up a solid Whig orthodoxy about the politics of the previous generation. Boyer and Rapin, significantly enough, were both Huguenots who had settled in England in the wake of the Revolution. The others, without exception, were Whig clergymen. Never before had there been access to such reliable (if biased) accounts of recent events, and the now unread tomes which in their day dealt with events through which their older readers had lived, have much to do with the self-consciousness and the confidence of eighteenth-century Englishmen. They knew, or thought they knew, more about their own recent history than any previous generation. When Stanhope tentatively began on the reform of Oxford and Cambridge—a project soon dropped—his first step was the establishment of the regius chairs of modern history, which remain memorials to the first great age of English historiography. The Whigs gained much from the support given to their version of history by contemporary historians—though Walpole once said that he knew by experience that history could not be true.

The threat of Jacobitism after 1715, when the Duke of Argyll had outfaced rather than defeated the Earl of Mar on the field of Sherrifmuir and the Whigs had been merciful according to their lights, remained a real one, domestically and internationally. The great Tories of Queen Anne's reign, though they were condemned to political twilight, had better powers of survivorship than the great Whigs. Harley lived until 1724, and the brilliant if meretricious Bolingbroke down to 1751. Nothing is more characteristic of Walpole's methods than the semi-toleration that he allowed these men. Perhaps they were not serious Jacobites; but Atterbury, the apologist of Convocation who had risen to be Bishop of Rochester, certainly was. The plot with which his name is associated was very far from being a rising on the tribal fringes of the kingdom. Twenty-three peers and eighty-three members of the House of Commons were said to be implicated in it.* The need for a substantial peace-time army, not only in Ireland, where most of it was always stationed, but in England and Scotland as well, was mainly dictated by the needs of internal security. The forces had been reduced to as few as 20,000 before the War of the Spanish Succession broke out. Under Walpole they never went below 30,000, and for much of the time they were over 40,000.

The army and navy, with their recent achievements and battle-seasoned officers, gradually became an accepted if disliked part of British life, and the provision of the Bill of Rights, forbidding a standing army without the leave of Parliament, became no more than a constitutional safeguard providing an opportunity for annual debate, instead of the expression of the idea that normality meant no army at all. The old hostility to the idea, however, survived in the strong disapproval of providing barracks for the soldiers to live in. The first barracks ever built in England was put up in 1722 (though, significantly enough, one had been provided in Dublin since 1703). No doubt a sense of economy encouraged this view, but Blackstone, as late as 1765, considered that barracks were unconstitutional, because 'soldiers should live intermixed with the people'. Commissions in the army (but never in the navy) were recognized as a species of property which

---

* The Jacobite documents also list 23 former M.P.s and 21 men who were to be M.P.s in due course as possible supporters. Sympathy seems to have been especially strong in the south west, where Cornwall showed 10 M.P.s or former M.P.s as Jacobites, Devon 9, Dorset 5, Somerset 7, Wiltshire 10, and Gloucestershire 5.

could be bought and sold, and George I issued the first Royal Warrant setting the tariff in 1720. The system was to endure for a century and a half, until Gladstone, unable to carry the abolition of purchase by Act of Parliament, discovered that it needed no more than another Royal Warrant from George I's great-great-great-granddaughter to sweep it away.

The close association between the Crown and the army was established under the first two Georges who, whatever their other differences, were both military men. George I had taken part in the storming of Buda in 1683, where he had captured his two influential Turkish body-servants, Mehmet and Mustapha, by whom his private finances were managed, and to whom he assigned the task of reading the English press for his private information. George II had also smelt powder as a young man, and became a peppery little martinet as an old one. Whatever other aspects of affairs these kings might leave to their ministers, in military matters they required consultation on the smallest details. George II was responsible for importing from Hanover the magnificent, if mysterious, military ballet of the trooping of the colour. British military pageantry is the creation of Britain's German dynasty.

The transition between the first two Georges was pretty noiseless politically; but neither monarch was a nullity. George I is a sombre almost secretive figure, himself isolated by the dark imprisonment to which he condemned his unfaithful wife. George II at least brought a queen to the throne beside him, and in Caroline the country had one of the cleverest and most engaging of consorts. If the new monarchy was never popular, and had lost much of the magic of the old, Caroline did more than anyone to make it pleasant and acceptable.

Apart from their regular progresses in the direction of Hanover, the first two Georges rarely left the south-eastern corner of their kingdoms. No British sovereign, indeed, visited Scotland, Wales, or Ireland, throughout the eighteenth century. The practice of visiting great local magnates, which even William III had kept up, quite died out. London was re-emphasized as a capital and a world apart, where the sovereign stood visibly at the centre of an official society.

The separation between the social and political aspects of the monarchy was already marked by the geography of St James's palace. Socially the palace was open to almost anyone wearing a decent suit of clothes entering through the ante-rooms and encountering the king when he received company in his drawing-room two or three times a week. More select guests were allowed into the room beyond, which was technically described as the bed-chamber, though the king did not sleep there. A wholly different entrance—'the back-stairs'—led to the office or 'closet' where the king spent several hours a day at his desk. Only ministers and other visitors by appointment were admitted there. In the language of eighteenth-century politics forcing the king's hand in the choice of ministers was known as 'storming the closet'. It had the flavour of an intrusion on privacy.

The king might no longer go to Newmarket, where Charles II had once projected a palace, but horses remained the passion of the land-owning classes. Moreover, since the arrival in the reign of Queen Anne of the famous Godolphin Arabian whose blood now flows in the veins of countless race-horses, stock had notably improved. The race meeting, hunting field and shooting party made the English squire a formidable cavalryman in war, and protection of these sports occu-pied much of his time as a landowner and magistrate in time of peace. The game laws, the most strictly enforced of all regulations, effectively denied hunting and shooting to all but landowners. It was not, as Blackstone observed, solely the desire to preserve the game that caused the law against poaching to be so strict. The desire to prevent insur-rections and resistance to the government by disarming the bulk of the people 'is a reason oftener meant than avowed by the makers of game laws'.

Walpole's England, then, was not quite the placid, easygoing country it seems from a distance. There was, it is true, a sense of detumescence after the immense achievements of the first years of the century, which had culminated in the commercial elephantiasis and disaster of the Bubble Year. But the inner explosiveness remained, even under Walpole's skilful design for calm. Fortunes were being made, and they were in a more lasting form than before. Foreign capital flowed steadily into the island, even though interest rates were low. Overseas trade increased. As the quiet years passed, a trickle of emigrants (to which the first Transportation Act of 1719 contributed) departed for America and silently increased its European population. Georgia, the last of the original continental colonies, was founded in 1734. Simultaneously the other two great city states of Europe, Holland and Venice, slid into political and economic decline. Holland had been mortally damaged by the war against Louis XIV; Venice surrendered her over-seas empire in 1718 by the Treaty of Passarowitz.

The designs for the monuments of English prosperity had already arrived. While the European conflict between the Venetians and the Turks was still in progress, a young English visitor to Italy brought home with him the recipe for rural urbanity by which Venetian business men had transformed their hinterland from a fen into an agricultural landscape decorated with elegant villas. Richard Boyle, 3rd Earl of Burlington, was only eighteen when, during a tour of Italy, he acquired Palladio's original designs, and thereafter devoted his life and fortune to aerating English architecture. His fortune, inherited by marriage with the daughter of the Trimmer Marquis of Halifax, was enormous. In 1716, at the age of 21, with the advice of the Scottish architect Colen Campbell, he began the reconstruction of Burlington House, and Vanbrugh's heavy Flemish grandeur was out of fashion before his chef d'oeuvre of Blenheim was finished. In 1725 the publication of Campbell's *Vitruvius Britannicus* was completed, and though the name on the title page of this great book, from which the designs of hundreds of country houses were taken, was Colen Campbell's, the inspiration was Burlington's. In 1736 Burlington's imitation of the Villa Rotonda, Chiswick House was finished—too small, said Lord Hervey, to live in, and too large to hang on one's watch—but one of the most charming Palladian creations that exists. Venetian villas came to England at the same time as a Venetian oligarchy.

Burlington was the patron not only of Campbell but of William Kent, who went on to build the Treasury and the Horse Guards, and of Flitcroft, architect of St Giles's, Holborn, and St John's, Hampstead. New churches now almost invariably marked new urban development rather than the piety of individual donors. Burlington House, indeed, was the central feature of an estate in the area north of Piccadilly into which London was now rapidly expanding. It was one of many. Hanover Square was built by a consortium of Whig generals which included Carpenter, victor over the Jacobites at Preston in 1715; Wade, the military engineer who was to give the Highlands their roads; and Pepper, who later dabbled profitably in the South Sea promotion. Further to the north still the Cavendishes and Harleys were creating the streets which still bear their names, and to the west the Grosvenors, whose marriages into wealth almost matched those of the Duke of Newcastle himself, started in 1725 to lay out the huge estate which centred on Grosvenor Square.

London was developed not by a king, like St Petersburg or Napoleonic Paris, but by speculators large and small. From the first they offered houses, each standing on its own land, rather than flats in which the families lived piled above each other—with important consequences both for the appearance of the streets and the social organization behind their façades. There were several reasons for this, including restrictions on the height of buildings which had been laid down by Parliament after the Great Fire. But the most important reason was probably that houses were easier to finance and to sell. The typical builder worked with the minimum of capital, renting his site for as little as he could and then running up a shell for quick sale, leaving the purchaser to fit it out according to his taste. The system was ideally suited for tempting private accumulations of capital into bricks and mortar without the need for either the machinery of mortgage or the existence of big contracting organizations.

Building standards, at least in London, were already a matter of regulation. Wooden structures were no longer allowed, and in the reign of Anne, Parliament had done much to create the typical Georgian façade by forbidding wooden cornices and insisting that windows should be set back from the line of the wall, rather than flush with it as in the past. Pattern-books ensured that such regulations were obeyed, so far as appearances went, but the absence of any system of inspection meant that jerry-building where it could not be seen, in party walls and foundations, was all too common. Combined, as it often was, with lack of maintenance, it led rapidly to slums. Nevertheless, even in an age when authority is supposed to have made a principle of not interfering in industry, Parliament showed a continuing interest in building matters. In 1739, it legislated that all bricks made in the London area should be the same size: an act whose consequences for the efficiency of building operations and the appearance of London, has lasted longer than any other of its period.*

In the year the first George died in his coach at Osnabruck, and his unloved son succeeded him, England's growing consequence in Europe was marked by a prolonged visit by the young Voltaire. Robert Walpole's brother Horatio, the ambassador in Paris, brought it about, and never has a private visit arranged through diplomatic channels had more lasting consequences. Voltaire, citizen of what was still the most powerful and populous country in Europe, was charmed and excited by what he saw in the island kingdom. He detected little of the manipulation that sustained the Robinocracy, and drank in the evidence of a far more open society than his own over-regulated, and over-ripe world. He sensed the dynamism and independence of

---

* A brick is still $8\frac{3}{4}'' \times 4\frac{1}{8}'' \times 2\frac{1}{2}''$. The price of Georgian bricks throws considerable light on transport costs as compared with costs of production. The grey and brown bricks produced from London clay cost only a little more than half the red ones, which had to be brought from Berkshire or Bedfordshire.

the English, and was led into an Anglophile attitude which was as superficial as it was permanent. 'England,' he wrote, 'is the only country in the world where . . . the Prince is all-powerful for good, but has his hands tied to prevent his doing harm; where noblemen are great without insolence . . . and the people share in the government without disorder. Each man pays taxation,' he went on enthusiastically, 'not according to his rank in society, but according to his income.'

Here, especially, Voltaire was misled by his Whig friends, for business escaped tax almost entirely, and it was Walpole's dearest wish to broaden the basis of taxation primarily by increasing the share borne indirectly. Only in this way, he considered, could the heavy burden of the land tax—a kind of national rate—which Voltaire so much admired, be reduced. In 1733 he made the effort in this direction which nearly ended his career. Nothing tells one more about a society than its convulsions over taxation. In introducing the celebrated Excise Scheme, the Prime Minister found himself faced by a combination of business men, Jacobites, and the lower orders of society; and the first Budget in English history became the 'dance that will no longer go'.* Its failure shows the nature of a tacit social agreement, which was for a long time fundamental to English social structure, about who should pay for the central government.

The year 1734 marked the end of the second of the three seven-year stints of Walpole's power. The era of the country gentleman was becoming institutionalized. Three years earlier Edward Cave, who had been a post office clerk and part-time journalist, had launched the *Gentleman's Magazine*, which was to have a life of nearly a century and a half. The idea of a miscellany of news, articles of topical interest, descriptive narrative, political reporting, letters to the editor, all designed as a *storehouse* of ammunition for social life, was as new as the name for it which Cave drew from military vocabulary. Other 'magazines' were soon to follow in the wake of Cave's archetype—a *Scots Magazine* and a *Manchester Magazine* began publication before the end of

* The proposals of 1733 for extending and reinforcing the Excise were not, of course, part of a formal annual review of the nation's finances, as the Budget has now become; but Walpole considered them important enough to require such a general review to put them in their context, and they were put forward in one of his longest and most fact-laden speeches. Rumours had preceded it, so that the speech was greeted by the Opposition as a revelation of the terrible truth and one of the Opposition pamphlets dubbed it 'The Budget Open'd'. For some years the phrase retained its imputation, but gradually, as with 'Whig' and Tory the slur was lost, and only the technical meaning survived.

the thirties: but none recognized so acutely the elements of hinterland and city state which characterized Britain. For editorial purposes, as a compliment to town and country readers alike, Cave christened himself at the top of his regular column 'Sylvanus Urban'.

Though the struggle for existence was still desperate, and there was no mercy for those who were trodden down, it is probably true to say that the early eighteenth-century Englishman felt he was living in a new and different world; and he was right. He perceived, though he was only half aware of the significance of what he saw, that society was no longer having to devote almost all its effort to produce for the purposes of immediate consumption. Increasingly, and before the impact of technology or (except in one or two fields such as brewing) large-scale industrial operations, the emphasis of the economy was on the productive processes themselves. The object of the agricultural improvers, above all, was to increase production and dispose of a surplus through trade. The huge fairs, of which Sturbridge is one example, and the steadily rising trend of both exports and imports, are evidence of a society aligned to production rather than consumption: a world in which, despite misery and squalor, the standard of living was rising.

Chapter 8   The Growth of British National Consciousness

Two of the long-term changes that were at work underneath the gross, apparently unchanging upper crust of the Robinocracy concerned the position of women and the development of philanthropy, or, as the times preferred to call it, benevolence.

Legally the woman was always thought of as dependent. If she were married, everything she possessed became her husband's, though prudent parents often provided for widowhood or a spendthrift husband by putting an income for a married daughter's benefit into the hands of trustees. If a woman were single she might own land, but she was almost never in a position to sell it or raise money on it, for it was always on its way through her hands to male heirs. But the reality was growing less oppressive. The advent of joint stock enterprise and the National Debt, by producing a form of capital which the law had not thought of, was almost certainly beneficial to the economic position of women, who could freely own, buy, and sell shares, as not a few of them, including Lady Mary Wortley Montagu, are found doing during the South Sea boom.

One profession, which happened to be rising in public esteem, was opening to women. This was authorship. Mrs Aphra Behn and Mrs Mary de la Rivière Manley had blazed the trail at the sensational end of the market in drama and fiction, and they had earned their livings. The dramatic personality and outstanding talent of Lady Mary Wortley Montagu, who was estranged from a dull husband, gave impetus, almost respectability, to the idea of a woman commanding intellectual and social influence without the excuse of a consort. Sarah, Duchess of Marlborough, was an almost equal political partner with her husband, and long survived him to enjoy the wealth they had jointly accumulated. On a more moderate scale Swift's 'little Irish muse', Mrs Laetitia Pilkington, managed to survive in London largely by her fluent pen, despite an unsavoury divorce. 'Nothing but poetry', she said brightly to a gentleman who asked her what she lived on. If it was not quite true, she certainly worked as hard as most poets.

97

Elizabeth Elstob produced the first Anglo-Saxon grammar, and was helped by Queen Caroline. The names may not be many, but it would be difficult to muster even a list this length for independent women of distinction from any earlier period of English history.

In a period when the criminal law was growing more barbarous, not less,* and sympathy for misfortune took a low place in comparison with the universal struggle for existence, it is strange to encounter such figures as General Oglethorpe and Captain Coram. Yet in 1729 Oglethorpe managed to get monstrous prison conditions in Newgate exposed by a parliamentary enquiry, and the keepers, Huggins and Barnes, prosecuted for extortion and cruelty. Oglethorpe's friend and fellow-trustee of the new colony of Georgia, Thomas Coram, lives on in the genial Hogarth portrait of him at the Foundling Hospital which he launched in 1739 to deal with the appalling problem of abandoned new-born children in London. The principle of the open door, on which the charity came to be based, proved disastrous, and led to overcrowding, epidemic, and almost to breakdown. Just the same it is in contrast to the fashionable commonplace of the times, which was expressed by the husband of Fielding's Amelia: 'that as men appeared to act entirely from their passions, their actions could have neither merit nor demerit'.

Almost all the great London hospitals (the main exceptions being the ancient foundations of St Thomas's and St Bartholomew's) have their origins in eighteenth-century benevolence. Guy's was founded on the profits from the well-managed speculations of Thomas Guy, a stationer, in the South Sea Company. Before the end of the century four more major hospitals—not to mention dispensaries for the poor—had been added to London: the Westminster, the London, St George's, and the Middlesex Hospitals. The movement was hardly less strong in the main provincial towns, where most of the 'infirmaries' go back to the middle of the eighteenth century, and very few of them further.

Even the selfish, complacent thirties had the sense of advance, of

---

* The multiplication of capital crimes (Blackstone in the middle of the century listed 165), and the hideous punishment for treason, are well known. For a number of offences, such as coining, a woman could still be burned at the stake, even after the disappearance of the Witchcraft Acts. The extraordinary punishment of pressing to death was last inflicted in 1735. A prisoner who stubbornly refused to plead was extended on the floor of a prison, and weights were then placed on his chest, 'as much as he can bear and more'. He was then left there until he died. This frightful procedure was in a way worse because it was based on a mistake in reading the Norman French requirement of 'prison forte et dure' *until* a recalcitrant prisoner agreed to plead. But there was no escape from the 'peine forte et dure', once it was incurred, even if the prisoner agreed to plead.

moving to a higher level of civilization than before, and parliament contributed a modest quota of reforms in this spirit. In 1730, against the protests of the Lord Chief Justice, English was substituted for Latin as the only language of the courts.* Six years later, this time against the vehement opposition of a Scottish judge, Lord Grange, who was reputed to have an unrivalled library of books on demonology, the Witchcraft Acts were repealed, and one of the most grisly chapters in the history of the island was brought to an end.

Before the thirties were out the new and powerful voice of Wesley would be heard, and a new class was to be brought to the light. He had already, as a young tutor at Oxford, taken up the tradition of the religious societies from the later years of the seventeenth century, had visited prisons, and even defended a man charged with sodomy. Like Berkeley, Oglethorpe and Coram, he had felt the call of America, and had spent three years in Georgia (1735–7) in spiritual and amorous adventure. His almost Napoleonic energy and powers of organization were to burst like an evening storm on the fading glory of Augustanism, and refresh levels of society it had wholly ignored. But well before that happened the apparently quiescent Church of England was presented with a discovery which has lasting significance for the study of society.

This was the work of a strong-minded cleric named William Warburton. Later in life, when he was safely a bishop and a literary pundit, Warburton observed that the Church of England, like Noah's Ark, was worth saving, not for the sake of the animals on board, who 'probably made most noise in it, but for the little corner of rationality that is as much distressed by the stink within as by the tempest without'. He owed much to the church. He had never been to a university, and had started life as an attorney's clerk in Nottingham. In 1734 he put forward the most ingenious solution to the problem of the relationship between Church and State that had yet been advanced. Each, he argued, was necessary to the other, and this necessity justified the benefits which each conferred on the other. The state payed and protected the church; and the church produced by its teaching a state of opinion which made government possible. But they differed in nature. The state was an inevitable accompaniment of society; but within any society there was a theoretically infinite number of groupings which might provide the basis for a church. Out of this infinity

* Chief Justice Raymond's argument that 'upon this principle, in an action to be tried in Pembroke or Caernarvon, the declaration and indictment ought to be in Welsh', was treated by the House of Lords as frivolous.

the state would select the grouping which commanded the widest support; but if some other religious grouping came to predominate, the state would abandon its former partner, and extend its protection to the new 'church'. This was more than toleration, it was pluralism, and as such a development of permanent importance.

Warburton spoke from observation of the existing state of affairs, and the existing 'compact between Church and State' had been well expressed by Gibson, Bishop of London, writing to Walpole a year before Warburton published his book. 'The distinguishing characteristic of a Whig for thirty years together,' wrote Gibson, who was speaking of himself, 'is the settled principle of maintaining the Protestant succession, the Church Establishment, and the Toleration.' The Whigs, in fact, were no longer the party of Dissent, however camouflaged, but of the church they had penetrated and brought into partnership. The great contribution of the Duke of Newcastle to politics was his management of ecclesiastical patronage in the interests of government.

As Bishop Hare of Chichester put it to the Duke, 'the clergy have their relations, friendships, interests and opinions, as others have.' In return for acknowledgment of this truth, the clergy offered a considerable stock of political information and influence, which could sometimes result in forecasting that would make a modern pollster green with envy.* As the century wore on it became steadily more difficult for poor men to advance in the church, and those who did were almost bound to attach themselves to a grandee as chaplain, tutor or secretary, with the aim of being provided for after services which were often murky. The alternative was perpetual curacy on a stipend that was not only low (£20 or £30 a year), but uncertain, for the curate was no more than the hired servant of the beneficed clergyman who paid him and could discharge him at any moment. To this clerical proletariat also belonged the shabby ushers and undermasters of schools; the Fleet parsons, who were available to celebrate unlicensed marriages until Lord Hardwicke's Marriage Act of 1753 put a stop to it; and journalists, such as Wilkes's rowdy friend Charles Churchill,

---

* The cathedral clergy of Chichester were asked by the Duke of Newcastle to provide a forecast for the result of the election for the county of Sussex. There were four candidates:

	Forecast by the Chapter of Chichester Cathedral	Result
Pelham (Whig)	2,262	2,271
Butler (Whig)	2,046	2,053
Bishop (Opp. Whig)	1,698	1,704
Fuller (Tory)	1,570	1,581

or the discreditable Paul Whitehead. Door after door was being closed to the young man without influence who had managed to make his way through the university.

John Wesley belonged to this class. When he graduated in 1724 and was lucky enough to be elected a fellow of one of the least important Oxford colleges—Lincoln—the choice before him was perpetual celibacy as a college fellow, or poverty as a curate. In the end it was Wesley's methods of organization, rather than his theology or his social teaching, that made him a man apart, and one of the most significant figures of his century. Those methods defied the parish system on which the Georgian church was based. The famous utterance 'the world is my parish' was not mere rhetoric but a repudiation, conscious or unconscious, of the system which denied him a voice. For him it was not a question of subverting the church, or of starting a rival to it. He lived and died, as he always insisted, an orthodox Anglican and a devoted supporter of King and Parliament. But he chose to preach and to organize over the heads of the entrenched clergy, and his strategy had the vast simplicity of ignoring the church as an organization. It was his gift of organization rather than the originality of his message that made him great. Methodism was not a theological position but the application of order and principle to personal life and socio-religious organization. To express it in military terms, Wesley had discovered the war of movement, leaving the established church in the position of static garrisons.

Wesley's great social achievement was to discover a public which the established church had hardly reached, but which was rising steadily in economic importance: the poorer town-dwellers and the workers in the industrial villages. One might almost say that Wesley did not so much preach to the lower-middle class as create it. His use of group pressure through his system of 'classes' for each locality where he planted his ideas, regularly meeting to discuss religion, made for social cohesion. Instead of gin, obscenity, and dirt, he substituted, for tens of thousands, tea, respectability, and personal cleanliness. His neat, well-washed figure was in sharp contrast to the malodorous grossness of most people. There should, he said, be no such thing as a ragged Methodist, and it was possible for the poorest to be tidy.

The drinking of tea appears on page after page of his monumental journal, as he travels round the country encouraging and recruiting his followers. It was the great lubricant of Methodism, and in fifty years moved from being an upper-class luxury to something very near a universal necessity. In 1706 the 54,000 lb. imported had sold for

16s. a lb. wholesale. By 1750 the sales had multiplied fiftyfold and the price was 4s. a lb. The effect on the prosperity of the East India Company was remarkable. England became a tea-drinking nation in the first half of the eighteenth century. It may be wrong to associate the turn in the tide of spirit-drinking, which rose to its peak in the 1730s, directly to the increased popularity of tea, but there can be little doubt that the impact of Methodism in general had a good effect on public health, in which Wesley himself was keenly interested.

As early as 1725 Wesley had decided where he stood on the controversy over rational religion. For him religion was not, and could not be, founded on reason. Only personal faith would serve, and the other road pointed out by Toland and Bolingbroke led by way of Deism and doubt to infidelity. Wesley himself had suffered paralyzing doubts and conflicts within his own nature—not least over women—but in 1738 they were resolved in a great spiritual crisis that decided him, in partnership with George Whitefield, to begin a campaign of open-air preaching at Bristol. His effect on the urban poor was electrifying. By 1743 the first rules of the Methodist Society were promulgated, and a year later its first conference was held. The dapper, tireless little preacher had become a wholly unpredicted national figure, capable of rousing huge audiences to fervent emotion, and orthodox clergy to violent indignation. He was barely forty. To claim inspiration of the Holy Spirit, wrote Bishop Butler, 'was a horrid thing, Sir, a very horrid thing'.

Other evidence was gathering about the silent growth of the new tea-drinking class to whom Wesley made his appeal. In 1740 Richardson produced the first novel of ordinary life, in *Pamela or Virtue Rewarded*, which was an instant success. Its lesson is the same as Wesley's: one does not have to be on the pedestal of high life to feel deep emotions. Pamela is a servant girl, and the theme of the novel is her successful marriage above her station. The origin of the novel is congruent with its contents, for Richardson himself could not lay claim to any literary education. He had risen through apprenticeship to be a jobbing printer, and no man could have been better placed to portray middle-class morality than a self-made man.

By the end of the 1730s Britain was moving into two decades of almost continuous war on the continent, at sea, and in the New World, and the social changes one can already detect with hindsight in the last years of Sir Robert Walpole's power were to be hastened. War developed a conscious national feeling and demonstrativeness that was novel, and was to be long lasting. 'Rule Britannia', produced by one of the earliest Scots to make his way in the south, James Thomson, belongs to the year of Wesley's spiritual crisis and the outburst of national indignation over Jenkins's ear. 'God Save the King' followed a few years later, when it was taken up spontaneously by a concert audience during the Forty-five Rebellion. Long before the end of the century it had been institutionalized as the first of all national anthems. The political convulsion that brought down Sir Robert Walpole was no victory for the parliamentary and literary Tories who had pined for it so long. It masked a Whig continuity that was to endure for another twelve years. By 1741 the great days of Queen Anne might be disappearing below the horizon for most people, but Walpole's successors in power were still men who had been formed in those times. Newcastle remained at the hub of patronage and electoral management; his brother, Henry Pelham, emerged as a second Walpole at the Treasury; Hardwicke, having attained the Lord Chancellorship in 1737, was to retain it for nearly twenty years; Ligonier, who had fought in all Marlborough's battles, held high commands at Dettingen and Fontenoy. George II soldiered on, to the bitter disappointment of his ambitious dilettante son, Frederick, Prince of Wales.

But the nascent note of patriotism, and even ascendancy, that sounds in 'Rule Britannia' marked a crucial change in the nation. It was in the early 1740s that the generality of the inhabitants of Britain became aware that the whole world was accessible to their sea-power, and that their home island, by virtue of the same power, had little to fear from foreign invasion. Between 1740 and 1744 Anson's squadron circled the globe; and the rebellion of 1745-6 was contained by the navy's ability to prevent French reinforcements from reaching rebel-held areas, while at the same time transporting large numbers of troops from the continent and southern England to the points at which they could be most effectively used against the Highlanders. Four of the greatest names in English naval history—Rodney, Saunders, Duncan, and Howe—served in the naval operations of the Forty-five, three of them as captains and one, Duncan, as a midshipman.

We never speak of the 'English' navy. The British navy (and it is significant in dating its prestige that at this point the adjective attaches itself without self-consciousness) had become one of the most formidable armed forces in the world. Even in peace-time it contained well over 300 ships. The conditions of service in it, as the reader of *Roderick Random*, Smollett's novel about the navy, can discover, were almost inconceivably brutal, and the press gang was freely used to make up the crews who would be summarily turned off without consideration as soon as there was no further use for them. Discipline was savage, and the captain of each ship was virtually a despot. Captain Fergusson of the appropriately named H.M.S. *Furnace* carried instruments of torture on board and was known as 'the black captain'. The food was usually bad, and the care of the sick and wounded was rudimentary. One is tempted to ascribe its fighting efficiency to desperation.

But there were other reasons for the navy's remarkable success. The capital equipment of ships and guns was of good quality, and on the whole was efficiently maintained. Although there was patronage on a large scale there was no purchase of commissions, as in the army, and it was almost impossible to rise to senior rank except through experience at sea. A command in the navy was more open to talent than it was in the land forces, as the career of Captain Cook, who was working in the thirties as a deck-hand on a Newcastle collier, was to show.* But even an aristocratic officer such as Boscawen had served at sea for years in junior rank. The sea was a way of life for both officers and men, and they often spent months or years on commission without seeing a home port. The men might hate and fear the officers, but they relied utterly on their superior experience and training. Nor were more material motives lacking to keep a crew together. Prize money was an important source of income to naval men of all ranks in time of war. The lion's share might go to the officers but all ranks in a victorious crew participated, and the inn kept by a retired mariner who had found the capital out of prize money is a typical institution of the times. Above all the sailor, while he might be ill used, was regarded by society with an affection which the soldier never commanded. The friendly expression 'tar', which had emerged at the beginning of the century, did not find its land-based complement in 'Tommy' until much later in history. Admirals on the whole were Whigs and made popular politicians on occasion—as when Admiral Vernon fought and won the great Westminster election of 1744. Generals, on the whole, went for safe seats, and tended to be Tories after 1750.

The Highland rebellion of 1745–6 seems so out of key with the rest of Georgian Britain (and has been so overwritten since) as to appear almost an irrelevancy. Bands of Celts intrude suddenly on the stage of history and are then bundled off. But much was in fact settled by the bloodshed of Culloden and the savage repression that followed—far

* The navy lists of the time contain very few aristocratic names in the ranks of captain and below.

more than the fate of Celtic tribalism in Britain. Lowland, Presbyterian Scotland, which was itself undergoing a revolution against the old narrow ways, became dominant north of the Border.* The north and west was missionized, improved, and mapped. The old feudal jurisdictions of the Highlands, compulsorily exchanged for money compensation, put capital into the hands of Highland landlords for the first time. In the years after Culloden, Colonel David Watson, of the engineers, and his skilful clerk William Roy, were preparing the first adequate maps of the Highlands, for possible future military use. Huge schemes of afforestation were put in hand by Highland landlords. Between 1716 and 1746 Grant of Monymusk is said to have planted 30 million trees; a little later Lord Finlater planted 11 million. The Highlands were tamed. National discontents ceased finally to focus round the cause of the old dynasty, and sought other outlets, which were soon to be provided.

Above all the failure of the Rebellion was a demonstration that the great majority of the British were reconciled to their German dynasty and their Whig political system. A generation of stability had done its work and David Hume, whose first book appeared in 1739, found the key to human nature in the power to form habits, and the road to truth in the question 'Is it probable?' Hume's is the philosophy of an age in which one expects to be able to predict on the basis of experience, and the prices and qualities of things are known: a world where knowledge can reasonably be equated with certainty.

Hume was one of many Scots who were beginning to make an impression on Britain as a whole, and to seek fame and fortune in the richer south. Pupils of Newton's protégé, Colin Maclaurin, who was elected to the Chair of Mathematics at Aberdeen at the age of nineteen and to the Royal Society at twenty-one, provided a stream of engineers to the British army; and during the Forty-five Maclaurin himself mobilized the students of Edinburgh to dig fortifications of his own design against the Jacobites. James Thomson had established himself by 1730 as a London poet with the help of his fellow-countryman David Mallett. In 1736, to the grief and sorrow of both her parents, Lady Mary Wortley Montagu's daughter insisted on marrying an obscure but good-looking Scottish nobleman who was paying his addresses to the court of the Prince of Wales with a view to a political career: John Stuart, Earl of Bute, who in twenty years was to be

---

* Except with regard to whisky, which was to be the gift of the Highlands to Scotland, and later to the world. Carlyle of Inveresk notes that whisky was unknown in Lowland Scotland when he was a young man, before the Forty-five.

Prime Minister. Perhaps the most impressive career of all was to be made by young James Murray, who chose the law as the way to rise to the highest places, and by the early forties was one of the leaders of the English bar. At Westminster with Pope, at Oxford with Pitt, James Murray is the prototype of the ambitious, successful Scot.

Lord Chancellor Hardwicke said Murray could not help being a Scot long before Johnson said it of Boswell. The thrusting of the Scots in the south, in fact, was bitterly resented, and the resentment is one of the leading features in British life in the mid-century. More than one Scotsman in the south tried to conceal his name—Malloch became Mallet, Millan the publisher dropped the tell-tale 'Mac'. Hume practised an accent that would pass muster as English. For an able politician, appreciating that at least 'Liberty' was still 'English', not 'British', there was a situation ready to exploit.

In 1744 four men met in the rising James Murray's chambers in Lincoln's Inn Fields: Alexander Pope, Bolingbroke, Warburton, and Murray himself. For Murray, at thirty-nine, the deadly controversies of the high Georgian era—Wilkes, Junius, and America, were still ahead, together with an unrivalled career as a judicial law-maker. Warburton was on the threshold of punditry. The two Augustans were almost spent. Pope died that year, and Bolingbroke, though he lived to haunt Whiggery for another ten years, was a man of the shadows. It was a meeting and a parting of generations. Prior, Gay, Arbuthnot and Vanbrugh were already dead. Swift, by now a pathetic mental invalid, was to die in 1745. Lady Mary Wortley Montagu had retired to Italy and obscurity to nurse a broken middle-aged heart. Sarah, Duchess of Marlborough, after dictating her own version of historical events at the Court of Queen Anne to a journalist who had been virtually kidnapped and brought to Blenheim for the purpose, had also died in 1744. Most inveterate of all his generation, perhaps, had been Bentley, whom only death, at the age of eighty, in 1742, could deprive of the mastership of Trinity College, Cambridge. For years the greatest Greek scholar of his century had lived without speaking to the members of his college, who had used every legal means, without success, to get rid of their tyrant.

The 1740s saw the disappearance of the cultural leadership of the previous thirty years, but spared the political leadership. Most people no longer remembered the great period of turbulence and change, for by 1746 no regime England had known since the Tudors had lasted longer than the Georges. The settlement of Church and State, the Union of England and Scotland, the parish and the justice, the infinite convolutions of patronage and obligation, had become hardened and enshrined. The differences between 1746 and 1715 are not in appearances, but in economic strength and social stability, marked by thirty years of low interest rates, light taxation, moderate increases in population. Between these two years the export of native products had increased by 50 per cent, and re-exports had doubled. London had not grown much in size. But it had become the greatest commercial city in the world. The cumulative effect was to nourish British self-confidence, and develop the financial base for the industrial age that was to follow.

For the industrial age, which transformed not only Britain but in due course the whole world, did not depend solely on technology, and still less on pure science. The world of invention and mechanical power needed a special set of conditions in which to strike its roots, and these conditions came into being in Britain during the first half of the eighteenth century. They included stability and freedom from external threat or internal convulsion; a sufficiently developed system of commerce, finance and law; substantial reserves of labour; accumulation of capital; a major urban centre; and a widespread sense of identification with a national society. The next three decades were to bring many pressures to bear on the society that was now emerging, and the sense of self-confidence and identification were to be severely shaken. But under the Robinocracy the roots of change had struck too deep for subsequent weather to weaken the growth.

Chapter 9

'God made these Good
Things for Us'

In the 1740s Shakespeare suddenly came into his own again. Some of
his plays had not been seen on the stage since they were first produced.
Others were known only through versions which had undergone
wholesale modernization, such as Davenant's rendering of Macbeth.
The brilliance of the early eighteenth-century stage had in any case
made the Elizabethan and Jacobean drama seem old fashioned, and
Shakespeare had no particular pre-eminence among the earlier
dramatic poets. To the audience of 1741 the performance of the unknown twenty-four-year-old Garrick as Richard III—his first Shake-
spearean part—was a revelation, and the enthronement of Shakespeare
as the national poet took place alongside the thunder of the War of
Austrian Succession, the defeat of the Rebellion of 1745, and the establishment of the National Anthem. Arne, the composer of 'Rule Britannia' for the Scottish patriotic piece by Mallet and Thomson, was
responsible also for setting Shakespeare's songs to music for Garrick,
and stamped the Elizabethan poet with the approval and taste of
eighteenth-century patriotism.

The renaissance of Shakespeare was registered by more than the
advent of Garrick. In the same year as his appearance as Richard,
Macklin, taking the part of Shylock, put on *The Merchant of Venice* for the
first time in more than a century, and a little later *All's Well that Ends
Well* appeared on the English stage for the first time since Shakespeare
himself had put it on. Only one edition of Shakespeare that could in
any sense be called modern existed: that of Nicholas Rowe, the pet
Whig poet of Queen Anne's time, who had divided the plays for the
first time into acts and scenes, and inserted stage directions.* A serious
text had to wait until the middle of the century, when it was provided
by the inevitable authority, William Warburton, in 1747. By 1750 the

* Rowe, among much else, was responsible for a version of Marlowe's *Tamerlane*,
in which the central figure, curiously enough, was supposed to be William of
Orange. For many years it was regularly put on for the anniversary of the Revolution of 1688.

two chief London theatres, Covent Garden and Drury Lane, had rival productions of *Romeo and Juliet*: one with Spranger Barry and Arne's sister, Mrs Cibber, and the other with Garrick and George Anne Bellamy. England had rediscovered a national poet equal to the greatest that French civilization could offer, and Shakespeare was very soon to be translated into all the principal European languages. It can rarely have happened that in a renaissance of patriotic feeling a poet has been placed at the pinnacle of European achievement nearly two centuries after his death.

Garrick, with his Lichfield schoolfellow Samuel Johnson, had trudged to London in 1737, like so many other fortune-seekers, and had become famous in four years. Johnson, in accordance with his obsessional nature, set himself a harder road and did not emerge on the platform of fame until his *Dictionary* was published in 1755. Until then it was a journalistic struggle, working on parliamentary reports for Cave's *Gentleman's Magazine* and establishing a name rather than a place in society with his two great poems, 'London' and 'The Vanity of Human Wishes'. *The Dictionary of the English Language,* when it at last appeared, was offered with embittered triumph, an achievement 'with little assistance from the learned and without any patronage of the great . . . amidst inconvenience and distraction, in sickness and in sorrow'. It was not the first such attempt, but it was incomparably the most successful; and it was Johnson's purpose not merely to provide a work of reference but to arrange and purify. He had found a language 'copious without order, and energetick without rules . . . perplexity to be disentangled, and confusion to be regulated; choice was to be made of boundless variety, without any principle of selection; adulterations were to be detected without a settled test of purity.' Though Johnson deplored the notion of an Academy, his aim was to place English on the pedestal beside French as a modern language co-equal in dignity with the two ancient tongues.

Though Johnson's purpose was to reduce the language to order, he probably did not foresee that such a work was the indispensable foundation for literacy on a wide scale, and for the multiplication of readers on which alone a prosperous book trade could flourish. Until orthography was settled, and the visual patterns of words finally established, rapid, habitual reading could never be widespread. The importance of Johnson's *Dictionary* lies not so much in its definitions as in its authoritative spelling.

By the end of the fifth decade of the century the flowering of English imaginative literature was unmistakable. In three years, 1748–51, three

major novelists published three of their major novels: Richardson's
Clarissa Harlowe, Smollett's *Roderick Random*, and Fielding's *Tom Jones*.
Each, with hardly a glance at the elegance of the Augustans, sought
to describe life as it was; and between them they registered once and
for all the category of fiction with its new middle-class public and
their leisure to read.

At the same time a new note was creeping into poetry. The glittering
irony of the *Dunciad*, Pope's poetical manifesto bearing witness to the
fools among whom he had had to spend his life, had already given
way in the popular taste of the 1740s to the turgid melancholy of
Blair's *Grave* and Young's *Night Thoughts*. It is strange to think that *Night
Thoughts*, the work of a rector of Welwyn who pined for preferment,
should have endured to the end of the century to provide the favourite
bedside book of Robespierre. But long before that the raw emotionality
of Blair and Young was distilled into something far greater by Gray,
whose *Elegy* ushers in the first year of the new half-century. Here the
reader is taken gently by the arm and asked to identify himself with
the poet as he gazes at a world left 'to darkness and to me'. It was not
a matter of expressing an insight into religion or love, which had been
the excuses of earlier poets for intruding themselves into their verses.
Gray asked his reader to sit beside him in Stoke Poges churchyard and
gaze at the world with a kind of sympathetic detachment.

The new sense of leisure which these works of imagination were
produced to satisfy, extended to what we would think of as only a few;
but they were not all landowners and clergymen. Increasing prosperity was bringing not only literature and tea, but newspapers, fashion,
the pleasure-gardens and theatres of London, and the life of the spas,
within the reach of tens of thousands. Bath, declared John Wood, its
creator, had room for 12,000 visitors in 1740. The social and economic
success of Bath epitomizes the progress of English civilization in the
first half of the century.

Bath was developed as a clean, well-regulated holiday metropolis
by municipal foresight and the collaboration of three diverse talents:
Beau Nash, an impresario; John Wood, an architect and town planner
of genius; and Ralph Allen, an entrepreneur and local politician, who
combined the contract for an important part of the postal system*
with the exploitation of the Bath stone quarries. Nash contributed his
skill and energy in providing a regular round of entertainment in

* Allen's part in the development of the postal system was significant. It consisted
in organizing a 'cross-country' mail service in supplementation of the service
based on London.

which the visitor could be happily ensnared, and a kind of social dictatorship which curbed any eccentricity of behaviour. Wood's triumphs in British Palladian provide him with a monument which can still be enjoyed long after Nash's rather melancholy formal dance music has been silent. Allen was the least dispensable of the three. His business acumen, his friendships in the world of politics and literature, his unpretentious philanthropy, and his immense financial resources, make him the father of Bath. Fielding commemorates him as Squire Allworthy in *Tom Jones*. Pope and Warburton, both of whom he helped with money and influence, were among his closest friends. And for a time he persuaded William Pitt to represent Bath in Parliament. He is one of the few influential men of his time not to seek a seat in either the Lords or the Commons, though he was politician enough to have summaries of debates sent to him privately. As Pope said of him, he did good by stealth and blushed to find it fame; and he quarrelled bitterly with the poet over the previous line, which referred to 'low-born Allen'.*

Both architecturally and socially Bath was a planned city in the age of *laissez-faire*. The round it offered was open to anyone who could pay the fees and was presentable, and was designed to enable people to meet on an equal footing. The rules forbade the enforcement of distinctions of birth and fortune, and Nash had a quick eye for the dancer in the assembly rooms who merely touched the hand offered in the country dance instead of clasping it, indicating thereby a sense of social superiority. Such an offender was dismissed from the floor. The corresponding social rule was that there was no obligation to keep up elsewhere an acquaintance made at Bath; despite which Bath undoubtedly served the turn of social mobility, and was, above all, a marriage market. 'Bath', wrote Johnson to Mrs Thrale, 'is a good place for the initiation of a young lady. She can neither become negligent through want of observers, as in the country; nor with imagination that she is concealed in a crowd, as in London.' The very formality of the programme which Nash provided made for easy introduction, as did the three main amusements—gambling, dancing, and mixed bathing.

By 1742, when Allen became mayor of Bath and Nash posted the famous code of etiquette which enshrined the principle of 'ladies first' for the first time, Bath was a fully established institution. Though the Royal Crescent was still to come, Queen Square, with its obelisk

---

* Warburton married Allen's niece, and by Allen's influence gained successively the deanery of Bristol (1757) and the bishopric of Gloucester (1760).

commemorating the visit of the Prince of Wales in 1738 and the qualities of Bath stone, crowned the town that the elder Wood had planned. Bath had the *imprimatur* of one of the greatest of urban aristocrats, Lord Chesterfield, and he had made it the headquarters of the opposition to Walpole in 1738. England had not only created a second centre for style and fashion: it had rediscovered the concept, lost since Roman times, of a holiday resort and a holiday society. Wesley, not unnaturally, made it one of the first targets for his campaign of open-air preaching, and though his confrontation with Nash was far from friendly, it brought together the two men who probably contributed more to the improvement of social manners than any others in the first half of the eighteenth century.

At the beginning of the century even the greatest had been gross, and manners in high life had been governed by a man's sense of his own importance, rather than by any notion of consideration for the feelings of others. Johnson might say that Chesterfield, in his letters to his son, taught the manners of a dancing-master, but even these were a great advance. 'The Graces, the Graces, remember the Graces,' he moans over the crude young man whom he hoped to polish into the most perfect of gentlemen. He should not blow his nose, except on his handkerchief, should not laugh openly, should cultivate older ladies as the surest way to success in society. It was a society that had moved from the heavy gorgeousness of Vanbrugh's palaces to the almost over-refined charm of Horace Walpole's Strawberry Hill, which launched the fanciful 'Gothick' style in the middle of the century.

It was also a society increasingly influenced by European thought and taste. Travel for pleasure outside England was still for the few, but it was especially important because most of the travellers were young. Unlike the modern rich tourist, who tends to travel for improvement fairly late in life, the typical pair in the first half of the eighteenth century is a young, unmarried man of means and a youthful tutor, usually a clergyman. Such posts were eagerly sought after, since they could lead to livings later on. France was the main country visited, but Switzerland, Italy, and Germany formed part of any tour that could reasonably claim the title 'grand'. Rome, where the industrious Pompeo Battoni painted huge numbers of aristocratic English tourists in the course of his career, was the usual southern terminus. There, at Florence and at Venice, where from 1740 to 1760 the indefatigable collector Joseph Smith was British consul, contacts were established with the agents and dealers through whom antiques and works of art were bought to adorn the galleries of English country houses.* Even from the comparatively remote counties, such as Northumberland and Durham, young men were going on prolonged continental tours as early as the second decade of the century, and by 1740 there was already an English coffee house in Rome. A call on Voltaire at Ferney was very soon to become one of the stations on the cultural pilgrimage. And the compliment to the continent was being reciprocated. In 1746 Canaletto found it worth his while to settle in England, and remained, recording the beauties of the new Venice on the Thames, for nine years.

The immediate surroundings of the great houses, and even of the more modest ones in which the country gentry dwelt, were changing. The formal geometry of gravel paths and interlacing box hedges, the topiary and avenues of neatly shaped trees, which seventeenth-century England had borrowed from French taste, were giving way to a smoother and more characteristically English sweep. Burke, in his first published work, laid down the rule clearly. 'Nothing long continued in the same manner, nothing very suddenly varied, can be beautiful; because both are opposite to that agreeable relaxation, which is the characteristic effect of beauty.' From the *Philosophical Enquiry into the Origin of our Ideas of the Sublime and the Beautiful,* indeed, one might almost infer that the supreme aesthetic pleasure consisted in going to sleep.† Kent and Lancelot ('Capability') Brown worked on the principle that landscape beauty resided in the sinuosity of the S shape, and in the blending of the cultivated garden with the contours of the surrounding countryside. They preferred in consequence, to eliminate the boundary wall, and to mark the end of the garden with the device of a concealed terrace, or ha-ha. Brown, who had risen from being kitchen gardener at Stowe to the status of a consultant, drew the wish from one of his customers that he might die before Brown

* Many treasures, and much rubbish came to England in this way. British diplomatists were not above art-dealing for their friends in England—Horace Mann, the British envoy in Florence and friend of Horace Walpole being a notable example. The notorious Bubb Dodington, who had himself been a diplomatist, used diplomatic contacts to acquire antiques—and other things, such as two enormous porphyry pillars, which were shipped from Italy to adorn his house at Hammersmith.

† 'When we have before us such objects as excite love and complacency, the body is affected, so far as I could observe, much in the following manner: The head reclines something to one side; the eyelids are more closed than usual, and the eyes roll gently with the inclination of the object; the mouth is a little opened, and the breath drawn slowly, with now and then a low sigh; the whole body is composed, and the hands fall idly to the sides. All this is accompanied with an inward sense of melting and langour . . . beauty acts by relaxing the solids of the whole system.' (1798 ed., p. 288.)

and so get to heaven before the great man had begun to discover and bring out its capabilities. Huge sums were spent, and whole villages were employed, on shifting earth and damming streams to make the sheets of artificial water across which one of Brown's favourite scenic bridges would gracefully carry the eye beyond the shrubbery to the downs or the woodlands beyond. Shenstone, when congratulated by Pitt on the natural beauties of his famous gardens near Birmingham, replied rather uppishly that he hoped he had done something for Nature, too. Nor was Pitt himself behindhand as a landscaper. Apart from advising others, his own grounds at Enfield possessed a pyramid, a bridge, and a Temple of Pan 'adapted with so much propriety to the thickets that conceal it from the view that no one can wish it to be brought forward.'

The very fruits, flowers, and vegetables in the gardens were changing —changing above all as a result of Britain's wider-ranging maritime trade. Up and down England eager amateurs with correspondents in America or in the navy were unpacking and experimenting with strange packets of seeds or carefully packed tropical plants. The dog-wood and the persimmon, the date-palm and the rhododendron, found their way into English gardens, and gardening books began to include directions for the management of green-houses and conserva-tories. Varieties rapidly multiplied, and it was a fitting thing that Brown himself should have been employed, just half-way through the century, to lay out the gardens at Kew where, above all, the living evidence of the expanding empire overseas could be planted and displayed.

The movement towards adequate systems of classification, to which the great English scientists of the Augustan period had given the impulse, had passed abroad when the generation of Newton had died away. Science was now, to a far greater extent than fifty years earlier, an international republic, and Buffon's *Histoire Naturelle* (1749) and Linnaeus's *Philosophia Botanica* (1751) were as influential in England as on the continent. It began to seem as if it might be possible to draw up a complete account of human knowledge. In 1751 Diderot published his proposals for a universal encyclopedia; and in 1753 the British Museum was established.

Yet the optimism of the mid-century, whether it took the form of domesticating the country gentry by subjecting them to a regular round of civilized pleasure at Bath or classifying Creation in books of reference, rested on shallow foundations. Of the five continents, one (Australia) was no more than an indication on the charts, and another,

Africa, was known only on its coastal strip. Even knowledge of India, whence fortunes were beginning already to percolate back into the estates bought by English 'nabobs', was rudimentary. Its languages, religions, and laws were barely touched upon, even by those who spent years there fighting and trading. The world that considered Newton had explained the universe understood little about the composition of matter, and was still, with Franklin's lightning conductor and Kleist's Leyden jar, only on the edge of speculating what powerful forces apparently inert matter might contain. Even steam power, the only source of mechanical power to be discovered since the windmill, remained much as Newcomen had left it in the reign of Queen Anne, driving pumps in the Cornish tin mines by an engine which required the cylinder to be drenched in cold water after every stroke in order to achieve the necessary condensation.

It is natural, but a mistake, to associate the transformation of the means of production—sometimes known as the Industrial Revolution —which enabled new multitudes to survive and to improve their standard of living, with the population explosion which was now on the point of occurring. All the probabilities are that the up-turn in the population, which almost certainly began in the 1740s, was wholly independent of any advance in technology or industrial methods. It preceded the effective application of steam power and the widespread adoption of factory methods by as much as a quarter of a century. It cannot indeed be said with confidence that the up-turn which most demographers assign to the 1740s did in fact occur, for there was no national census, and no effective registration of either births or deaths.* A census was indeed suggested in 1753, but the proposal was howled down in a storm of protests which ranged from quoting the fate of Saul when he numbered the people to claims that the government would use the data for political or fiscal purposes.† But although the up-turn of population is unverified, and some contemporary observers supposed that the population might actually be declining, the grounds for placing it in the 1740s are very strong. The best estimates suggest that between 1740 and 1750 the population of England increased by

---

* Christenings and burials, which were of course recorded locally, do not necessarily correspond closely to births and deaths—though burials correspond more closely with deaths than christenings with births. The matter is further complicated by the exclusion of Nonconformists and Catholics from the parish records.
† There was, however, a most effective census in Scotland in 1755; but it was not conducted by the government. It was conducted by the Kirk. See J. G. Kyd, 'Scottish Population Statistics', *Proceedings of the Scottish Historical Society*, 3rd Series, vol. 44 (1952).

about 4 per cent (to 6·25 million) after several decades of almost complete stability. The cause may have been temporary, even trivial, but the upward movement, once started, was never halted. The Scottish and Irish populations had been moving upwards very steadily since the beginning of the century, while that of America had already exploded; so that by 1756 Pitt was not far out in speaking, during the debate on the Treaty of Westminster, of 'twelve millions of his countrymen' provided he included the Irish and the Americans. But he had no figures to rely on, and the more likely significance of his utterance is a dramatic example of the general ignorance about the size of the population of Great Britain.

The proposed census in 1753 was not the only attempt at social legislation in the mid-century. Though the way of the social legislator was hard, there was more done to improve matters by Act of Parliament in the age of *laissez-faire* than is often credited to it. Governments, indeed, did not usually take the initiative on such measures, partly because they knew there was virtually no machinery to carry them out; but legislators, many of whom were themselves magistrates, dearly loved to pass bills against the evils of the day as they saw them— as witness the succession of acts against gin and gambling, most of which were ineffectual for lack of enforcement. Legislation on social questions in the age of the Pelhams only had a chance of effectiveness if it was virtually self-enforcing, and even then it had to contend with vested interest and the innate conservatism of the ordinary citizen.

Lord Hardwicke's Marriage Act satisfied the condition of self-enforcement, and by requiring adequate publicity for a marriage to make it valid, it protected family wealth from the perils of elopement and marriage to a fortune-hunter by a down-at-heel parson. It was certainly the first lay regulation of marriage. Lord Chesterfield's interference in the calendar (much against the wishes of the timorously conservative Duke of Newcastle) was another such venture into a field which till then had been considered the preserve of the church, and by legislating eleven days out of the month of September 1752 in order to catch up with the Gregorian Calendar used on the continent, it caused uncomprehending riots against the reduction of the human life-span by Act of Parliament.* A third piece of social legislation, which

* Harmony of the time of day in all parts of the kingdom had to wait until the next century, when speeds of communication began to make it desirable. But Chesterfield's Act was a notable step away from insularity, and a sign of the bond with Europe. It not only established the Gregorian Calendar, but set 1 January as the beginning of the calendar year, instead of 25 March. The Treasury had to bow to the omission of eleven days, and made up a full year by moving the end of 1751/2

was in fact engineered by the government itself, and not by a private legislator, is especially instructive about the state of public opinion and the possibilities of its manipulation in the middle years of the century. This was the so-called Jew Bill.

Even in 1753, when the Jewish Naturalization Bill was proposed, there were only about 5,000 Jews in England, and it is likely that not many Englishmen had ever met one.* Most were in business in London, and a few were wandering, exotic pedlars. One or two men of Jewish race but Anglican religion, such as Sampson Gideon, had risen to considerable financial and social heights; but no professing Jew could be British, for the simple reason that even the expensive procedure for naturalization by Act of Parliament required that the naturalized person should take Communion according to the practice of the Church of England. The Jews, therefore, remained aliens, and the Bill first proposed in 1747 and revived in 1753 sought no more than the removal of the religious test to give them access to naturalization.

The Whigs had always favoured an open door to English citizenship, and even a comfortable post-Walpolian like Pelham still felt the influence of the old doctrine which had once been used to help the Huguenots and the Palatines. The government's weight was thrown behind the Bill; but opposition poured in from all over the country, with the City of London in the lead. At a time when the Tory party is generally supposed to have been quiescent, the old alliance between church and squire, amplified by a furious newspaper campaign, showed more unanimity and vigour than at any time since the impeachment of Sacheverell. The Bill did indeed pass, but it was very soon repealed. The demonstration of exclusiveness and insularity—for this, rather than any feeling against Jews as such was the main feature of the opposition to the Bill—was clearly still one of the Englishman's strongest traits: it did not matter whether that Englishman was a rural landowner, a parson, or a town-dweller. One of the Bill's most inveterate opponents was the leading M.P. for the City of London, Sir John Barnard, who had been brought up a Quaker, but had developed into a staunch Anglican and unrelenting Tory, an opponent of the 'moneyed interest' and the Stock Exchange, and an eager representative of the small merchants and tradesmen of the

---

* M. Dorothy George, *London Life in the Eighteenth Century,* p. 128. The number had risen considerably by the end of the century, in the wake of east European persecution.

---

forward. But they shrank from a change to the new calendar year, so our financial year still begins on 5 April.

City which he represented for nearly forty years. Though he was himself a very big business man he had all the instincts and prejudices of a small one: instincts which were to be turned in the next decade from insularity to radicalism.

Yet this still insular community was now, after years of accumulation, the repository of huge funds from abroad, and was on the verge of ruling half the known world. In 1723 the foreign holdings of British securities in the three great public companies* came to £4·3 million; in 1750 they amounted to nearly £7 million—one-fifth of their entire capital. Altogether the foreign holdings of British stocks, including government issues—what we would call today the sterling balances —were estimated in the 1740s at over £10 million, or 15 per cent of the stock issued. There can be no doubt that foreign investment was vital to the success of the British wars between 1739 and 1763, and that without it the subsidies to Britain's continental allies—first Austria, then Prussia—would hardly have been possible.

The social consequences of this expanding debt were as important and as lasting as the political and military ones. On the continent, especially in Holland, and at home, increasing numbers of individuals and societies were coming to depend on the British economy and the stability of the British government for their incomes. The pastors of the French Church at Basle, Marguerite Girardot de Préfond of Paris, John Tamesz 'Esq of Moscow', Nicholas Salisbury, barber, of Boston Mass., Major John Penvaise of the King of Prussia's Horse Grenadiers, Bertrand de Jonge of Middleburg, surgeon: were all holders of British government stock in the mid-century. Many schools, colleges, charities and local authorities for whom land was the traditional investment, now held part of their assets in the stock issued by either the government or one of the three great companies. Stock, moreover, was a convenient way for a woman to hold assets and the growth of female property in securities is especially significant. At the beginning of the Robinocracy women had owned about one-fifth of the principal stocks. By the middle of the century the fraction had risen to about a quarter of a much larger market, and much more than this quarter was owned on behalf of women by trustees and executors.

This is the context in which Henry Pelham, the skilful under-estimated Prime Minister of the early 1750s must be judged. His great reorganization of the National Debt, which in its details appears so

* The Bank of England, the East India Company, and the South Sea Company. Until nearly the end of the century the London Stock Exchange was virtually limited to dealings in these three companies and, of course, government securities.

technical an operation, in fact concerned the pockets of many thousands, ranging from Moscow to Boston, Massachusetts. By investing in securities backed by the British government one was sure of a regular income—even if the yield was only 3 per cent.* The reduction in the rate of interest, which pleased the squires in Parliament and was bitterly resisted by the City, was a significant enough index of the general state of confidence. It increased the flow of capital, but even more significant was the apparently technical rearrangement of administration by which the old concept of debts secured on particular taxes was abandoned, and a large part of the debt made to depend on a single or 'consolidated' fund to which all the duties were carried, and from which all the interest on the debt was paid. For such a system was perpetual, and envisaged the National Debt as a permanent part of British administration. There was no longer to be a Sinking Fund dedicated, at least in name, to paying it off; and the new 3 per cent stock, which rapidly came to be known as 'consols', was no more than an income guaranteed by the British government. It could be transferred from one person to another, but there was no question of the government ever repaying the original loan. The price of 'consols' was consequently the most sensitive of all indices of British credit. The genius of Pelham lay in discovering a respectable method of borrowing money without any obligation to pay it back.

King George II reached seventy in 1753, and his Prime Minister was still under sixty, looking forward, as he told his old crony Bubb Dodington, to a successful election in 1754, a thorough Whig Parliament, and a period of office long enough to see the old king quietly into his grave and put the new one on to the right road. Then, in March 1754, with the election only a month ahead, Pelham died, leaving the headship of affairs to his indefatigable, fussy elder brother, the Duke of Newcastle. The Robinocracy was beginning to draw to a close, and a new, more emotional era lay ahead.

* Professor T. S. Ashton, *The Industrial Revolution, 1760–1830* (Oxford University Press, 1948) p. 11, places particular emphasis on the downward trend of interest rates as a factor in capital formation.

Chapter 10   The Rise of Efficiency and the Hardening of Class

As Lord Hardwicke remarked, very few people could remember a time when the House of Commons had not been dominated by either Henry Pelham, or Robert Walpole before him. The age into which the Duke of Newcastle, an increasing anachronism, was permitted, unlike his brother, to survive, was one of mounting conflict, of grappling in the dark with new issues whose outlines were only half perceived, of internal questioning, and bold adventure. But it is enriched by being also a period of manifest flowering and achievement. The humdrum sanity, genial acquisitiveness, alcoholic grossness of Hanoverian Whiggery are quite abruptly succeeded by the neurotic aggressiveness of Pitt, the raucous libertarianism of Wilkes, and the purposeful meanderings of Sterne.

People were becoming more mobile, both geographically and socially. It was no unusual thing for a servant-maid, having lost her job in County Durham, to turn up in London looking for work a month or two later, having travelled down on a collier with her box. Laurence Sullivan and Robert Clive, who for years disputed the control of the East India Company, had both started as clerks. The horizon was filling with new possibilities. The impact of successful conquest in India and America, one densely populated by an old and chaotic civilization, and the other wide open to exploitation by European slave-owners and pioneers, was being felt in every corner of British life, at the very time when the possibilities of mechanical power in its application to industry were being unlocked. But to contemporaries the gathering clouds of industrialism did not, for a long time, suggest anything new. India and America were the dominating themes of politics during the twenty years of High Georgianism that followed the death of Pelham.

The generations that had passed since the union of the island had brought a great measure of consolidation to the country as a whole, and as the old Celtic culture of the Highlands was destroyed the level of Lowland Scottish civilization rose steadily towards English standards.

The rotting heads of the rebels of Forty-five, impaled above Temple Bar, were a reminder, but a reminder of something that was finished. In the northern half of the kingdom the link between unionism and higher standards was explicit; and when King George III opened his first Parliament (with a speech written by the first of Scottish Prime Ministers) glorifying in the name of Britain, union, as much as patriotic pride and the acclimatization of the monarchy was in mind.*

Carlyle of Inveresk chronicles the development of a civilized life in Scotland which by the end of the century was to make Edinburgh and its New Town 'the Athens of the North'. The struggle was long and deliberate, fought in the church, in the theatre, on the golf links, and at the card table, against the old fragmentary narrow theocracy whose heroism and absurdity are so vividly described in *Old Mortality*. Carlyle and his allies in the General Assembly tirelessly pressed for broader churchmanship and better pay for the clergy. By personal example he tried to substitute a middle-class style of living for sanctity as the clergyman's source of prestige. To the general scandal he played golf,† sat down at cards without locking the door, and ostentatiously attended the first night of Home's *Douglas*.

That Carlyle should have been the first clergyman to attend a theatre in Scotland (attempts were made to deprive him of his living in consequence) is perhaps less surprising when one considers that until the 1750s theatres were not permitted in Scotland at all. But the production of *Douglas* on 14 December 1756 was more than a pioneer performance or an opportunity for clerical protest: it was, and was meant to be, a national intellectual manifesto of a new kind. For months previously the manuscript had been circulated among Home, Carlyle, Robertson, and their friends of the 'Select Society' so that the tragedy on a Scottish theme was almost a collective work. It was meant to show that Scotland had arrived on the intellectual scene, and the cry of 'Whaur's your Wullie Shakespeare noo?' from the back of the audience, which followed the thunderous applause, showed that it had succeeded.

The drift of Scots to the south in search of careers as authors,

* Junius did not fail to take the point: 'When you affectedly renounced the name of Englishman,' he wrote in his letter to the king, 'believe me, Sir, you were persuaded to pay a very ill-judged compliment to one part of your subjects, at the expense of the other.'

† Carlyle also took part in what must have been one of the first games of golf ever played in England. In 1758 he and five other Scots played on a ground at Garrick's house near Hampton Court. On their way to the course, carrying their clubs, they were cheered by the Coldstream Guards, on duty outside Kensington Palace.

politicians, journalists or gardeners, was no longer a matter of the exceptional few. Well educated and pushing, they were watched with increasing suspicion and jealousy by the English. John Douglas, who took Anglican orders, entered the Pulteney family as a tutor, 'acquired a very exact knowledge of the Court and of both Houses of Parliament', and finished up as Bishop of Salisbury while his sister continued to keep the Scotsman's favourite gathering place in London, the British Coffee House. Murray, blenching at the prospect of leading the House of Commons against the opposition of Pitt, stepped on to the Bench as Lord Chief Justice. Allan Ramsay emigrated from Edinburgh to paint portraits in London in 1756, and became court painter to George III. In 1762 the youthful Boswell, after canvassing half London in his efforts to get a commission in the Guards, met his literary destiny in Cave's bookshop in the shape of Samuel Johnson, and braved his hostility to Scotsmen.

The hostility was not an eccentricity of Johnson's, but something he shared with the majority of his countrymen. As late as the 1770s Junius was writing of the

> characteristic prudence, the selfish nationality, the indefatigable smile, the persevering assiduity, the everlasting profession of a discreet and moderate resentment . . . We shall soon be convinced *by experience*, that the Scots, transplanted from their own country, are always a distinct and separate body from the people who receive them. In other settlements they only love themselves;—in England they cordially love themselves, and as cordially hate their neighbours.*

Pitt's embodiment of Scottish regiments in the British army for the third and greatest of the conflicts with France which the century had so far seen, brought Highlanders into Wolfe's force for the capture of Quebec but was by no means a sign of Scottish acceptability in England —or of the desirability of giving arms to more than a few Scotsmen. Despite Carlyle's suggestions, Pitt's plans for a popularly based militia were limited to England, and the idea was not extended to Scotland until the early nineteenth century. As for acceptability, Highland officers fresh from service in America in 1762 were hissed by the audience when they took their seats in a London theatre: an incident which made Boswell wish 'from my soul that the Union was broke and that we might give them another battle of Bannockburn'.

Edinburgh in the fifties might be already glowing towards brilliance,

* Preface to *Letters of Junius.*

but Glasgow, prospering as never before from the sugar and tobacco trade which the Union had opened, was the seed-bed for developments which were to be more lasting for Britain and even the world. There Adam Smith, as honorary member of a businessmen's club, began to find in the conversation of tobacco merchants the trains of thoug which were to lead him to *The Wealth of Nations*; and Joseph Black defined the principles of latent heat which underlay an effective technology of steam power. In 1764 his technician assistant, James Watt, constructed the first separate condenser, making use of Black's principle to achieve the decisive economy in fuel, and the possibility of a reciprocating engine.

Pelham had left behind him a financial situation which was almost unprecedented, and was never to be repeated. With the conclusion of peace in 1748 he had brought expenditure on the armed forces down from £9 million to £2 million a year, and the land tax to two shillings in the pound. By reducing the interest on the National Debt he cut the transfer of money from the taxpayer (mainly the agriculturist) to the stockholder by more than a quarter. Never again were the squires to see such a happy moment. Five days after Pelham's death the level-headed Hardwicke summed the political situation up in a letter to Archbishop Herring. 'The opinion, therefore, which I with my friends in the Cabinet have formed, is that there is at present no person in the House of Commons fit to place entirely in Mr Pelham's situation with safety to this administration and the Whig Party.' With great skill he had straddled not only the landowners and the great 'monied interest', but the increasingly vocal and important middle class of the towns—above all of London: narrow, jealous, ambitious, nationalistic and turbulent, searching for a political leadership which the system did not yet provide.

By 1754 all these three ingredients of society had altered and developed, both within themselves and in relation to one another, since Walpole had first come to power. Enclosure of open fields and waste had gone rapidly ahead: under George II nearly 319,000 acres were the subject of Enclosure Acts, compared with 18,000 under George I, and only 1,500 under Queen Anne. Much enclosure, of course, was carried out by agreement, and acreage enclosed by statute measures only cases where enclosure was opposed. The pace of advance is impressive. The social change wrought by enclosure was considerable, even though (contrary to what is often assumed) no provable rights were abrogated. The established cultivator of a few strips in the old open field received his allocation when enclosure took place, though he often lacked the capital to fence his new holding, sold out, and became a labourer or migratory employee, or perhaps a tenant. But there were many with no ascertainable rights, who had literally picked up a living on the fringes of the village economy, and enclosure swept away such primitive independence as they had. On the whole the effect of enclosure was to make the substantial properties larger, with the largest of all gaining most. By the middle of the century England was well on the way to being alone among European countries in having eliminated the peasantry as a class. The peasantry survived only in such remoter areas as the Lake District or in Scotland and Wales; and, above all, in Ireland.

The gain in agricultural efficiency and output per man was very great, and continued to improve over the next twenty years. Drainage schemes, systematic rotation of crops, improved strains of wheat, organized breeding of stock, became possible on a scale that could not have been contemplated earlier in the century. Above all a population was released—painfully, perhaps, but less painfully than when peasantries were liquidated in later centuries—to provide the hands for new industries and the peopling of America. Landlords increasingly turned to the exploitation of non-agricultural sources of wealth yielded by their lands—to coal, china clay, stone, timber, copper and tin. Not surprisingly, rising rents reflected rising yields. During the quiet days of the Robinocracy rents had remained remarkably stable—and this was not merely because productivity did not increase very much. Sometimes because of social conscience, but more often to preserve good relationships and political support, the great landlords had been shy about asking a higher rent when renewing a lease. Over the sixty years between the Revolution and the middle of the century the maximum movement in rents had been less than 1 per cent per annum, and commonly the increase was much less. But between 1750 and the end of the century an average of 2 per cent per annum was typical.

The result was a new, hitherto untapped source of capital, part of which remained to improve the land (or often to burrow beneath it for minerals) while part flowed through the hands of urbanized aristocrats to swell the resources of the City. There the 'monied interest', based on the three great privileged companies—the Bank of England, the East India Company, and the South Sea Company—now controlled very large capital sums through a comparatively small group of established City magnates. When Pitt failed in his populist attempt to raise a war loan in small sums from a broadly based open subscription, Sir Joshua Vanneck, Sir John Gore, Sampson Gideon, and the three great companies raised in a few days almost the entire £2 million required. The companies' contacts were international, and they were pre-eminently the channels through which foreign funds flowed into the English Exchequer. The charters on which their monopolies were based had been renewed from time to time for long terms of years in return for further loans to the state— in the case of the East India Company the next renewal date fell in 1780. In the three Indian Presidencies of Madras, Calcutta and Bombay business and political influence was quietly expanding as the Mogul Empire and its weakly ruled princely dependencies decayed. Occasionally, at home, there were movements in shareholders meetings which in retrospect have some significance; but in general, until the 1750s, the caucuses maintained a tight hold, and a few hands ensured orderly progress.

But the flood-waters were rising against the monopolists of the 'monied interest', and in the 1750s the dams burst, and the smaller business men of the City began to come into their own. In William Beckford, whose huge fortune came from Jamaican sugar, the smaller men found an energetic spokesman whom they returned to Parliament for the first time in 1754. It was in appealing to this new element, which was willing to use the politics of the streets as well as the influence of the counting house, that Pitt's special gifts resided; and in a measure those of Wilkes also. Drama, and a dramatic personality, were what the rising class demanded. Pitt's 'power without doors', Wilkes's 'patriotism' and non-specific emphasis on 'liberty', captured the imaginations and crystallized the ambitions of the Londoners— or rather of the inhabitants of the urban area stretching from Chelsea to Bermondsey.

It has been pointed out that during the whole of the eighteenth century only three governments enjoying the full support of the Crown were overthrown: Walpole's in 1742, North's in 1783, and Newcastle's in 1756. In each case failure in war, savage journalistic attacks, and popular clamour had been enough to tip the scale; but the fall of Newcastle's government in 1756 is the only instance where these 'out of doors' pressures were stronger than both the Crown and a substantial loyal majority in the House of Commons. Parliament never withdrew its confidence from Newcastle's shortlived attempt to carry on the system he had inherited from his brother: its Members had been returned only two years before in one of the quietest and least contentious elections of the century. The novelty of the situation and the strength of Pitt's 'power without doors' or 'popularity' sufficed. His programme was largely designed for the platform, and not for execution when in office: disentanglement from continental commitments; a citizen army; reliance on small subscribers for national loans; continued denunciation of a Jacobitism that was now dead as a political force; and a forward policy in America.

Behind the demonic figure of Pitt (and behind Wilkes, also, until he went too far) stood the great landowning cousinhood of Grenvilles and Temples, centring on Stowe. Pitt had grown up under their protection, and they provided Wilkes with a seat in Parliament, the sheriffdom of Bucks and a commission in the 'popular' Bucks militia. But neither Pitt nor Wilkes could claim either land or gentility. As 'Leonidas' Glover proudly told Pitt's City supporters, he was 'without the pride of birth'.* Wilkes's father had made his fortune from gin. Pitt had received his higher education at Utrecht, Wilkes at Leyden. Both were capable of unlocking popular enthusiasm on a scale which had not been seen for several generations.

The Seven Years War, in which Pitt was the architect of victory in three continents, differed profoundly from Britain's earlier wars. Not only was it on a vaster scale, geographically and militarily, making greater calls on money, manpower, and industry: it was the expression of the thrust and vigour of the new urban class. Dynasticism and religion, the balance of power in Europe and the old Whig alliance with the Hapsburgs, moved into the background, and of the victories of 1759 Minden, which was almost in the class of Ramillies as a land battle, took second place to the capture of Quebec in the popular mind. If it was already determined by the course of world history that European civilization in one form or another should spread over the globe, the large share of it that would be English was decided by the Seven Years War.

For the development of British society this enlargement of horizons was very important. To the confidence of the rulers securely based on their landed rights and their mastery of the political system, it superadded a confidence among the ruled. 'Empire' and 'Liberty' were curiously blended, not opposed. When Johnson said that patriotism

* There is an element of propaganda in this statement, but it is mainly true. Pitt inherited no money from his grandfather, the celebrated 'Diamond' Pitt, whose career belongs to the first age of English enterprise in India. His father, Robert, was wholly undistinguished. Both Robert's and William's generations, however, married energetically into the peerage.

was the last refuge of a scoundrel he could as well have been referring to Wilkes as to Pitt.

Into the noisy success and increasing prosperity of High Georgian-ism a new, and more self-conscious style of literature was being laun-ched. Models, authority, expertise, were being overthrown in the process. By 1760, though laboured over long before that, appeared the fantastic, rambling novel—if novel is the word for it—offered by an obscure Yorkshire clergyman, Laurence Sterne. The immediate success of *Tristram Shandy* contradicts the cliché which describes the eighteenth century as the Age of Reason, for nothing could be less rational. It has no message, no story, no point except to etch personality and feeling. Sterne does not tell, or narrate; he describes and re-creates, and it is often forgotten that *Tristram Shandy* is one of the first of 'period' novels. It is set in the second decade of the century, a generation earlier than its readership. Uncle Toby's background is King William's war, and Mr Shandy's politics are those of Queen Anne's time. Defoe had re-created the atmosphere of the past under the colour of truth: Sterne re-created its personalities under the colour of fiction.*

Interest in the past, indeed the sense of the past, which finds its flowering in Scott half a century later, was spreading and deepening. In 1762 Warburton's friend Hurd published his *Chivalry and Romance*— a juxtaposition of words whose utter novelty it is now hard to recap-ture; and three years later Thomas Percy, in *Reliques of Ancient English Poetry,* put before an enthusiastic public a poetic tradition wholly different from the one to which they had been conditioned since the beginning of the century. Before the decade was out the genius of Chatterton was to be wasted and destroyed in exploiting the market for antique literature, and the first preposterous medieval blood-curdlers, such as Horace Walpole's *Castle of Otranto*, were reaching the public.

Not surprisingly, when minds were on the turn, there appeared almost at the same moment an expression of the conventional view so abject as to be almost a parody. In his *Free Enquiry into the Nature and Origin of Evil* Soame Jenyns came close to demonstrating there was no such thing as evil. 'Evils of imperfection are in truth no evils at all, but only the absence of comparative good.' 'Moral evil . . . could never have been admitted into the works of a just and beneficent Creator, if it had not some remote and collateral tendency to universal good, by answering some ends beneficial to the immense and incom-

---

* Sterne might have chosen the sub-title 'Tis Sixty Years Since' with almost as much justification as Scott chose it for *Waverley*.

prehensible whole.'* Yet even the complacency of Jenyns contained the germ of the utilitarianism that was soon to come. He wrote:†

> So far as the general practice of any action tends to produce good, and introduce happiness into the world, so far we may pronounce it virtuous; . . . by this we may be enabled not only to determine which are good and which are evil, but almost mathematically to demonstrate the proportion of virtue and vice which belongs to each, by comparing them with the degrees of happiness or misery which they occasion.

Bentham was then a nine-year-old pupil at Westminster.

Politics and business might be taking on the tinge of lower middle-class radicalism, but a reverse tendency was at work in the Church of England. The grandees might be in retreat before the mob, and the Duke of Newcastle mutter about the wretched Admiral Byng that 'he shall be tried immediately, he shall be hanged up directly'; but in the church the upper classes had got the upper hand. 'Reckon upon it,' wrote Warburton to his friend Hurd in 1752, 'our grandees have at last found their way back into the Church. The only wonder is that they have been so long about it.' When Warburton, the attorney's son, was himself installed as Bishop of Gloucester in 1760, Bishop Newton who conducted the ceremony indicated that he regarded it as an exceptional occasion. He pointedly remarked:

> Though the Apostles, for wise reasons, were chosen from among men of low birth and parentage, yet times and circumstances are so changed that persons of noble extraction, by coming into the Church, may add strength and ornament to it; especially so long as we can boast of *some* who are honourable in themselves as well as in their families.

A comparison of the origins of those who became bishops in the first half of the century and in the second bears him out. Since the considerable increase in episcopal incomes no longer enforced any approximation to apostolical poverty, they were becoming too valuable to

---

* Jenyns offers, among other illustrations of this thesis, that 'adultery may bring heirs, and good humour too, into many families, where they would otherwise have been wanting' (*Works*, 1790 (new ed., Gregg International, 1970) vol. 3, p. 85). He spoke here from personal experience. 'Mrs Jenyns, under the pretence of a journey to Bath for her health, made an elopement with one Mr Levyns . . . with whom it was supposed she lived very familiarly, even when that gentleman used to be at Mr Jenyns's house . . . ' (See William Cole's letter quoted in the article on Jenyns in *The History of Parliament 1715–1754*).
† *Ibid.*

use as rewards for any but the ablest of those who had climbed from obscurity to a chaplaincy in a politically influential household.*

An even more remarkable transformation was overtaking the Dissenters. On an increasing scale they were abandoning belief in the Trinity. In 1753 the Rev. Samuel Davis, of Hanover County, Virginia, left his Presbyterian congregation and his beloved wife Chara, to cross the Atlantic for a fund-raising tour of Britain on behalf of what was to become Princeton University. The young clergyman found it a distressing experience. The English Presbyterian ministers were learned, candid, regular in their morals, and 'friends to the liberty of mankind'. 'But what shall I say? They deny the proper Divinity and Satisfaction of Jesus Xt . . . They ascribe a Dignity and a Goodness to human Nature in its present State, contrary to my daily Sensations.' They had discarded the mystery of the Trinity and the determinism of Calvin, in favour of Unitarianism and a belief in the perfectibility of human nature.

On the whole the congregations were generous to the American visitor, and such a substantial sum as £20 was a not uncommon offertory. But he found some chapels were committed to other causes. Mr Milner, the Presbyterian minister of Yarmouth, refused to allow Davis to make an appeal in his chapel, explaining 'that he had engaged to use all his influence to promote a Presbyterian academy in Lancashire'. Duly established at Warrington in 1757, it was to be the most important institution of higher education to be founded in Britain during the entire century. Among the Warrington Dissenting Academy's staff at different times were numbered Joseph Priestley, the discoverer of oxygen, Reinhold Forster, the botanist who accompanied Cook on his greatest voyage, and Jean-Paul Marat who no doubt taught French, but was also interested in electricity.† The accent was not on theology but on liberal studies, and only one student in eight entered the ministry. Besides the normal course, which lasted five years, there was a commercial course lasting for three. The tone of the dissertation subjects set is unmistakable: 'Show how far the several forms of government which have been introduced into the

---

* It was to Bishop Newton that George Grenville observed that there were two kinds of bishoprics—'bishoprics of business for men of learning and abilities, and bishoprics of ease for men of family and fashion.' *Life of Dr Thomas Newton*, Alexander Chalmers, 1816, (ed.), vol. 2, p. 54.

† Marat (born 1744) seems to have taught at Warrington for a time after 1770. His first book, *Chains of Slavery*, appeared in 1774 in English, with an Edinburgh imprint. It was followed by a series of works on electricity in French, but published in London.

world are calculated to promote the happiness of mankind, which is the great end of government'; or 'Enquire into the effect of civilization on the real improvement and happiness of mankind, in relation to the principles of Rousseau.' Burke was in due course to stigmatize such academies as 'arsenals in which subversive arguments and doctrines are forged'. Certainly Warrington, where the course was infinitely more taxing and vigorous than contemporary Oxford and Cambridge, produced a very different kind of graduate. He was a critic of society as it stood, and an admirer of the new society on the other side of the Atlantic.

By 1760 the population of Great Britain had increased by about a million, or 17 per cent, since the beginning of the century, compared with an increase of some 600 per cent, to 1·6 million in America. The political nation, that is to say the electorate, had increased only slightly more quickly than the population, at any rate since the accession of the House of Hanover, when the number entitled to vote had been in the region of 284,000. In 1754 it was 315,000. But in some constituencies the electorates had actually declined under the influence of borough-mongering and restrictive decisions on election petitions. Scotland had sunk from 3,000 to 2,500; Calne's 60 in 1715 had become 25, Marlborough's 42, 12; Gatton's 22, 2. But in some towns, where the right to vote was on a fairly broad basis, growth in electorates is an indicator of the growth of urban populations. In the six cities of West-minster, Bedford, Canterbury, Carlisle, Liverpool and Bristol forty years saw the addition of 7,000 electors. In the five constituencies covering the metropolitan area (London, Westminster, Southwark, Middlesex and Surrey) the electorates increased between 1715 and 1754 by about 20 per cent, from 24,000 to 29,000.

Lower down in the structure the native vitality of the parish and other traditional basic units of political organization was beginning to show signs of strain from the demands that were being placed on it. Unions of parishes to provide workhouses, Turnpike Trusts and Paving Commissioners to provide roads and streets, brought new managerial bodies into existence and left the work of many parish overseers and surveyors—already unwanted and unpaid—unnecessary as well. There was an increasing tendency to employ paid officers. The London par-ishes alone employed 143 beadles by the middle of the century. Parish and vestry meetings tended to become formalized, and attendance fell off. At Gateshead, for instance, the twenty-four vestrymen had attended frequent, vigorous meetings early in the century, fixing rates, punishing nuisances, enforcing house repairs. But as time went on attendances declined until by 1745 only one meeting a year, with three vestrymen present, was considered enough. At a higher level the old county court was no more than an antiquarian survival, though one had to be assembled at a public house in Holborn by the Undersheriff of Middlesex to outlaw Wilkes in 1763.

Expanding trade and better communications were making the nation more closely knit. Wages and prices had changed surprisingly little since Defoe's time, but figures leave no doubt about the expansion of the economy. Between 1700 and 1750 the output of coal almost doubled. International trade moved from strength to strength. Total imports rose from £6 million in 1700 to £9·8 million in the year George III came to the throne; and exports, even more strikingly, went in the same period from £6·5 million to £14·7 million. The growth in tonnage of British shipping is the most impressive index of all. In 1709 the tonnage engaged in both coastal and overseas trade was put at 171,120 tons. By 1751 the shipping based on London overseas trade alone amounted to nearly 120,000 tons, and the total national tonnage came to over 400,000. Much the greater part of this expansion in the fleet was due to the increase in overseas trade.

Internally the development of natural rivers for navigation, which had reached its limit by 1730, was merging into the era of canal-building. Brindley's great work, the so-called Bridgewater Canal, was begun in 1759 to facilitate the movement of the Duke of Bridgewater's coal to Manchester. The piecemeal but persistent development of turnpikes made land travel and the movement of letters and news more expeditious than it had been since Roman times. The main roads were now good enough to allow the private traveller who could afford changes of horses to move at something like 100 miles a day—double the speed of fifty years earlier.* Boswell, in 1762, travelled comfortably from Edinburgh to London in five days, and Bubb Dodington, in the late 1750s, was able to be at his country palace in Wiltshire without spending a night on the way, provided he made an early start from his Hammersmith villa. But coastal shipping still carried the poor slowly from north to south, as well as hauling the heavy loads to London.

How did increased prosperity show itself in the standards of life?

* Down to 1720 no visitor to Bath had travelled by carriage except Queen Anne. Pope, inviting Warburton from Newark in Lincolnshire to Bath (a distance of ninety miles) in 1741, assures him that the journey will not take more than three days on horseback. The authority for this assurance being Ralph Allen, the postmaster, makes it reliable.

Housing certainly improved, brick taking over from stone and clay, tiles from thatch. In farmhouses the ladder to the loft was being replaced by the staircase to the attics. In the homes of the better-off wall-paper was appearing instead of hangings or panelling, carpets instead of bare wooden or stone floors, sash windows instead of immoveable casements (*Tristram Shandy* is anachronistic in its description of the infant Tristram's accident). Silver was now within the reach of much greater numbers of people. Imported porcelain was a significant subsidiary trade of the East India Company, and was making its appearance on the tea-tables of squires and coal merchants. With the new market in mind Wedgwood founded his first works in 1759, and ten years later had created 'Etruria'—his factory with annexed housing for the workers.

Yet industrialism in the later sense of urban factory production was still a rarity. As often as not an organized workplace would be in the country, near the water-power or the coal or the clay that it consumed. Textiles, still the central industry, were still firmly on a domestic basis and the spinning jenny, while it had made the spinning wheel obsolete in hardly more than a decade, simply multiplied the efficiency of the domestic worker. Country landlords still bargained with gangs of miners much as they bargained with gangs carrying out other work on their estates. Boswell found Boulton, the great Birmingham factory owner, a romantic figure, 'an iron chieftain', corresponding, one suspects, to memories of a hero from Ossian's alleged poems. No one yet speculated about where industrial organization and technology might be carrying the nation.

Nobody had designed the lines on which the society King George III came to preside over in 1760 should develop. Straddling the Atlantic, bursting with ambition, governed still by landlords who were not only the traditional masters but the traditional setters of style, men were beginning to acquire a sense that other styles, and other sources of satisfaction, might be within reach. In spite of the limits of the franchise, the savagery of the criminal law, and the banked-up authority of privilege, Britain felt itself to be a free society, possessing institutions which symbolized that freedom, and which it was outgrowing.

King George III was twenty-two when he was called upon to rule. He had been brought up entirely in England—the first king for more than a hundred years to be so—and felt himself identified with his people. Neurotically conscientious, courageous, loyal to those on whom he relied, hostile to change, he was far from being suited to an age of transformation which for him became a personal tragedy. He rejected as corrupt the 'system' which the Duke of Newcastle survived to represent; but at the same time he was unwilling to envisage political development. His aim was not autocracy, but the operation of the mixed constitution of king, Lords and Commons which he thought he had inherited.

He was a literalist who placed duty above expediency, and paid dearly for it. Even actions which were in themselves beneficial and constructive helped in the march of his political tragedy. He considered, for instance, that the independence of the judiciary needed to be completed by abolishing the requirement that judges should vacate their offices on the death of the king who appointed them, and promoted an Act of Parliament for that purpose: and the newly found judicial independence was rapidly exercised in the unpalatable judgments of Pratt and Mansfield in the case of General Warrants. George was equally anxious to give some sort of reality to the executive government and legislature of Ireland, insisting that the Lord Lieutenant should actually reside in Dublin throughout his two-year term, and that the Irish Parliament should, like the British one, last only for a set period. The Octennial Act of 1767, which gave effect to the king's wishes about the Irish Parliament, ended a quiescent period of Irish politics, and opened a new and turbulent one.

With all his faults and failures King George was loved by most of his subjects as few of his predecessors had been. His character chimed with the new sense of nationhood and the more closely knit society; and it comforted those who felt threatened by impending change—not all of them, by any means, members of the upper classes. The British throne as an institution owes more to him than to any of those who have occupied it since the Restoration except his granddaughter Queen Victoria. It is difficult to imagine an Anglican clergyman going into the field behind his rectory and firing a solemn blunderbuss in honour of the birthday of George I or William III, as Parson Woodforde regularly did for George III.

The most unusual innovation of the new reign was a Scottish Prime Minister: a Jewish one would have been almost as startling. John Stuart, Earl of Bute, possessed favour without fortune. For those who equated respectability with loyalty to the House of Hanover his background was tarnished. Had not his wife's aunt married the leader of the Rebellion of 1715? Did he not himself bear the name of the exiled family? He owned no land in England, and possessed no political interest with which to serve supporters. He stood for peace with

France and the end of the heady series of victories. There was, in fact, much about the new Prime Minister and the new king which could be exploited by an able journalist. In 1762, the year in which Jean-Jacques Rousseau proclaimed that man was born free and was everywhere in chains, John Wilkes began the publication of the *North Briton*.

Chapter 11 The Beginnings of Change

For thirteen years after the Peace of Paris in 1763 Britain was externally at peace. It was the longest such period for a generation, and the most turbulent since the beginning of the century: a period of violence, protest, and disorder as the shift from a rural to an urban society gathered way. Greater numbers of people were crowded together, and exposed to speedy communication, above all in London, but also in expanding Bristol, Manchester, Birmingham and Liverpool. Greater numbers, notably in the towns, but also in the country, were coming into direct dependence on money wages and prices. For the majority it was still true that the bread they ate, and almost every article they consumed, was home-made, and the village shop represents a higher standard of development than rural Britain had so far achieved. Occasional visits to the market town, supplemented by the rounds of travelling pedlars was the limit of what we would describe as shopping, even for the comparatively well-off, whose household servants were themselves an important source of production. Nevertheless there were now far more people for whom the gentle upward slope of prices, let alone the sudden seasonal variations in them, could make the difference between a tolerable livelihood and destitution.

Although agricultural production had considerably increased, the end of England as a net exporter of cereals was now in sight. She had had an export surplus of more than 3 million quarters over the decade 1740-9, but during the corresponding ten years in the eighth decade of the century there was to be a net importation of 400,000 quarters, in spite of the protective duty and the bounty on exports when the domestic price fell below a certain level. The time was coming when the hinterland of Britain would no longer suffice for the city state first fattened by trade, and now becoming still more populous with the growth of manufacture.

In the great towns the merest sketch of government was superimposed on a population which for the most part had put down no urban roots. The aristocracy and their dependants, who provided most of the membership of Parliaments and Cabinets, were mainly based in the country, and still regarded London as a place where they were called by business or social duty. The same was true of the major business men who constituted the 'moneyed interest', who had long ago made substantial investments in land, and established themselves in estates and country houses in the home counties or even further afield. Even such a City patriot as William Beckford, Pitt's adviser and spokesman in the corporation of London, and an adversary of the reigning financial establishment who said he never measured the patriotism of a man by the number of his acres, had his main base in Wiltshire, at the magnificent house he christened Fonthill Splendens.*

As for the poorer Londoners, now nearly three-quarters of a million in number, it is almost enough to say that until the end of the century more were buried every year than were baptised: and baptism did not promise long life. In 1750 it was estimated that the chances of a child born in London surviving to the age of five were three to one against. The average death-rate in the mid-century was one in twenty-one—slightly worse than it had been in 1700. The population was perpetually topped up by newcomers, and Dr Bland, who kept a record of patients attending his dispensary between 1774 and 1781 found that only a quarter of them had been born in London. A sixth came from Ireland or Scotland—rather more from the first than from the second; and the rest from the English or Welsh hinterland.

The capital was even freer from parish, parson, and squire than the other big towns. Within the old London boundaries the City Corporation still maintained a vigorous autonomy, over which governments could exert only a precarious influence through such friends as they could muster on the Court of twenty-six aldermen. The Common Council, or lower chamber of the Corporation, with its 240 members, was elected by the 'Common Hall' of over 7,000 freemen, and was virtually outside the range of government influence. The Councillors, and still more the freemen who elected them, were overwhelmingly of 'the middling sort'. As craftsmen, shopkeepers, and owners of small businesses, they were in strong contrast to the bank directors and commercial magnates who formed the majority on the Court of Aldermen. Shopkeeping in the City was rigorously reserved for freemen; but other kinds of business activity were open to all.

* Beckford's enemies, and they were many, did not hesitate to point out the contrast between his enthusiasm for Liberty and his huge West Indian sugar estates, mainly worked by slave labour.

Outside the City a medley of authorities formed originally on the rural pattern, presided over packed streets which petered out in urban sprawl. In Westminster nominal authority lay with the Dean and Chapter, operating through their High Constable. Beyond it, but still included in the metropolitan area grimly described as 'within the Bills of Mortality' lay the rest of urban Middlesex, taking in the built-up (and more heavily industrial) areas to the north and east of the City,* and governed, so far as it was governed at all as a whole, by the justices meeting at Brentford. Development had not advanced so far to the south of the river—though there were now three bridges across it, compared with one at the beginning of the century†—but outside Southwark, which was in some respects part of the City, the seat of authority for the Surrey bank lay at Guildford. Altogether the urban area was divided into nearly two hundred parishes, liberties, and precincts, each with its own officers, its own rights, and possibly its own Act of Parliament. Beyond it lay a disagreeable belt of brick-kilns, market gardens, dairying establishments, stock-yards and rubbish dumps, intersected by heavily polluted ditches.

Yet what struck contemporaries about London was not its squalor or its inefficiency, but its vigour and variety. It had none of the stately squares and processional routes that make continental capitals impressive but mark them as the creations of autocratic planning. Karl Philip Moritz, a young German clergyman, commented on the immense, purposeful, well-dressed crowds, the sense of activity and independence, the absence of beggars. 'There are few subjects of general conversation,' he observed, 'on which the workers are not able to form an opinion.' Johnson's remark that the man who was tired of London was tired of life referred above all to the intense sociability and ease of communication that marked London life. His own club, founded in 1764, was only one of hundreds of gatherings, usually on a fixed day each week, which brought individuals with common interests together in a convenient tavern or coffee house.

The opinion formed by the London worker was not always accurate or well informed. Sometimes it was based on myth or prejudice, as witness the almost indelible belief that George III's mother was the

* The phrase 'The Bills of Mortality' had been drawn to describe the greater London of the later seventeenth century. It was the area within which all deaths were supposed to be reported and covered the City, Westminster, Southwark, and the twenty-two 'out-parishes' of Middlesex to the east and west. Urban Middlesex also extended, however, to certain parishes outside 'the Bills'.
† Westminster Bridge (1750) and Blackfriars Bridge (1760) had been added to London Bridge against the protests of the boatmen.

Earl of Bute's mistress. The symbols of this particular legend—a boot and a petticoat—were hoisted as late as 1770, during the last of the Wilkes-inspired riots. But right or wrong the ordinary Londoner considered himself to be concerned in politics, and was not willing to leave such questions to his betters. In Wilkes he found his hero.

Wilkes was a man of almost demoniac ugliness, a poor orator, and claimant to no coherent political philosophy. Effrontery, courage, and skill in choosing his ground, were his great assets. Like the lightning conductor which Benjamin Franklin had recently invented, he caught the electricity in the London clouds, and set the bells ringing.

Of Wilkes's three great campaigns the first, in 1764, primarily concerned the executive, though Parliament became involved in it. The other two were fought primarily against Parliament—a Parliament which over the years had been permeated by the executive power. It was the parliamentary system as inherited from Walpole and the Pelhams that was the target, not some novelty of management introduced by George III or Bute. The 'King's Friends' about whom Burke was so indignant were not a party of neo-monarchists bent on restoring the autocracy of the Stuarts, but the increasingly professional managers and manipulators of majorities—the Robinsons, Jenkinsons, Barringtons, and Webbs—whom Namier has characterized as the 'permanent ins'. They were not the less bureaucrats and defenders of the system through being themselves almost to a man, Members of Parliament.* The venom of the *Letters of Junius,* Junius being the other great Opposition journalist of the sixties, is derived from the fact that they were written about the 'permanent ins' by someone—almost certainly Philip Francis—who had been ejected from their charmed circle before reaching the rank he aspired to.

The Wilkes campaign of 1764–5, which started with the attempted prosecution of 'Number 45' of the *North Briton,* and led to riots in the course of which the Austrian Ambassador was held upside down by a

---

* John Robinson (1727–1802), M.P. successively for Westmorland and Harwich 1764–1802; Secretary to the Treasury 1770–82. Charles Jenkinson (1727–1808), M.P. successively for Cockermouth, Appleby, Harwich, Hastings, and Saltash 1761–86 (when he was raised to the peerage); Under-secretary of State 1761–3; Secretary to the Treasury 1763–5. William Wildman Barrington (1717–93), M.P. successively for Berwick and Plymouth 1740–78; in office continuously 1746–78. Philip Carteret Webb (1700–70), M.P. for Haslemere 1754–68; Solicitor to the Treasury 1756–65. Webb, who gave the fatal advice on general warrants brought down immense odium on his head by saying of the Earl of Bute (then Prime Minister), 'He is my master.' It is interesting both that Webb, like a modern civil servant, considered this a harmless remark, and that most contemporaries thought it a scandalous one. For Burke's views see p. 149.

crowd while the sacred number 45 was chalked on the soles of his boots, destroyed the machinery by which successive governments had been able to keep a tight hold on the political press. The disappearance of the Licensing Act in the wake of the Revolution had allowed the press to multiply, but it had not deprived the executive of the power to suppress objectionable papers by administrative act. The launching of a general warrant by a secretary of state against unnamed publishers and printers was not an unconstitutional novelty but a well-tried expedient which Walpole had regularly used against opposition papers. Its purpose was not to achieve a successful prosecution for libel before the courts, but to put the paper as such out of commission by locking up its staff and closing its plant. Wilkes, though in the course of the struggle he was discredited, outlawed, and expelled from Parliament, established the illegality of general warrants in the courts, and became a popular hero on a scale unknown since Sacheverell. But now the hero came first, and the concept second, in the popular cry. The slogan had been 'High Church and Sacheverell': now it was 'Wilkes and Liberty'.

After an interval spent in exile, Wilkes launched his second and most spectacular campaign by presenting himself as a candidate for Middlesex at the general election of 1768. Through his hold on the electors of the metropolitan area this unacceptable man faced the House of Commons with the choice of either accepting him as a member or defying the electorate which had returned him by 1,143 votes to 296. They chose the latter in the celebrated resolution that his opponent 'Henry Lawes Luttrell Esq. ought to have been returned a member for Middlesex, and not John Wilkes Esq.' The thing now went to the heart not only of Wilkes's dispute with the 'permanent ins' (of whom Luttrell was a typical minor specimen) but of the representative character of Parliament. The power of the machine had been shown too nakedly, and thousands who abhorred Wilkes and in some cases had even voted against him at previous elections, signed the petitions of protest which were eagerly organized by Burke and the Rockingham Whigs up and down the country in 1769.

Finally, when Wilkes had forced his way into the Court of Aldermen in 1770, he was presented with an opportunity of fighting once more for the freedom of the press. Having destroyed the government's machinery for silencing political comment, he now proceeded to attack Parliament's precious privilege to prevent publication of reports of its debates. As recently as 1728 the House had renewed its ban on the public reporting of speeches, and there had been open defiance only in the last few years, during which Almon, Wilkes's old publisher, had been printing parliamentary reports in the *London Evening Post*. The so-called 'printers' case' has even more of the elements of farce than the rest of Wilkes's achievement—officers of different authorities arresting one another, courts treating as innocent those denounced by Parliament as criminals—but in some ways Wilkes's third victory contributed even more to the transformation of Parliament's relationship to society than the dispute over the Middlesex election. The idea that Parliament was not only a representative assembly but an opportunity for the public expression of conflicting views was wholly foreign to the conventional politician of the eighteenth century. He was more inclined to think that *because* Parliament consisted of representatives, their contributions should be protected from publicity. Such, at any rate, was the view of Speaker Fletcher Norton, who considered—not without some reason—that members would speak less frankly and fearlessly if their speeches were publicly reported.

For the third time Wilkes was victorious. He had no principles, and Wilkism had no programme, and the Wilkites were not by any standards a party. The Society for the Bill of Rights, formed to give some kind of principle to the Wilkes agitation, broke up in disorder on the question of how far Wilkes's private debts should form a first charge on its funds. The hero of liberty in due course developed into a conventional City figure, a Lord Mayor, and a vehement enemy of the French Revolution. Wilkes's allies Sawbridge and Beckford, for all their radical roarings, never contemplated not remaining the very rich men they were. The Opposition politicians treated the whole issue as an eruption from which they would draw such tactical advantage as they could. Of all the supporters of Wilkes only the renegade parson, Horne Tooke, can be treated as an ideological radical.

Benjamin Franklin, the intellectual Pennsylvanian postmaster, who had been living more or less continuously in London since 1757 as a kind of unofficial ambassador of the American colonists, was disgusted and apprehensive about the commotion caused by Wilkes. In 1768 he wrote to a friend:*

Mobs patrolling the streets at noonday, some knocking all down

---

* A. H. Smyth (Ed.), *The Writings of Benjamin Franklin* (Macmillan, 1908), vol. 5, p. 133. It is interesting that Franklin should have sympathized so little with Wilkes who, though outrageously, did so much for the freedom of the press. Franklin himself had crossed swords with the Massachusetts assembly, which had used language about the *New England Courant* that was almost as high-handed as Parliament's utterances about the *North Briton*.

that will not roar for Wilkes and Liberty; courts of justice afraid
to give judgement against him; coal-heavers and porters pulling
down the houses of coal merchants that refuse to give them
more wages; sawyers destroying saw-mills; sailors unrigging all
the outward bound ships and suffering none to sail till merchants
agree to raise their pay; watermen destroying private boats and
threatening bridges; soldiers firing among the mobs killing men,
women, and children; which seems only to have produced a
universal sullenness that looks like a great black cloud coming
on, ready to burst in a general tempest . . . Some punishment
seems preparing for a people who are ungratefully abusing the
best constitution and the best King any nation was ever blessed
with.

Franklin was to change his view of George III.

Nevertheless the Wilkes agitation found a ready response on the
other side of the Atlantic, where 'English Liberty' and the American
cause were quickly matched. The legislature of South Carolina voted
a substantial sum for his support—a gesture which cannot have been
lost on King George III as a telling commentary on the real attitudes
of American assemblies; and in 1765 between the first outbreak of
Wilkism and the second, Franklin himself had used defiant language
to a Committee of the House of Commons when he was examined on
the subject of Grenville's attempt to make the Americans pay for
their defence: the Stamp Act. Even if the stamp duty on business
documents were reduced, Franklin told the Committee, it would not
be paid, nor would any other tax designed to produce revenue and
relieve the English land-tax payer. But would the Americans really
defy the writ of Parliament, asked puzzled members of the Committee? Yes, they would; could they really do without British textiles?
Yes, they could. Did they not need British troops to protect them
against the Indians? They could deal with the Indians very well themselves.

In this celebrated exchange with the Commons Committee, which
he subsequently published, Franklin was very careful to appear as a
detached observer, not a partisan. He was one of the very few men who
had thought deeply about America, and although his public position
changed, his fundamental outlook was remarkably consistent. He
already foresaw that continental America would have a large population and yield unprecedented wealth, while Britain was a 'pretty
island, which compared to America is but like a stepping stone in a

brook, scarce enough of it above water to keep one's shoes dry'. Even Lord Shelburne, one of the most intelligent of ministers, had to be reminded that a superintendent of Indian affairs covering the frontier from Nova Scotia to Virginia would necessarily be remote from some part of his responsibilities. The European population of America had already increased tenfold since the beginning of the century. By 1770 the majority had been born and brought up there, and had never known the rule of squire or parson. The weekly admonition to pray for the king was unheard in their chapels, and no test excluded Dissenters from public office. The notion of a peerage as a distinct order of men was foreign to them. Since 1763, when the French threat had been removed, they saw an open frontier to the west, and they were restive at the restraints on settlement beyond the Alleghenies which the British government, for reasons of economy, tried to impose.

Franklin considered that the colonies, which in his view should be united, possessed natural rights independently of Britain, even though at the same time they formed part of a community owing allegiance to the British Crown. When he used the phrase 'no taxation without representation' he was not suggesting that America should send members to the Westminster Parliament—an idea he described as 'Union', and in his heart considered impracticable. The American assemblies, emanating, like the British Parliament, from the natural rights of the inhabitants, were to him the sole legislatures of America, and the relevance of the non-representation of the Americans in Westminster was that it showed their proper legislators were on their own side of the Atlantic. Parliament was the legislature of Britain and of Britain alone. 'The sovereignty of the Crown I understand,' he wrote in 1768, 'the sovereignty of the British legislature outside Great Britain I do not understand.' His quarrel, and eventually America's quarrel, was not with King George III but with a Parliament which regarded America as no more than an unenfranchised dependency of Britain. It is one of the bitterest of history's ironies that the king, who sought, according to his lights, to support his Parliament over America, should have been pilloried by posterity as a king who tried to defy Parliament, and to cling to an autocratic authority across the Atlantic.

The prestige of the judiciary was now reaching its zenith, and under the guidance of Mansfield the law was systematically being adapted to the needs of a business community. But what was the law? It was buried in black-letter tomes and terse reports of past judicial decisions.

The age of Johnson's *Dictionary*, and Linnaeus's classification demanded a comprehensive statement of the origins, principles, and nature of English law. Towards the end of the fifties a young fellow of All Souls, William Blackstone, had delivered a series of lectures on the laws of England, and in 1765, now Professor of Jurisprudence at Oxford, he published his *Commentaries*. They stand as Oxford's greatest contribution to human knowledge during the entire century—perhaps her only one of major importance. The book, complacent though it is, must rank as a synthesis and codification of genius, indispensable to an expanding society.

Blackstone was no critic of his times. To him the British constitution had just reached a final state of perfection* and he was lucky to live at such a moment. The idea of property elicited some of his most enthusiastic writing. 'There is nothing which so generally strikes the imagination,' he wrote at the beginning of his second volume, 'and engages the affection of mankind, as the right of property.' It was 'the sole and despotick dominion which one man claims and exercises over the external things of the world, in total exclusion of the right of every other individual in the universe'. Blackstone did not mean by this apparently absolute statement that an interest in a piece of land or other property was indivisible. One man might own the bank of a river and another have the right to fish from it. One man might have the right to live in a house till he died, and another the right to inherit it after him. Blackstone saw property (by which he meant 'property rights') as a kind of atomic structure, which determined legal relationships. While the *right* of property was always absolute, the application of these rights to the *objects* of property could be complex and subtle, since it involved isolating abstract, partial, and even qualified rights as the atoms making up any particular property situation.

The only limitation Blackstone placed on English property rights —and it was a significant one—was that they could not extend to persons. Slavery imposed by the law of other countries (it was unknown, as the judges had already held, to the law of England) might, he thought, confer a property right on the master which the English courts would enforce; and with the same characteristic emphasis on the topographical limits of legal systems, he took no notice of the

* An interesting characteristic of the British constitution is its perfection at each successive stage of its development. Whether the commentator be Blackstone in the eighteenth century or Dicey in the nineteenth, it has always just reached the stage at which no further changes are required. Such commentaries are usually at their most lyrical when the constitution is in fact on the brink of dramatic change.

fact that coal miners in Scotland were still juridically serfs (or 'necessary servants') who could be, and were, sold along with the collieries in which they worked.* But serfdom, so far as England was concerned, along with all other feudal tenures, had disappeared, and he described the statute of Charles II, to which he attributed this decisive event, as a 'greater acquisition to the civil property of this Kingdom than even Magna Charta itself'. So Blackstone chased feudalism out of the law at the same moment as chivalry, under the aegis of Hurd and Percy, galloped into literature.

The *Commentaries* were far more than a technical work for lawyers. In a country where the administration of justice was largely in the hands of landowners, and the general population was increasingly conscious of its rights, they had a wide public. Grenville quoted them in the Commons debate on Wilkes. Gibbon, already under the spell of Rome, not only read Blackstone three times, but made 'a copious and critical abstract' as well.

Gibbon had been inspired among the ruins of the Roman Capitol in 1764, twelve years before the first volume of *Decline and Fall* was published. His learning, his irony, his extreme intellectuality should not blind us to his essentially middle-class characteristics. He was an indoor man, devoting the same care and effort to his chosen task as his grandfather the linen-draper and thousands of others devoted to business. Restraint and precision, which marked the lives of successful eighteenth-century entrepreneurs and manufacturers, are the very qualities that strike any reader of Gibbon's *Memoirs*. He feelingly describes having to sell 'a delicious morsel', in the shape of a share in the New River Company, to pay his father's debts. Above all, the self-sacrifice and concentration that went into achieving fame in the case of Gibbon was the same as went into the nail business in the case of Samuel and Aaron Walker, allowing themselves 'ten shillings a week for wages to maintain our families', or into wholesale grocery in the case of Samuel Smith, father of the Dissenter M.P. The Walkers finished up with a business worth a quarter of a million, and Smith with one yielding an annual income equal to the capital he had started with.

Why should a work on the Roman Empire have been such an

---

* The Scottish statute of 1701, which has been claimed as the Scottish habeas corpus, and was designed to prevent wrongful imprisonment, contained the proviso 'and sicklike it is hereby provided and declared that this present act is noways to be extended to colliers or salters.' In 1775 Parliament enacted that serfdom should not apply to new recruits to the Scottish mines, and a procedure for gradual liberation of existing serfs. Final liberation of all the Scottish serfs was not achieved until 1799 by 39 Geo. III: cap. 56.

enormous success—'on every table, and almost on every toilette . . . crowned by the taste and fashion of the day'? Several thousand copies were sold within the year of publication. The reason is simple. It provided the educated British public with a connected and intensely dramatic account of their adopted ancestors. The notion that across a huge void ('the middle ages of barbarism and ignorance') Britain was the continuator of Roman civilization, had for years been a subconscious assumption of formal education. As Gibbon himself reflected in 'the awful interval' before publication, the book was sure to succeed because 'Rome is familiar to the schoolboy and the statesman'. Familiar, yes, but in a disconnected and incomplete form. Gibbon's work was like presenting a son with a full biography of a father he only knows through a few household possessions.

Gibbon also personified the growing penetration of the English educated classes by the ideas of continental Europe. His subject was a past that Europe and Britain shared. His manner was sceptical and cosmopolitan, not British and robust. Hume, Buffon, Voltaire, were his intellectual masters, Tillemont and Mosheim his scholarly predecessors. Fifty years previously it would have been inconceivable that an Englishman should have written such a book, striking as it did at deeply held certainties about religion—and none the less effectively because this was done under the colour of history.

Just as it is easy to lose sight of Gibbon's middle-class virtues because his achievement was intellectual, it is possible to overlook the social process that was at work in Johnson's Literary Club underneath the stimulating conversation that Boswell records. As in other clubs up and down Britain, which brought together people with a common interest, the world of professionalism was being developed. The *Spectator*, at the beginning of the century, had canonized 'the three great professions of Divinity, Law, and Physick'; and the very word 'professional' is a creation of the first half of the century. In 1768 Joshua Reynolds, in the foundation of the Royal Academy, took a major step in professionalizing the artist.* Garrick had raised acting from bohemian dependency to gentility, and crowned the achievement with the great Shakespeare Jubilee at Stratford in 1769, for which he was painted by Gainsborough. In William Chambers appeared the first professional architect—distinct alike from the amateur designer such as Burlington, or the official employee, such as Wren. Johnson himself symbolized

---

* The Academy was designed to be even more than an organization for established artists: its primary purpose was to serve as a school of art.

the author who owed nothing to patronage and everything to his professional skill and resolution.

A significant but little-known name links together the intellectual world of the High Georgian period: that of William Strahan, the printer. Strahan had published Johnson's *Dictionary* and went on to publish Hume and Adam Smith, Blackstone and Gibbon. He acted as Benjamin Franklin's agent for the supply of printing machinery and type in Philadelphia and became one of the American's closest friends. On the strength of his success he became the first publisher to sit in the House of Commons. Even the great Tonson, for all his political connexions, had never got further than the secretaryship of the Kit-Cat Club and the right to print parliamentary proceedings.

Such flourishing literary and publishing success implies a substantial reading public and consequently a rather better educational system up to thirty years earlier than England is usually given credit for. Literacy, certainly, was surprisingly widespread. In the Westminster petition of 1769 in favour of Wilkes there are 5,137 signatures, and only twelve of these are by mark. Yorkshire's petition contained only 297 marks out of over 11,000 signatures. Many had learned to read and write at the charity schools of which there were over 1,300 by the third decade of the century; and innumerable curates and underemployed clergy kept little schools to eke out wretched incomes. The custom of painting the ten commandments in village churches for the edification of the worshippers would hardly have been undertaken on such a scale if the congregation had been predominantly illiterate; and the elaborate inscriptions on the gravestones of even quite humble villagers were intended to be read. A serious parent—and there were many in all classes, notably among the Dissenters—believed that truth was to be found by study of the Bible, and the commonest of all roads to literacy was probably puzzling over the book which was repeatedly being read aloud in the child's presence, in church, chapel, meeting-house, and at the fireside.

Once a child was literate there were few attempts to graduate or guide his reading, and no sense of barriers to what it was suitable for him to read. Very little, in any case, was published for children, or for the less educated, and what a child was likely to find was usually challenging. The ten-year-old Benjamin Franklin browsed in his father's collection of theological controversy, and devoured Defoe's *Essay on Projects*, Plutarch's *Lives*, and an odd volume of the *Spectator*. Since even those who went to school were taught almost nothing except Latin, it is safe to say that in the England of the 1760s almost everyone who was educated at all beyond the rudiments and the classics had in large measure educated himself. Karl Philip Moritz found that his landlady was a regular reader of Milton, and considered that the ordinary English were greater readers than the Germans. Cook learned the science of hydrography entirely by private study.*

But the use of literacy and of the ability to do simple sums was primarily in business, and not cultural at all. The contribution made by education in this way to the efficiency of the economy during these years, though incalculable, was certainly great. The bills which Lord Torrington preserved as mementoes of nights spent on his tours of England and Wales show practised sloping hands and precise business methods, even in remote village inns. Some degree of literacy was needed to handle the privately issued paper money—notes on the now numerous country banks, bills of exchange for small amounts backed by local business men, tickets and vouchers issued by employers in lieu of cash wages—which were becoming more and more common.

For one of the most striking symptoms of the changes that were coming over the country was the shortage of ordinary currency. In 1718 the Gateshead coal-owner, William Cotesworth, was advising his undergraduate son to keep track of his expenses 'by putting twenty shillings into your pocket at a time, and at night reckon what remains'. By the 1770s Cotesworth's successors were scouring the countryside to find small change for their wage-packets. For half a century silver had been in heavy demand for other purposes: to satisfy the rising demand for tableware, and to meet the adverse balance on the trade with India.† Copper change was even scarcer, and innumerable employers and tradesmen were driven to issue their own small change, or 'tokens' which circulated freely. The central government had no economic or demographic indicators to guide it on the amount of coin that was needed. But the main reason for insufficiency of the coinage was the increasing number of money transactions as greater numbers of people were concentrated in the towns, as wages increasingly took the place

---

* Scott, in *Waverley*, Chapter 3, describes how his hero, as the child of a landed family in Yorkshire, 'was permitted, in a great measure, to learn as he pleased, what he pleased, and when he pleased' by simply roaming through a miscellaneous library. Many upper-class young men must have been educated on these principles; but others, even when educated at home, were subjected to formidable time-tables of study.

† Since British exports to India were few, the huge imports required settlement in bullion. It was otherwise with the trade to America. In the eighteenth century British tea was paid for in silver, but sugar in slaves.

of provision in kind, and as wage-rates and prices themselves moved upwards.

Throughout society standards, and with them expectations, were mounting. Though the lower classes in the towns had as yet no specific aims or organization, they were beginning to become conscious of their power. The political system, and above all Parliament itself, though it was calibrated and organized more efficiently than ever to serve the ends of its managers, was coming under criticism from people who had been educated outside the conventional framework, either at dissenting establishments or by their own efforts. At an even deeper level, the attempt to find a rational religion was giving way, as Wesley had foreseen it would, to openly expressed scepticism and 'infidelity'.

Under this 'great black cloud' of which Franklin had spoken, successive Prime Ministers laboured through the 1760s: the angular, tactless Grenville, the ineffectual Rockingham, the burnt-out Chatham, and the juvenile, unconvincing Grafton. At last, in 1770, with the storm about to burst, the king found in Lord North a chief minister on whom he felt he could confidently rely.

Chapter 12

'Present Discontents'

Suddenly a whole range of assumptions about society was being questioned. 'All the solemn plausibilities of the world,' wrote Burke in 1770, 'have lost their reverence and effect.' *Thoughts on the Causes of the Present Discontents* was conceived during the last stages of the struggle over the Middlesex election and professed, with tremendous quotability, to give an explanation of what seemed to be a general loss of confidence in the political and social system. The trouble, according to Burke, was that 'distributed with art and judgment through all the secondary, but efficient departments'* there were the agents of an irresponsible, permanent cabal, exercising power under cover of a succession of dummy politicians. 'They bear themselves with a lofty air . . . like Janissaries they derive a kind of freedom from the very condition of their servitude.' These timorous, cunning, incompetent conspirators, said Burke, were the people who described themselves as 'king's friends' and were responsible for the general failure of confidence. Since they were interested primarily in the survival of their own organization, and not in the national welfare, their influence on society and on politics was essentially destructive.

Even Burke never suggested that King George III himself directed his 'friends' in a plan to re-establish some kind of Stuart autocracy. On the contrary, his complaint was that they were not an open political party but a covert system of influence using the king, as they used Parliament and the politicians, for their own selfish ends. He did not name any of them, but it is clear that the target of his pamphlet was the system of 'permanent ins' which had taken root under Walpole and the Pelhams. This system was now confronting problems of a scale and complexity that the Robinocracy had never had to contemplate.

---

* 'Efficient' in eighteenth-century usage was the equivalent of our 'operational'. 'Efficient' offices were those with duties to discharge, as distinct from sinecures or honorific appointments. 'Efficient' in the sense of adequately skilled appears to be an American usage—Harriet Beecher Stowe's phrase 'an efficient workman' would have been incomprehensible to Burke.

An interesting change was taking place in the Whig tradition. The Rockingham Whigs, for whom Burke was the spokesman, were no longer, like Newcastle's Whig caucus, the national party of government. Far from being 'permanent ins', they were close to being 'permanent outs', the embryo of an opposition in the modern sense. They laid claim to 'the name of whig, dear to the majority of the people', but Burke's remedy for the evils he described was anything but revolutionary. To him 'the natural strength of the Kingdom', which ought always to predominate in the political system, consisted of 'the great peers, the leading landed gentlemen, the opulent merchants and manufacturers, the substantial yeomanry'. The adjectives are the important part of that sentence. Burke was the spokesman not for a class, but for the leading members of each class.

> He who has not sway among any part of the landed or commercial interest is a person who ought never to be allowed to continue in any of those situations which confer the lead or direction of all our public affairs; because such a man *has no connexion with the interest of the people.**

Burke's diagnosis of the malaise was inadequate even in strictly political terms; and it ignored altogether the social forces which were working towards irremediable change. Dissenting ministers agonizing over loss of faith in the Trinity as they pursued their chemical experiments; obscure excisemen agitating for higher wages; military doctors interested in the development of sanitation; lairds and men of means concerned with social statistics and zoological nomenclature; junior naval officers with a self-acquired knowledge of hydrography; the growth of the great provincial towns: these did not enter into Burke's scheme of things.

The challenge which Wilkes had exploited rather than represented came mainly from areas which lay outside the range of Burke's experience and sympathies. It was, above all, a novel challenge, made up of variegated, even contradictory elements, yet homing always on the themes of discovery, opportunity, and secularism. After the curtain-raising farce of Wilkes the seventies begin the earnest drama of radicalism, scientific progress, and the struggle for institutional reform. It is not too much to say that with them a new dimension opens up in society.

'Rational religion' in its new form of Unitarianism formed one sub-

---

* *Thoughts on the Causes of the Present Discontents.*

stantial ingredient in these newly generating forces. The old narrow dissenting sects, and especially the Presbyterians, increasingly rejected the central mystery of the Trinity which the Toleration Act had made the touchstone of social acceptability. A religious view which lay outside the whole design of the Williamite settlement was becoming respectable. Price, the mathematician and moralist, was a Unitarian; so was Priestley, the scientist. In 1774 Theophilus Lindsey established the first openly Unitarian congregation in Essex Street, off the Strand. And not only Nonconformity was being eroded by the new rationalism. The established church was shedding minds to the movement. Lindsey himself had been in Anglican orders, a fellow of a Cambridge college, and a beneficed clergyman. Among those he drew to his congregation were two dukes—one of them Grafton, the former Prime Minister; and Bute's former Chancellor of the Exchequer, Dashwood, who had himself tried his hand at rewriting the Prayer Book. Even one or two bishops were beginning to betray unorthodox opinions: Bishop Watson of Llandaff said openly that he thought the Athanasian Creed was nonsense.

Embedded in the theological position of Unitarianism was an even more potent secular doctrine which its inventor David Hartley, the friend of Warburton and Butler, had dubbed 'necessarianism'. Hartley, who was a doctor by training, had reached the view that the brain functioned by tiny vibrations—he called them 'vibratiuncles'—which in a mechanical way produced thought. In the hands of Belsham, the principal of the Daventry Dissenting Academy, necessarianism received a theological dress which gave it enormous influence. Since all things had been set in motion by the Divine Will, they must of necessity improve; and since, as Newton had shown, all things moved according to ascertainable laws, mankind, in discovering these laws, was furthering the inevitable working out of the Divine purpose. The doctrine not only gave a motive to scientific enquiry which was more respectable than either curiosity or commercialism: it contained elements both of nineteenth-century belief in liberal progress and of Marxist determinism.

The science of the seventies, unlike Newtonian science, was concentrated on the nature of matter rather than the laws and forces of the universe. The emphasis was on experiment, not theory; on chemistry, geology and electricity rather than on physics and astronomy. The famous experiment at Lansdowne House, in which Priestley first isolated oxygen in 1774, was conducted under the influence of a wholly erroneous theory that all combustible matter contained a substance ('phlogiston') which was consumed in the burning process; so that Priestley described the gas he had discovered as 'dephlogisticated air'.* Yet in the course of his numerous experiments with wholly inadequate theoretical equipment, Priestley succeeded in isolating no fewer than nine gases. No commercial or academic motive possessed him, though he benefited for much of the time from the patronage of Shelburne. He did not even seek to patent his discovery of how to manufacture soda water, which over the years was to contribute to the decay of that characteristic British institution, the spa.

Geology, with its urge to arrive at the origins of the earth itself, was a second characteristic science of the seventies, with the great Edinburgh geologist, Hutton, as its chief British exponent. Here was a science which, even more than chemistry, had one foot in theological controversy about the mystery of Creation, and the other in severely practical industrial applications. For the scientific world of the seventies was far closer to industry than Newton's had been. In Cornwall and South Wales the exploitation of tin and copper and the search for more mineral deposits was transforming landscapes and enriching landlords, and practising geologists were in demand. In Birmingham the new partners Matthew Boulton and James Watt, on the threshold of developing steam power, and Wedgwood the potter, supped monthly at the full moon with Withering and Erasmus Darwin the botanists, in the so-called Lunar Society. The possibilities of research and development, which had been beyond the Newtonian age of pure science, were now within reach.

One other branch of science was already attracting the devotion of investigators, though its results for society were still far in the future. This was electricity. Electrical experiment was peculiarly the mark of the man with advanced opinions. Franklin, who had not only constructed one of the earliest devices for storing electricity, but had given it its name of 'battery', acquired much of his prestige from his publications on electricity. Priestley conducted electrical experiments. And the obscure Jean-Paul Marat published several books on the subject.

Even steam power, despite the business acumen of Boulton and the mechanical genius of Watt, was slow to affect ordinary life. For many years after the seventies its use was confined to mining and to one or two other industries which traditionally required the concentration of labour, such as brewing. Down to the turn of the century water power normally sufficed for the new textile machinery. The

---

* The word 'oxygen' was coined very soon afterwards by Lavoisier who also, a little later, produced the generic term 'gas' in place of the confusing 'air'.

factory,* where it existed, was more characteristically a feature of the countryside than of the town, with its location chosen for the water power or coal deposits on which it depended and the accessibility of water transport. The town worker was still overwhelmingly one who worked in his own home or in a small workshop, though he might well be using modern equipment owned by someone else. But as between the domestic worker and the factory hand there was a striking difference in earnings. In a copper-smelting works clear wages of twelve or thirteen shillings a week (for a twelve hour day) were considered reasonable. For a domestic weaver a shilling a day was common.

Progress in chemistry, leading to new and far more effective processes, was probably more important in these earlier stages of industrial change than either steam power or factory organization. But most important of all was progress in the precision of engineering in all its departments. In the last resort all the inventions of the Industrial Revolution depended for their fulfilment on master craftsmen such as Jesse Ramsden, the optical-instrument maker and engraver, or James Harrison the horologist who manufactured the chronometer by which the calculation of exact longitude at last became possible. Watt himself had started his career as an instrument-maker. In every department where precision was needed, whether astronomy, engineering, navigation, or cartography, the contrast in standards between the first decade of the century and the eighth is spectacular.

Patient, accurate work underlay the achievements not only of industrial innovation but of navigation. The charts of James Cook had been a major factor in Wolfe's campaign against Quebec in 1759, and in 1768 his reputation as a hydrographer caused him to be selected for the expedition the Royal Society was sending to the South Seas. The primary object of the voyage made by the *Endeavour* in 1769–71 was not discovery but an observation in the southern hemisphere of a transit of Venus which had been predicted by Halley. The series of voyages which followed, and led to the opening up of Australia and New Zealand, is in lineal descent from the Newtonian age of science, and its prime movers were the men who were gradually rescuing the Royal Society from the status of a noblemen's club to which it had descended in the previous two generations: Pringle, the military

---

* To a man of the eighteenth century 'factory' meant a trading station, usually abroad. The word hardly comes into use for an industrial establishment until the next century. In the eighteenth century a large workshop would be a 'manufactory'.

doctor and pioneer in hygiene; and Joseph Banks, the naturalist. The world revealed on Cook's return in 1771 was almost as astonishing and unsuspected as the world that had been revealed to Leeuwenhoek by the microscope: a completely new flora and fauna, of which numerous specimens were brought back by the indefatigable Cook. They included a new kind of man, the native Tahitian Omai, who impressed Dr Johnson by his good manners and elegance. New Zealand and the eastern coast of Australia had been charted, and a continent annexed to the British Crown.

Cook's second, and even more astonishing voyage—this time in the *Discovery*—lasted for three years, took the first men to the edge of the Antarctic icecap, and for the first time encircled the globe from west to east. But in some ways the most remarkable feature of the voyage was the contrast in cost with its predecessor, in terms of human life. From the *Endeavour* Cook lost thirty men out of a crew of eighty-five, mainly from scurvy and fever. From the *Discovery* he lost 1 out of 115. The difference was due to systematic study of health at sea. That a naval officer should concern himself with such a matter was in itself novel.

Almost simultaneously the first great investigation of the interior of Africa by a British explorer was taking place. Raids, coastal trading, and piracy, had long been features of the European presence on the west coast, but there had been virtually no penetration of the gigantic land mass, either on the west or the east. While Cook was skirting the Antarctic one of the greatest of land travellers, James Bruce, reached one of the sources of the Nile, having started from the Red Sea coast, and returned across what is now the Sudan after a journey which lasted nearly seven years.*

Minds sensitive to change were vibrating, questioning states of affairs which had held good for generations. A minor civil servant, Granville Sharp, grandson of Queen Anne's Archbishop of York, had in 1765 met and befriended a destitute Negro called Jonathan Strong. Negroes were already quite numerous in London—Dr Johnson was

---

* Although Rider Haggard removed the geographical scene of *King Solomon's Mines* to southern Africa there can be little doubt that its inspiration was Bruce's *Travels in Abyssinia*. Many of the elements, including the involvement of the European traveller in the politics of an African kingdom are directly borrowed. Even the continuation of British habits of mind in inappropriate surroundings are to be found in Bruce, who carried the spirit of an improver into the Ethiopian highlands. At Mai Shum he received a present of vegetables from a peasant who kept 'a neat little garden on both sides of a rivulet . . . Such instances of industry are very rare in this country, and demanded encouragement. I paid him therefore for his greens.'

one of many to have a black servant—and not a few were slaves who had escaped from American or West Indian masters on visits to England. Strong was one of these, and Sharp's attempt to defend him against re-enslavement by his pursuing master failed in the face of the doctrine which had been handed down by the courts in 1729, that although the condition of slavery was unknown to the law of England, it could be enforced in England on behalf of masters living in a country where slavery was lawful. Sharp fought on, and in 1772, in the case of James Somersett, another escaped slave, he succeeded in getting from Lord Mansfield one of the most remarkable instances of judge-made law that the bench of England has ever provided. Mansfield said:*

> The state of slavery is of such a nature, that it is incapable of being introduced on any reasons, moral or political, but only of positive law . . . It is so odious, that nothing can be suffered to support it but positive law. Whatever inconveniences, therefore, may follow from the decision I cannot say this case is allowed or approved by the law of England; and therefore the black must be discharged.

The campaign for the abolition of slavery, on which Sharp had now started, was to be a very long one, occupying the energy of liberals for over half a century. The slave trade, indeed, continued to expand even after the Somersett case, bringing additional prosperity to Liverpool and Bristol, the two great slaving ports. The question whether the loss of slaves thrown overboard to lighten a ship in a storm could be recovered under marine insurance as jettisoned 'cargo' was yet to be debated in the English courts. The Somersett case was nevertheless a landmark, and not only as the first victory of the abolitionists. This was a new kind of cause, in which neither religion nor property provided the motive power. For although most of the slave trade abolitionists were earnest Christians, the basis of their campaign was political equality.

The association in particular minds of ideas not in themselves consistently related to one another, but making up collectively a recognizable political position, is conspicuous in the case of Sharp. For he was also one of the earliest advocates of another great cause—parliamentary reform; as well as a passionate supporter of the rights of the American colonists. In 1774, two years after his victory in Somersett's

---

* *State Trials,* vol. 20, pp. 80–2. Quoted in D. B. Horn and M. Ransome (eds.), *English Historical Documents 1714–1783* (Eyre & Spottiswoode, 1957), vol. 10, p. 262.

case, he published a pamphlet arguing for 'the People's natural right
to a share in the legislature', which he took as equal representation
in annual Parliaments. The notion of topographical franchises, in
which election by few or many voters was at bottom no more than
an incidental procedure for settling the minority of cases in which
there was a question of who should occupy a given seat, was deeply
engrained. The member of an eighteenth-century House of Commons,
whether he sat for Westminster or Old Sarum, did not represent
people: he represented a place with a franchise; and in so far as he
had a master to give him directions it was the dominant interest in
the franchise, as Lord Lonsdale, that most brutal of borough owners,
often made clear to members who were unfortunate enough to depend
on his electoral influence. The member for one of his boroughs who
voted contrary to his instructions could expect to be treated in the
same way as a disobedient servant.

Sharp's pamphlet, a speech by Wilkes in 1776, and in the same year
the publication of Cartwright's *Take Your Choice* were the first straws
in the wind which became a gale. In this, as in so much else, the 1770s
saw the beginnings of a great liberal cause; and a cause caught up, in
the minds of its first advocates, with the greatest progressive cause of
the time: the freedom of the American colonies. It was Charles Lee,
an American Wilkite, who in 1771 produced the first attempt to pledge
British parliamentary candidates to support 'a free and equal representation of the people'. When the final attempt to negotiate a compro-
mise between Britain and the colonies broke down Fothergill, the
physician, and Barclay, the Quaker, told Franklin that 'the salvation
of English liberty depended now on the perseverance and virtue of
America.'

Nascent radicalism was to find its most characteristic exponent of
all in a man drawn from the lower-middle class which had provided
Wilkes's most eager supporters. Except that he was an East Anglian,
not a Londoner, Tom Paine would have fitted into any Wilkite demonstration. Journeyman stay-maker, deck-hand, schoolmaster, excise
officer organizing a campaign for better wages, he was to become the
most formidable political pamphleteer since Swift. Paine was almost
entirely self-educated, and the leanings of his education were to the
new worlds of science and America. 'The natural bent of my mind,'
he wrote of his own childhood, 'was to science . . . I happened, when
a schoolboy, to pick up a pleasing natural history of Virginia, and my
inclination from that day of seeing the Western side of the Atlantic
never left me.' In 1774, through the agency of Benjamin Franklin, he

was sent there, and promptly began the career of a propagandist which was to carry him to membership of the Convention, and very nearly to the guillotine.

Franklin's letter on behalf of Paine was written in bitterness of spirit. A few months earlier, in one of those rare scenes when some kind of fate seems to draw together a diverse yet significant group into a single room on a great occasion, Franklin's long and influential stay in England had been virtually brought to a close. The instrument was Wedderburn, the Solicitor General, and the scene the Cockpit, at Westminster, where the Privy Council Committee for Trade met. Priestley and the young Bentham, Burke and Shelburne, Dunning and Dashwood, North the Prime Minister and Strahan the publisher, were among those who heard Wedderburn accuse Franklin of secretly undermining the authority of the Governor of Massachusetts. The Solicitor General's vitriolic diatribe was designed publicly and deliberately to destroy Franklin's towering reputation:*

> I hope, my Lords, you will mark and brand this man, for the honour of this country, of Europe, and of mankind . . . he has forfeited all the respect of societies and of men . . . I ask, my Lords, whether the vengeful temper attributed, by poetic fiction only, to the bloody African, is not surpassed by the coolness and apathy of the wily American?

On the following day Franklin was deprived of his main source of income—the Deputy Postmastership of North America.†

Franklin was the key figure, not only in building up sympathy for the American cause, but in the emerging progressive movement as a whole. His formidable scientific reputation, his skill as a propagandist, and the fact that he depended on no interest in the English scheme of patronage, all contributed to this influence. Before a shot was fired at Lexington or Concord, Franklin had won battles for American independence by ensuring that a large section of the most articulate and forward-looking English would support it. Britain entered its first imperial crisis as a deeply divided nation, with the critics opposed not only to the war but to the political structure in which it had occurred.

---

* *The Autobiography of Benjamin Franklin.*
† The impression this made on Franklin is marked by a well-authenticated anecdote. He put aside the suit he had worn at the Cockpit and did not wear it again until he signed the treaty of alliance with France on behalf of the United States. He then never wore it afterwards.

The crisis which became overt with the Boston Tea Party and the dismissal of Franklin reached the whole imperial position that Britain had established in the wars of the mid-century, and not the American colonies alone. The tea thrown overboard in December 1773 had crossed the Atlantic in the first place in an effort to relieve the liquidity crisis of the East India Company by disposing of its excessive stock at an artificially low price. This gigantic company, which already dominated Bengal and was a major Indian power besides providing the most important commercial investment London had to offer, was in serious financial and administrative difficulties. The system—if it can be called that—by which its political responsibilities in India were treated as merely incidental to its commerce, and not even distinguished in its accounts, could no longer be sustained. Government intervention, unwelcome as it was to the government itself, was inevitable.

North's Regulating Act of 1773 took the first tremulous steps towards the Raj of the next century—steps important for the fact that they were taken at all, rather than for any effect they had on the immediate situation. Under the Act the new Governor General, and the new High Court were appointed, not by the Company, but by the Crown. The struggle of the immediate future was to be the share that Parliament and the politicians should have in Indian patronage.

Life in the Indian settlements is vividly described by William Hickey in his memoirs. In the sweltering heat of Bengal the English, wearing clothes even more gorgeous than the court costumes at St James's, led a social life that was distinguishable from the one they led at home only by its exaggeration. In Calcutta, as in London, there were sheriffs and coffee houses, bewigged lawyers and whist parties, visits of ceremony and dependence on interest. From the first the new men and their womenfolk (for English women were already settling there with their husbands, or looking for husbands in India) established themselves in the already stratified society of Bengal as a new caste.

There were nevertheless profound differences from the behaviour of the British settlers in America. Never for a moment did the British in India—confronted as they were with an existing sophisticated civilization—establish their own constitutional framework or contemplate the notion of independence. Though the voyage home was longer, their hope was always to return and spend the rest of their lives in Britain. Because they lived in an Indian context, and their purpose was trade, not settlement, they were beginning to be more interested in Indian civilization than any American settler was concerned with the sparse and strange natives of his continent. In 1771 William Jones, the first, and in some ways the greatest of the English orientalists, published his Persian grammar, and in 1774 his *Commentaries on Asiatic Poetry*. He had established himself in a career which was to carry him to the high Court Bench in Calcutta and an absorption in every aspect of Indian life.

The prelude to the Regulating Act had shown the new chapter it was to open. Clive, now in his fifties and an addict of opium, but also an Irish peer, a Member of Parliament and a big owner of borough interest, was assailed for past maladministration by a parliamentary committee led by Burgoyne, who was soon to surrender decisively to the Americans at Saratoga. Within a year the victor of Plassey had committed suicide. The tradition of buccaneering in the East Indies which he had supremely represented was fatally damaged, even though not destroyed, and the conscience of Parliament was aroused on the subject of India in the way that was impossible in relation to America. Even Lord Rockingham, who was a strong defender of the Company's chartered rights, was conscious of the change of climate. 'Many men of tender feelings,' he wrote, 'on the dismal accounts of rapine and oppression in the Company's servants in Bengal, join in the cry that some stop must be put to it.'

Conscience had followed quickly on consciousness of Empire, whether in the East or the West. Yet the enthusiasm of the progressives for the American cause, and the attacks in Parliament on the mis-government of Bengal, were in a way contradictory. One denounced intervention by the British Parliament in the affairs of free colonies, and the other demanded its intervention in the empire acquired by a company. There is another contrast also. Franklin and the Americans had indeed established a powerful and deep-rooted lobby in Britain. The demand for the reform of administration in the East appears to have been spontaneous: at any rate it owed nothing to the agitation of those most affected, the Bengalis themselves.

Franklin left the idea of empire like a barb in the consciousness of the country from which he and the Americans cut loose. The notion which he was one of the first to express, of self-governing nations under the British Crown inheriting the British concepts of representative government, remained to haunt the nation which was on the brink of dominating southern Asia. At almost the same moment the banners of progressive reform are unfurled so that one can read the slogans to which the nineteenth century was to give practical reality: parliamentary reform; the end of the Anglican monopoly; change in Ireland; the abolition of slavery as a first step towards the acknowledgment of racial equality. Without the conflict with America, which irreversibly divided opinion in Britain, these issues could hardly have come to occupy the centre of the stage so quickly.

The nation of squires and parishes, for which George III was such an appropriate ruler, was by 1776 faced with the certainty of profound and lasting change. Change was not merely disagreeable to the average Englishman. The very idea of it was unfamiliar. To most people it still seemed as if their destiny was to repeat their parents' lives, and they had never noticed that even during their parents' lifetimes society had changed a great deal. The pace of change had been slow. Yet one has only to compare Defoe's travels through England with those of Arthur Young, or Celia Fiennes' side-saddle tours with the journeys which John Byng lovingly recorded in the *Torrington Diaries*, to sense the changes there had been. The purpose of the last chapter will be to indicate how Britain had changed by 1776, and where those changes seemed likely to lead.

Chapter 13   Britain on the Eve of the American Revolution

The year of American Independence stands out in high relief in almost every aspect of British life. Gibbon's first volume was published and swept in triumph through the educated and fashionable world. Hume, Gibbon's predecessor, who had laid the axe at the root of the tree of easy-going faith, died; and in doing so set a shocked world an example of how an infidel could meet the end calmly. In the same few months Adam Smith, Hume's colleague and Gibbon's friend, opened the principle of the division of labour and stated the logical case against restrictions on commerce. In the clear, closely wrought prose of *The Wealth of Nations* he dealt a blow to the old concepts of economic organization from which there was to be no real recovery. The young Jeremy Bentham launched his anonymous *Fragment on Government*, staking a claim for a scientific jurisprudence against Blackstone's traditionalism, and uttering the tremendous principle of 'the greatest happiness of the greatest number'. Beside the Strand, facing on to the Thames, the building of Somerset House—the first major building in England planned for purely administrative purposes—was begun. Mrs Siddons was playing her first season in London opposite the ageing Garrick, who was playing his last as Shylock and Richard III. Yet the event of 1776 which probably attracted the most attention at the time was the preposterous trial, before the House of Lords, of the retired beauty Elizabeth Chudleigh for bigamy with two successive peers. The drama filled Westminster Hall for weeks. Mrs Garrick, who attended the public gallery enthusiastically, swore her husband was not nearly so good a performer as the famous prisoner. The melodrama ended in farce. After Elizabeth had been unanimously found guilty by a House of more than a hundred peers, they were told there was no appropriate punishment for a peeress convicted of bigamy, and she was set free to exercise her middle-aged charms on the Czar of Russia.

Yet the trial of Elizabeth Chudleigh is not insignificant in social history. It is an example of the fact that throughout the eighteenth century the careers of aristocrats and criminals (she having the good fortune to be both) provided the main standards of mass entertainment and so of popular aspiration. Religion—the other main source of spectacle and style before mass media were developed—did not in its British forms lend itself to these purposes. One's wonder at the deference paid to the aristocracy and at the ghoulish interest in crime and executions is lessened when one realizes that for most people in the eighteenth century there was no public figure but the aristocrat to model oneself upon, and no public show comparable to a trial with a hanging at the end of it. The theatre reached few, and other forms of public spectacle were hardly above the level of the fair-ground.

1776 was the year in which the Britain launched in the reigns of William and Anne began to falter. There was a growing loss of confidence in many of the institutions and methods which had brought the country so far. Within five years this loss of confidence was to bring the country to international isolation and the verge of revolution.

One of the most significant symptoms was financial. The flow of funds from abroad, notably from Holland, which had been so marked a feature of the past eighty years, was beginning to evaporate. The obvious channel for them—the British National Debt—had ceased to expand since the year 1763 introduced an exceptionally long period of peace. Dutch funds, indeed, were already beginning to find an alternative outlet in America. Very soon it was to be not merely a drying up of new funds but a withdrawal of old ones. In 1777 Lord North estimated that the Dutch held about £59 million of British government securities. By 1780 the estimate had sunk to £29 million out of a much larger total swollen by the demands of the war in America. By 1786 the Dutch bond-holders had so redistributed their portfolios that they were drawing almost as much income on them from France as they were from England.

The era of American independence therefore coincides with a decisive shift in Britain's financial and economic relationship with the continent of Europe. It was soon followed by a degree of political isolation that would have been impossible under William III and have horrified all those responsible for British international affairs from James II to William Pitt the Elder. The patterns they had favoured had been many: *entente* with France had dominated Walpole's thinking; to 'be well with the Emperor' had been a precept of Whig foreign policy down to 1757; the symbiotic relationship with Holland was a habit of mind for generations of statesmen; Prussia had helped William III to the throne of England, and Pitt to his imperial triumphs. By the end of the seventies Britain was to be at war with France, Holland, and Spain, and scarcely had a friend in Europe.

The change in Britain's international standing was accompanied by, and to some extent was due to, the mood of profound internal questioning. Questions of the kind which once asked produce a radical change in the climate of opinion and eventually in institutions themselves, were being raised about almost every major aspect of British life: about Parliament, about the Anglo-centric system of commercial regulation, about the church settlement which still excluded Dissenters and Roman Catholics from the full rights of citizenship. Longstanding compromises of practice which had made life tolerable without the need for formal change suddenly became no longer acceptable. Christopher Wyvill, the Yorkshire parliamentary reformer, denied the ingenious doctrine of 'virtual representation', which sought to defend the freakish franchise by arguing that it did not particularly matter provided it produced a House of Commons which was reasonably representative as a whole.* Adam Smith destroyed the intellectual basis of the Navigation Acts. Dissenters who had for years been content to hold municipal office in the knowledge that no one would invoke the Corporation Act against them, or to depend on the annual Indemnity Acts excusing them from the consequences of the Test Acts, were beginning to agitate for the abolition of all disqualifications. Unitarians, technically outside the scope even of the Toleration Act, were arguing that they should still be treated as Christians.

Anglicanism had failed to master either the city state of London, the new industrial towns of the provinces, or the overseas empire that had been created. It had never struck root in Ireland. It remained fundamentally the religion of the countryside and the small towns of England. Of the fifty churches which Queen Anne's enthusiastic Tory Parliament had voted should be built in London only eight were ever completed. Birmingham, one of the most rapidly growing towns in the country, received two new churches in the first seventy years of

---

* Soame Jenyns had unwittingly put a torpedo into the Lockean doctrine of virtual representation some years earlier, in trying to refute the American argument that there could be no taxation without representation. 'If the towns of Manchester and Birmingham, sending no representatives to Parliament, are there represented, why are not the cities of Albany and Boston?' The inference he drew was that the notion of taxation depending on representation was nonsense. (*Works*, vol. 2, p. 193.)

the century.* The huge new urban parishes had little of the community spirit which was Anglicanism's main support in the villages such as Nettlebed, in Oxfordshire, where the tourist Karl Philip Moritz spent an idyllic Sunday admiring the pure and patriarchal Anglican worship. At the same time the self-interestedness of the higher clergy was becoming painfully apparent. 'The life of a prebendary,' the Rev. E. Pyle had written in the 1750s, 'is a pretty easy way of dawdling away one's time: praying, walking, visiting; and as little study as the heart could wish.' He was not only Archdeacon of York but a canon of Winchester, and divided his year between the two cathedral cities and London, where he always spent three months.

Political patronage and the ties of birth had become increasingly important factors in promotion, and there was less of a leaven of bishops from humble backgrounds than there had ever been before. Even the loyal Parson Woodforde, returning from dinner with his bishop, noted in his diary that 'being with one's equals is much more agreable'. By 1775 Samuel Johnson himself—and there were few more energetic defenders of things as they were—commented that preferment could now only be achieved by parliamentary influence.

Yet a new religious force was coming to the established order's aid. Wesleyanism had been the most formidable challenge the established church had had to face since Cromwellian times, and by the seventies it had well over 100 congregations in England and Wales alone, not to mention its large following in the American colonies. In some manufacturing areas, and in South Wales, it was by now the dominant faith. Wesley himself was still alive, and had not ceased to be a controversial figure, dominating the organization he had created and engaging in fierce battles with the Calvinist wing of Methodism. There were now some fifty Methodist circuits, with over 35,000 faithful. His views, said the evangelical Anglican Augustus Montague Toplady, the author of Rock of Ages, 'are an equal portion of gross heathenism, Pelagianism, Mahometanism, popery, Manichaeism, ranterism, and antinomianism, culled, dried, and pulverised ... mingled with as much palpable atheism as could possibly be scraped together.' But Wesley never wavered in his support of the dynasty, the constitution as it was, and his conviction that he remained an orthodox Anglican. He had denounced the rebels of 1745, and he

* In 1818, when the population of Birmingham was estimated at 80,000, its eight Anglican churches, several of which had been recently built, had accommodation for only just over 11,000 people. See R. K. Dent, The Making of Birmingham (1894) p. 280.

denounced the Americans in 1776, just as he was to denounce, in their turn, the French revolutionaries of 1789. His influence had damaged the old comfortable church, and even caused Anglicans to incorporate hymns in their services, but by the seventies Methodism was a source of stability. Wesley identified himself with only one of the great new liberal causes: the abolition of slavery.

By the middle of the seventies the population of Britain was fully embarked on its irreversible upward trend. Dr Richard Price, the mathematician, argued strongly that it was not so, pointing to the appalling mortality which was still evident in London; but by the best estimates available the total population of Great Britain and Ireland had reached about 10·5 million, compared with about 8·5 million at the beginning of the century. Between 1770 and 1780 a million was added to the population. But even this rapid rate of increase could not compare with the rate of expansion in the American population, which in the year of independence was more than one-fifth of the British and Irish combined. At the beginning of the century it had been one-twentieth.*

Even within the British Isles the growth had been uneven, and had altered the proportions of the component parts. The populations of both Scotland and Ireland had more or less doubled since the Revolution, while that of England and Wales had grown by only about 50 per cent. The inhabitants north of the Border were therefore about one-fifth of the number south of it, against what had been one-sixth in 1690; and the Irish were about one-third the number of the English, as against perhaps one-fifth. Such growth as there had been in England had been mainly in Lancashire, the Midlands and London.

There could be no doubt that London in its broad sense was now much the largest urban area in the world, with well over three-quarters of a million inhabitants. Here, too, the distribution of population had changed since the beginning of the century. The old 'City within the walls' had only half the number that had been packed there in Defoe's time and the walls themselves, which had still been a recognizable circuit at the end of the seventeenth century, had now almost vanished. The population of Southwark had also shrunk. These deficiencies were more than made good by the huge growth in the 'out-parishes' of Middlesex and Surrey, and in Westminster. The

* The population of England and Wales may be estimated in 1776 at between six and seven millions; of Scotland at nearly 1·5 million; and Ireland at 2·5 million. See appendix 1.

development of Mayfair in the first part of the century and Marylebone in the twenty years after 1750, had carried the townscape north and west, and the construction of the 'New Road' from Paddington to the Angel in 1756–7 marks the first gesture towards an outer circular highway. The densest population of all, probably, was still concentrated in the hovels and shanties to the east of the Tower. Of the seventeen new parishes in the London area established since 1660, nine were in what is now the East End.*

The London of 1776 was better paved, better lit, better drained, and probably better policed, than it had been in the middle of the century. Sedan chairs, which had been in demand to avoid the filth rather than relieve the legs, were now less often seen. Whether it was a pleasanter place to live than it had been still earlier, in the days of Queen Anne, is more open to question. The two Fieldings, successively magistrates at Bow Street, had produced the first paid police force for Westminster, and the first attempts to combine summary justice with social improvement. The second Fielding, especially, interested himself in schemes which went beyond the mere repression of delinquency: in the Marine Society, for instance, which trained and equipped delinquent boys to be sailors, and the Orphan Asylum for Deserted Girls. Already, in 1766, John Gwynn, in his *London and Westminster Improv'd,* had envisaged a better-planned London, with wider and more purposeful streets, bigger squares, more bridges, and an embankment.

But in many ways London was a more terrifying place than it had ever been. As it grew older, it grew denser and dirtier. Until the great Building Act of 1774 there had been little control over either standards of construction or town planning, so much of it was jerry-built or worse.† Structures such as booths or stalls, which had originally been temporary, had been allowed to become permanent, narrowing down streets that had been planned as broad. Extra, often illicit, construction made courtyards and open spaces into closes through which thread-like filthy lanes led to the entrances of the houses. Underneath the pavements cellars had been scooped out to provide lodging for the very poorest. Large numbers, only slightly better off, lived in

---

* See M. Dorothy George, *London Life in the Eighteenth Century,* appendix 3.
† The Act of 1774 marks an era in social legislation and in the appearance of the British townscape. It categorized buildings into 'rates' (on the analogy of ships) and laid down standards of construction for each, including the thickness of external and party walls, and the depth of foundations. It also provided a considerable measure of standardization. The vast terraced development of London during the last quarter of the eighteenth century and the first half of the nineteenth reflects the standards of the legislation of 1774.

common lodging houses, four or five to a room, paying 2*d.* or 3*d.* a night, and 'what with the nastiness of these wretches', wrote Saunders Welch, the magistrate, after visiting such a house, 'and their number, such an inconceivable stench has arose from them that I have hardly been able to bear it the little time that my duty required me to stay.' A rung above these on the social ladder were the families occupying a single room—often a garret—for which two shillings a week was a typical rent: a large proportion of a twelve shilling a week wage.

Dublin, with 100,000 inhabitants, was not only the second biggest city in the British Isles but one of the largest in western Europe. Its courts were even more densely packed and more filthy than London's. Bristol, now with some 60,000 inhabitants, came next in size, as it had done at the beginning of the century. An admirable position and the American trade had favoured growth. But it was otherwise with many of the other older English towns which had still held their heads high under Queen Anne. Encumbered by their privileges, which were used to restrict trade to native citizens, such towns as Lichfield and Lancaster became relative backwaters. It was not an accident that economic growth occurred where regulation was least and representation in Parliament which went with privilege, was absent. Manchester, Birmingham and Leeds had no corporate or guild structure to prevent outsiders from settling and starting in business.

Birmingham can reasonably claim to be the characteristic urban creation of the first half of the century: a town of design and manufacture, not of fashion and sociability. By 1776 it had more than 30,000 inhabitants, and in the Soho Manufactory, with its thousand workers, Matthew Boulton had assembled an unrivalled number of workmen under one roof. 'I sell here, Sir,' he said to the astonished Boswell, 'what all the world desires to possess: POWER.' In Baskerville Birmingham had produced one of the greatest designers, typefounders, and printers so far to appear in England.* Never before in England had a major centre of trade been sited so far from the sea, or even from a navigable river. But by the end of the century Birmingham was the centre of a radiating system of canals. The sagacious Boulton followed London taste carefully in the interest of his main

---

* Like so many industrial designers of the eighteenth century Baskerville started life in the decorative arts—in his case japanning: Caslon started as an engraver on gun-barrels. Baskerville was a convinced sceptic and directed that he should be buried in a tomb (which he designed himself) with the epitaph: 'Stranger, beneath this cone, in *unconsecrated* ground a friend to the liberties of mankind directed his body to be inurn'd. May the example contribute to emancipate thy mind from the idle fears of superstition and the wicked arts of Priesthood.'

line of business, which was the manufacture of all kinds of orna-mental metal-work; but there was little fashionableness in Birmingham itself. 'I have laughed twenty times,' wrote Catherine Hutton to her friend in London, 'after your idea of enquiring about fashion in Bir-mingham, a place celebrated for neither fashion nor taste.'

The most spectacular flowering of urban life, perhaps, had been in Scotland, where both Glasgow and Edinburgh had become unrecog-nizable by comparison with their state at the time of the Union. The sugar and tobacco trades which the Union had opened to Scotland had brought prosperity and expansion to Glasgow, which had risen from a modest cathedral and university city of perhaps 12,000 inhabi-tants to a powerful commercial port of over 30,000. The case of Edin-burgh is even more striking because the economic causes are less obvious. At the time of the Union it had perhaps 30,000 inhabitants, on whose poverty and dirtiness all visitors remarked. By 1776 it must have rivalled, if not actually exceeded Bristol's 60,000, and it was for the time being superseding London as the intellectual metropolis of the island.

James Craig published his plans for a new Edinburgh in 1767, and in the years that followed few towns have more dramatically burst their bounds and changed their character. Conceived in the medieval wynds and seven-story 'lands' of the Old Town, the plan for a modern city on the other side of the valley was to take thirty years to execute. But already, by 1772, the draining of the marsh which separated the rocky spine of the old city from the new site had been accomplished and a bridge had been thrown across the resulting ravine.

The New Town of Edinburgh is the great monument to the success of the Union and the labours of Carlyle of Inveresk and his moderate friends in bringing Scotland into the main stream of British life. Carlyle himself was so proud of his achievement that as he grew older he became a passionate upholder of things as they were, especi-ally south of the Border. The Test Act, because its preservation was part of the bargain struck at the Union, had his energetic support. It was, after all, the law 'which has paved the road to office and prefer-ment . . . the key that opens up all the treasures of the South to every honest Scotchman.' Wilkites, and when they arrived on the scene Jacobins, did not command much sympathy from the intelligentsia of Scotland; and while in England the emergence of a radical left wing embraced many members of the governing and intellectual classes, in the north Toryism had a strong hold on both. Scotland's golden age was to be dominated by Pitt's crony Dundas, and the Tory tradition was to be uppermost down to the period of Walter Scott and the *Quarterly Review*.

No king had visited Scotland since the reign of Charles II*, and the stamp of the Union's final cultural success was left to the Great Cham of literature. Johnson's visit in 1773, which took in not only the Hebrides but the principal towns as well, was an event of great cultural— almost of political— significance. It is true that his account of it in his *Journey to the Western Islands of Scotland* emphasized a Celtic side of Scotland which was already in the decline, though it has ever since been the image presented by the Scottish tourist industry. But it would hardly be an exaggeration to say that Johnson's tour marks a stage in the relations between England and Scotland which is comparable to the Union itself in importance. By the last quarter of the century the hostility to the Scots in England, on which Wilkes had battened, was vanishing.

The vigorous intellectual life of Edinburgh and of Scotland in general had been built on an educational foundation which had no equivalent in England. Just as Scotland had little by way of a local Poor Law, so England had nothing to compare with the Scottish system of parochial education, which had been established by a statute of the Scottish Parliament in 1696. There is a curious alternative relationship between the two parochial systems: each, though falling short of its professed aims, was a form of social provision which was rare in contemporary Europe and had a powerful influence on social development in the island as a whole.

Anglicanism, despite its monopoly of education, had never organized a systematic network of schools. In Scotland the Kirk was required by law to maintain a school in every parish. The law was not everywhere obeyed, especially in the Highlands, and even where it was observed the school was often a hovel presided over by an underpaid and half-starved dominie.† System, however, it was, and it led to

---

* And even he, while the southern kingdom was in the hands of Parliament. One has to go back to Charles I's unacceptable visit in 1639 for an example of a king reigning in England visiting his kingdom of Scotland. The first king after the unions of the Crowns in 1603 to pay an ordinary royal visit to Scotland was George IV, who in return conferred the first literary honour—on Walter Scott, who organized it.

† The wages were indeed wretched. In 1748 the schoolmasters, in a petition to the General Assembly for more pay, pointed out that their average income was about £11 a year, or 7*d.* a day, 'which is less than the lowest mechanic can earn'. By 1782 it had risen to about £13 a year, and in 1802 Parliament was persuaded to offer a minimum wage of £16 13*s.* 4*d.* plus a house containing at least two rooms *including the kitchen.* One Scottish M.P. was heard to observe that this was overgenerous, and that he was against 'erecting palaces for dominies'

opportunities of higher education on a far better ratio than in England. In the obituary of William Strahan, the printer, the Edinburgh literary paper the *Lounger* spoke of how the elder Strahan—a minor official in the Customs—had been able to give his son 'the education which every lad of decent rank then received in a country where the avenues to Learning were easy, and open to men of the most moderate circumstances'.

What was still more important (though it was not in any way intended by those who had established the system) was that the parish and burgh schools had a virtual monopoly, which was vigorously defended. This discouragement of private enterprise in education had nothing to do with any class-conscious principle: its object was to prevent diminution of the income from the fees which the official schools were entitled to charge. But as a result the son of the laird and the son of the ploughman were often educated in the same school, and the tradition of boarding education for the children of the better-off never took strong root in Scotland.

The fruits of Scottish education were not harvested in Scotland alone. The Scots contributed, out of all proportion to their numbers, to improving the general sources of information which were now becoming widely available. Ephraim Chambers, an Englishman, had produced the first encyclopedia that can be called modern in 1728, and by 1746 his *Cyclopaedia or Universal Dictionary of the Arts and Sciences* had run to five editions and implanted the idea of a more comprehensive work in the mind of Diderot. But the *Encyclopaedia Britannica,* which began to appear in sixpenny weekly parts in 1768, was an entirely Scottish production, emanating from Edinburgh. The second edition, which came out only six years after the first was completed, ran to 8,500 pages, and had 340 plates: a work of reference on a scale never equalled before.

Scotland had prospered by a Union which recognized its religious and social diversity from England: Ireland had stagnated in a shadow of independence which did neither yet had the effect of excluding the smaller island from the economic progress of Great Britain. Irish commerce was still regulated by the British Parliament as if Ireland had been a colony, while the internal affairs of Ireland were still settled by Anglo-Irish Anglicans on principles which had been swept away in England by the Revolution of 1688. The costs of British troops in Ireland were met from Irish revenues—a fact which strengthened the conviction of British politicians that the same should apply to America. The Dublin Parliament, for which only Anglicans could vote, was a caricature of the Parliament at Westminster: an assembly which expected to be manipulated by the 'undertakers' or managers of Irish politics, and existed largely as a market for the distribution of patronage to its Members. Until the Octennial Act election to the Irish House of Commons was an investment tied to the survival of the reigning king, whose death dissolved it. '*Four thousand pounds* for a seat in the House of Commons of Ireland when his majesty is seventy years old!' wrote one of Lord Charlemont's correspondents in 1754. A single trio of political organizers controlled forty of the 300 seats.*

The English were anxious and guilty about the exclusion of Ireland from the benefits of the British economy. Dr Johnson, who saw nothing wrong with the traditional relationship between Britain and America, turned fiercely on a defender of English economic policy towards Ireland. It would be better, he declared, 'to restrain the turbulence of the natives by the authority of the sword, and to make them amenable to law and justice by an effectual and vigorous police, than to grind them to powder by all sorts of disabilities and incapacities.' That had been in 1770, but those few who understood Irish politics had been sensitive to the basic instability much earlier than this. All depended upon the acquiescence of the Anglo-Irish to Westminster policy, and even a relatively trivial disagreement between Dublin and London, such as occurred in 1753, had been enough to alarm a shrewd politician such as Bubb Dodington. 'Dangerous event!' he wrote in his diary, on hearing the Dublin Parliament was unwilling to accept Westminster's decision on the disposal of the Irish revenue surplus, 'and productive of more mischiefs than I shall live to see remedied.' By the sixties even the sluggish Dublin Parliament was showing signs of life. Ireland found her first great parliamentary orator in Henry Flood, who entered the Dublin Parliament in 1759 for Kilkenny and began building up a national—though necessarily Anglican—opposition.

The evolution of events in America decisively upset the long-maintained stability of Ireland. Many reasons contributed. For the first time in a century Britain was on the defensive. The commercial system from which Ireland and America suffered in common was under attack. The British garrison of Ireland had to be reduced to

* The organization of patronage through the Irish House of Commons can readily be studied in Chief Secretary Blaquière's 'Catalogue of the Irish Commons in 1775' (ed. William Hunt, privately printed, 1907). 'ALLAN, Thomas: Borough of Killybegs. Purchased his seat—was Commissioner of Customs—upon reuniting the Boards he was pensioned at £600—formerly Taster of the Wines, for which he received from Mr Beresford £800.'

meet the needs of the war. And an important component of the colonists themselves was of Irish origin, for Irishmen had been crossing the Atlantic at an annual rate estimated at 6,000 for many years past. There were not many Catholics among them: far the greater number were northern Presbyterians, whose economic and religious disabilities in Ireland were hardly less than those of the Catholics. During the epoch of the American Revolution and the Volunteer Movement in Ireland the mutual encouragement across the Atlantic came from Protestant voices. It is a facile and partial view of history that associates Irish patriotism exclusively with the Catholic and the Celt.

In 1775 the young Henry Grattan had been returned to the Dublin Parliament for the Earl of Charlemont's pocket borough and a beginning was soon to be made, under the pressure of events, on the liberalization of the worst features of Georgian Ireland. The next five years were to see the legislative basis of Westminster's supremacy swept away, an end to the enforcement of mercantile restrictions, and a cautious beginning with religious toleration. What Lord North in his years of desperation felt bound to concede to the heady demonstrations of the Volunteer Movement, Rockingham, as the guardian of 'Revolution Principles', completed. Something like what England had achieved in the post-1688 settlement now became the constitution of Ireland. But it was a solution that hardly touched the position of the native Catholic Irish peasantry, just as the Scottish settlement of 1707 had left out of account the feudal Highlands of Scotland.

Paradoxically, foreign confidence in Britain was shaking and she was about to lose her American empire at precisely the moment when her population and her internal economy were thrusting irresistibly forward into new orders of magnitude. By the 1770s the value of British manufacture was estimated at £56 million a year, and the value of exports was £15 million compared with about £5 million at the beginning of the century. Exports from England had more than doubled in three-quarters of a century, and those from Scotland had almost quadrupled. Since there had been hardly any inflation there can be no doubt at all that general prosperity must have increased, and the upward trend of wages, which is perceptible in the last quarter of the century, represented higher real standards of consumption.

But much of the gains—perhaps even the lion's share—went into the formation of capital assets: the canals of Brindley, the Carron

Ironworks, Boulton's Soho Manufactory, and the thousands of small labour-saving machines, mostly in the textile industry, which had raised output without as yet bringing the workers together under one roof. On the land enclosure was essentially a capital-intensive movement. This did not necessarily spell rural unemployment, for the hedging and ditching, drainage works and marling, still implied a large labour force. But it did mean a different way of living for many country-dwellers who had been subsistence farmers and were now wage-earners. And the perquisites of country life, such as fallen wood for fuel and common pasture for one or two animals, were now less accessible. For the poor man there was less to choose between the country and the industrial town.

The most massive investment of all was not going into agriculture or industry, but into communications. The traditional system of road maintenance, which depended on the parish and its statutory labour, had been breached early in the century by the first Acts constituting turnpike trustees. More than 1,200 such Acts had followed, and two-thirds of them were passed in the twenty years before 1770. The turnpikes were unpopular, inefficient, and complicated. They never applied to more than a small proportion of the total mileage of highway, and often only a few miles of a particular route would be turnpiked, followed by a stretch of communally maintained road before the next turnpike was reached. Nevertheless the system extracted finance for the roads which could have been found nowhere else. Certainly the trusts did more for the roads than Parliament's endless legislation seeking to enforce wider wheels for heavy wagons, in the hope that land transport could be made to move on rollers, repairing the road as it passed.*

The roads, so far as it is possible to judge, had been as bad under Walpole and the Pelhams as they had been under Charles II. Passenger coaches then moved at four miles an hour in summer and at half that rate in winter. The improvement set in during the sixties, and in the course of the next half-century, before the railways put the coaches out of business, average speeds of ten or even twelve miles an hour

---

* For the lovers of odd, ineffectual, and labyrinthine legislation there is almost nothing to touch the long succession of statutes trying to enforce transport on wheels three, six, nine, and even sixteen inches wide. Preferential tolls and arbitrary penalties were tried in vain to secure popularity for such strange vehicles. W. T. Jackman's *Development of Transportation in Modern England* (Frank Cass, 1962), one of the most laborious and exhaustive of works, devotes many pages to describing the folly of legislators who insisted on concentrating on the wheels, rather than on the surface of the roads.

were being attained between the principal towns. Even by the mid-seventies the average summer speeds had reached six miles an hour. The golden age of the horse-drawn stage coach was approaching.

The change may not seem remarkable to us, but it cut the time from Leeds to London by nearly two days, and from Birmingham to London by nearly a day, compared with what it had been in the fifties. 'There never was a more astonishing revolution,' wrote a contemporary, 'accomplished in the internal system of any country, than has been within the compass of a few years in England.'* In 1773 the observant Robert Morris, posting with his child wife across Germany, compared his progress at two and a half miles an hour most unfavourably with what he was used to in England.† 'Our roads, in general, are so fine; and our speed has reached the Summit,' wrote the indefatigable traveller John Byng, some fifteen years later. Contemporaries might well be impressed. The improvement, proportionately, was almost equal to the substitution of steam for horse-power, or jet propulsion for piston engines.

Speed was not the only advantage from the better road surfaces—'the firm well-made road' as Karl Philip Moritz described the highway from Dartford to London. More passengers could be carried with the same horse-power, thus reducing costs. Until the seventies it was impossible to carry travellers 'outside' because wheel resistance and vibration would have made the load too heavy and the seats unsafe. But now it was possible to carry eleven passengers instead of the previous six. The demand more than justified the new practice, for more coaches were finding business. The list of regular passenger and goods services leaving London each week took up twenty-five pages in the 1740 edition of the *Guide to London*. In the 1772 edition it took up forty-four pages.

Simultaneously the opportunities for the highwayman were vanishing from the roads. This can hardly be attributed to improved policing or the savagery of the law. Perhaps enclosure played its part, for horses were not yet trained to jump, and the highwayman depended on rapid retreat into open heathy country. But the more important factor was the growing prosperity of the coaching inns, which provided not only the refreshment of travellers but the relays of horses. In the past the highwayman had depended on the inns for information, and with the growth of a travel industry it was no longer

---

* H. Homer. *Enquiry into the Means of Preserving and Improving the Public Roads* (1767).
† See J. E. Ross (ed.), *Radical Adventurer: The Diaries of Robert Morris* (Adams & Dart, 1971).

in the interest of the innkeepers or their staffs to destroy a blossoming trade. Growth reduced risks.

The canals, though designed primarily for goods traffic, also carried passengers. Morris travelled on the Duke's canal from Warrington to Manchester in 1774, covering twenty miles in five hours, which was not much slower than the coach and cost only a shilling. By coach the fare would have been almost three times as much. 'The surprise and wonder,' wrote that acidulous traveller, 'everyone is continually expressing about the canal &c becomes tiresome from its sameness and repetition.' But even he admitted, 'ye canal is not to be despised.' By 1778 most of the great waterway across the Pennines was open, joining Liverpool to Leeds by ninety-two locks, and winding through Wigan, Blackburn, Burnley and Skipton down Airedale to take in Keighley and Bradford on its way. Further south the seventies saw the creation of the Grand Trunk from the Mersey to the Trent, passing through Stoke, and bringing new life to the Potteries. Wesley was enthusiastic. 'How the whole face of the country has changed in about twenty years,' he exclaimed on a visit to Stoke in 1781, 'since which inhabitants have continually flowed in from every side . . . the wilderness is literally become a fruitful field. Houses, villages, towns, have sprung up; and the country is not more improved than the people.'

The canals were much the greatest public works the British had ever attempted, and required a scale of planning, finance, and confidence that was altogether new. The Grand Trunk represented an investment of £200,000 to which Wedgwood was an important contributor. The Pennine link, with its mile-long tunnel, and climb to nearly 700 feet, cost well over the £320,000 originally estimated. Such achievements brought not only economic and social benefits, but a new sense of power over nature.

The new topographical mastery, and the new precision are nowhere more sharply reflected than in the improved maps which were now becoming available to anyone with a few shillings. As recently as 1752 the old plates of Saxton's maps of England, first cut in Tudor times, were still being reissued and finding a market. But in 1759 the Royal Society of Arts, as almost its first enterprise, offered an annual award for accurate county maps on a scale of one inch to the mile, and the result was a series far more accurate and useful than ever before. By the 1780s John Cary was publishing cheap road atlases for the whole of England. In what has been thought of as the classic age of *laissez-faire* this was an area in which the government, for its own purposes, took a leading part. The greatest impetus for map-making was the military effort which was to culminate in the Ordnance Survey. As part of the programme for the final domestication of the Highlands after the Forty-five, Colonel David Watson was commissioned to prepare a survey of Scotland on a scale of one inch to a thousand yards, which was duly completed in eighty-four magnificent sheets. To a great extent it was the work of Watson's assistant, William Roy, a surveyor and organizer of genius, who laid the foundations of the Ordnance Survey as a permanent map-making organization, and conducted the first international survey which determined the exact longitudinal difference between Greenwich Royal Observatory and the Royal Observatory of Paris.

The English were being brought closer together than they had ever been, and there was an assault on isolation which was now never to cease. The remoter parts of England from London were still lonely and primitive, but they were no longer, as they had been only fifty years ago, almost foreign. Byng, the indefatigable tourist of the eighties and nineties, felt deeply that he was describing an England that was vanishing and needed to be caught for his grandchildren. It is difficult to think of an earlier period in which such a thought is expressed so clearly, or a later one in which it has not been powerfully felt. In Caernarvon, at the Boot Inn, he listened to a Welsh harper 'by name Erasmus', and reflected on the scene's association with 'former hospitality and ancient minstrelsy. I pity my grandchildren, who will only hear its merits, and fame, in their grandfather's, and other, pages.'*

Two strong themes then hang, like two pillars of smoke, one white, one black, over British society in the 1770s, like the smoke that was already beginning to appear above Birmingham, Manchester, Stoke-on-Trent, and the booming copper-mines of the Cornish peninsula: Industrialism, and romanticism. Often the leading motifs are found in the same mind, such as that of Sir John Sinclair of Ulbster, the agricultural improver and compiler of statistics, who was also an inveterate defender of the genuineness of the alleged poems of Ossian.† The two themes may seem opposed to each other both in content and intention, and they have contrasting heroes: the bour-

* C. B. Andrews (ed.), *The Torrington Diaries* (Methuen, 1970), vol. 1, p. 161. Byng (in the last few months of his life he was Lord Torrington) was a nephew of the unfortunate admiral who was shot in 1757, and grandson of one of the most effective conspirators in the 1688 Revolution. His travel diaries are among the most delightful accounts of late eighteenth-century England.

† Sinclair (1754–1835), besides his remarkable career as an agricultural improver, can claim two records. He was the first to use the word 'statistical' in the sense of a compilation of figures, and no Member of Parliament has sat for two more widely separated constituencies—Caithness and Lostwithiel.

geois entrepreneur, seeking profit and practising domestic and commercial virtue; and the dedicated poet, outdistancing convention in
his search for truth and beauty. But they had a common enemy in
the old regulated society of kings and priests; and the inheritors of a
black country were driven for the antidote to the figments of Byron
and Scott, pouring from steam-driven presses in the largest editions ever
printed.

Both conflicting yet complementary themes were peculiarly the
province of the new class which was now struggling out of the crowd
of small tradesmen, craftsmen, and out-workers. Defoe had begun to
idealize the 'upper station in low life' to which they aspired, in the
first chapter of *Robinson Crusoe*,* but the ideal offered was horatian rather
than economic or social. By the end of the eighteenth century the
notion of a middle class was firmly established. Its distinguishing
characteristics were the possession of a modest capital, usually sunk
in a family firm such as a wholesale grocery or a family bank, a broking
house or an exporting agency, an auction room such as Sotheby's
(founded in the 1750s) or a publishing house, such as Longman
(which went back to 1723). Its numbers were constantly being recruited
as smaller units gained enough size to lift the participants into comfort and respectability which did not aspire to power and honour.
Their pervasive presence, with family roots going back over one or
more generations, gives the society of 1776 a character which is utterly
different to that of a hundred years earlier. The members of the new
middle class did not look for patrons, and they disliked the lordly
system of influence. They sought customers for their goods and services who would pay cash. On the whole these people were outward-
looking, energetic, and acquisitive. They were quick to sense new
opportunities, and although the old ambition to own land was still
strong, they were on the whole better contented than their predecessors to transmit no more than a sound business and a comfortable
house and garden to the next generation.

They might not possess land, which was still the security for power,
but they shared, to an extent that the lower classes as yet did not, in
the advantages of the rapidly developing capital investment in roads,
canals, harbours and public buildings. It was not merely that they
enjoyed a higher standard of living, but that they had access to benefits

* 'The upper station of low life, which he [Crusoe's father] had found, by long
experience, was the best state in the world, the most suited to human happiness;
not exposed to the miseries and hardships, the labour and sufferings, of the
mechanic part of mankind, and not embarrassed with the pride, luxury, ambition,
and envy, of the upper part . . . ', *Robinson Crusoe*, Section 1.

which earlier generations had never known.* The sense of confidence in the early years of the century had arisen from the feeling that Britain, was in a position to exploit new resources. The confidence at the end of the century, and to a great extent ever since, has had its foundation in a sense of superiority in fixed investment and technological strength.

The first generation of the eighteenth century had looked to the Dutch in emulation and to the French in anxiety. Their successors of the 1770s felt they had outdistanced the one and were at least on an equal footing with the other; and they were no longer in a mood to take their styles from either. But the English, in spite of their reputed insularity, have always looked to the continent for inspiration, and at this moment a new window was opening for them in Europe, with startling results for England. Germany was undergoing a cultural revolution. The English had been used to thinking of Germany as a country, or rather a region, 'overrun by hussars and classical editors ... we had never seen a German name affixed to any other species of writing than a treaty by which some serene highness had sold us so many head of soldiers.'† Britain's German kings had, if anything, encouraged the British to avert their eyes from Germany. Very few Englishmen knew its language, though James Watt was one of those who took pains to learn it. Even fewer attended German universities. But it was difficult for the British to resist the charm of German literary men who enthused over English cultural achievements and, as Herder did in 1773, proclaimed Shakespeare as the bard of the northern peoples. In 1779 the compliment was returned with the translation of Goethe's novel *Werther* into English, and although the full effects of the new direction were not to be felt in full for more than a decade, the mutual admiration was already present by the time of American independence.

It was high time that Britain should have new admirers in Europe, for the old system of international relationships was spinning out of control as a result of the American War; and internally the war had set the country bitterly at odds with itself for the first time for nearly a hundred years. For such a situation the old mixed constitution of

---

* This is why comparisons in the value of money over long periods of time are meaningless unless very closely qualified. Travel by railway, or even by coach at five miles an hour, was not available to anyone in 1750, so that the 'value' of money in 1750—i.e. the lien it represented on society—cannot strictly be compared with its 'value' in 1850. To a very great extent this change in value by change in the range of economic choice reflects the progress of investment.

† *Edinburgh Review*, 1816, referring to the view taken of Germany 'Some twenty five years ago'.

king, Lords, and Commons, as established in 1688 and, as it were, dutifully renovated by George III, was almost pathetically inadequate. A Parliament whose centre of gravity was the squirearchy; a government without an effective machine for carrying out its will; found themselves committed to a trans-oceanic war which in its nature could not be won, for a purpose which was negative rather than constructive. War always hastens social processes. For Britain the American war was to be almost the equivalent of a second Revolution.

Forces were introduced into British life which would have been unrecognizable to the makers of the Revolution Settlement, to Sir Robert Walpole, and to the Pelhams: secular radicalism, industry organized in relation to mechanical power, and all the pressures of massive urban development. It is in this sense that G. M. Trevelyan intended his statement that the eighteenth century was an age of transition. Not transition as all history is movement, but transition in that society at the end of it was pointed in a direction which could not possibly have been foreseen at its beginning.

The most important completed development in society between 1688 and 1776 was the coming into coherent and conscious existence of the country called Britain. Even in the first half of the century the word had had an archaic, unfamiliar ring which we now find difficult to recapture, and it remains today a political, uncoloured word by comparison with the older 'England' and 'Scotland'.* The expressions 'North Britain' and 'South Britain', which enthusiasts for the Union tried to popularize, never caught on, and the old names retained their patriotic overtone. Yet Britain, England, Scotland, and Wales were not the only entities which rose to the islander's mind when he spoke of 'his country', and round this word 'country' the British sense of nationhood most closely entwined itself. Besides expressing the whole kingdom and its historic parts separately, the word could, in eighteenth-century usage, refer to no more than the county or district from which the speaker came. Lord Rockingham spoke of Yorkshire as 'this country'. For others 'my country' could be Devon or the Fens, the Welsh Marches or Kent, east of the Medway. 'Culprit, how will you be tried?' ran the time-honoured question to the prisoner at the beginning of a criminal trial. 'By God and my Country', was the reply that claimed trial by jury: not a trial by a national authority but trial by men of the district.

* Two such contrasting patriots as Wilkes and Nelson both avoided the term British for their most stirring utterances. For Wilkes it was always 'English Liberty', and for Nelson it was 'England expects . . . .'

'Country' then had the meanings which are expressed in French by two separate words—'patrie' and 'pays'; and it acquired further emotional charge through its association with rural, as contrasted with urban Britain, and above all with Britain outside London, for it is no misuse of the English language to speak of a 'country town'. So the picture which came into the mind of the man who spoke of 'his country' was of a native, rural setting for his citizenship of the nation as a whole. Even for Londoners the picture was usually there, for many of them had started as villagers.

The formation of a British national consciousness took place alongside advances in technology and commerce, a decisive upturn in the rate of population growth, and the penetration of the British in considerable force into America, Asia, and even Australia. Their view of themselves had become worldwide. The island which a century previously had been a virtual dependency of France, and in 1688 had been taken over by France's great opponent as his base of operations, had become an oceanic and intercontinental power. There is a sense in which the Channel and the North Sea were more important barriers in 1776 than they had been in 1688, since they stood between Britain and a continent whose standards she no longer envied.

This sense of national power, coherence, and growth, which is already noticeable in the middle of the century, preceded by several decades the effective onset of industrial concentration, which did not begin to make its mark on large numbers of English lives until the 1790s. But the elements of an industrial society of a kind the world had never known before were already present in Britain—and in Britain alone—in 1776. For decades past the economic climate had been favourable to the accumulation of funds for the necessary investment. Agricultural rents and profits, which had moved upwards only imperceptibly in the first half of the century, were advancing at an average of about 2 per cent per year after 1750, with dramatic effects on rent-rolls. The exploitation of coal and other minerals on an increasing scale brought landlords—among them the Bishop of Durham—enormous new sources of revenue. Population, technology, and improved communications all conspired with the accumulation of capital towards the utter change in society which industrialism implies.

And yet, if the period between the English and American Revolutions is one in which great changes for Britain and the world were matured, it was also an age in its own right, with its own rise, plateau, and decline. A happy coincidence has resulted in the placing outside the National Gallery of statues of the two men who set its boundaries: James II, who was the victim of the Revolution of 1688, and Washington, the victor in the war which followed 1776. During the period bounded by these two figures Britain was a trading emporium dominated by a land-owning aristocracy and gentry. Trade was worshipped and protected with the same enthusiasm as the wild game which the squires preserved so zealously on their estates by very similar methods. The jungle of commercial regulations which Adam Smith attacked is the product of the same minds and attitudes that produced the game laws chronicled by Blackstone. The British customs were the gamekeepers of eighteenth-century commerce, and the smugglers its poachers.

The rulers of England in the eighteenth century thought selfishly. But they were, in a curious way, self-critical. The unworthy motives which actuated so much human behaviour were frankly enough admitted, and even denounced—to an extent indeed that was to become unfashionable in the nineteenth century. The savagery of Hogarth and Rowlandson is as typical of the times as the bland optimism of Soame Jenyns or the tradition-worship of Edmund Burke. But though the times were surprisingly clear-eyed, the mood was acceptance of evils which were beyond curing, rather than any consistent feeling that effort could eliminate them.

Nowhere is this more obvious than in the universal system of patronage. Not only was it accepted, but it was operated through a minutely regulated and almost infinitely complex code which all understood and many despised, yet very few were prepared to defy. This system, not of class or of hierarchy, but of dependency, clientship, and obligation raised by favours received or in prospect, reaches its full maturity in what I have called the High Georgian age, and so deeply rooted was it that it was to survive the abrasiveness of the gospel of self-help and the invigorating blasts of competition for nearly a century.

The Anglican Church had survived the Revolution as an organization rather than as a spiritual force. It had produced philosophers and literary giants, useful pastors and talented pamphleteers, and the Georgian scene would lack an essential element without the black Geneva gowns and comfortable doctrines of its clergy. But rationalism had soon entered its soul, and by 1755 Archbishop Herring was firmly refusing to draw any moral from the Lisbon earthquake preferring, as he said, 'to regard as a good man he who is steadily so upon contemplation of the regular course of nature, the rising and setting of the sun, the return of the seasons, and the stability, not the shaking of the earth.'

The fact that Britain was soon to become involved in war, economic progress, and the conquest of world power on a scale undreamed of even by such minds as Chatham's, should not be allowed to conceal the fact that the characteristic confidence of Augustan and post-Augustan Britain ends at Saratoga Springs and Yorktown. Johnson and Warburton, Chatham and Rockingham hardly survived the decade. Wilkes, having achieved the momentary glory of Lord Mayor and the permanent salary of City Chamberlain, became domesticated. Burke settled down to pitying the plumage (in Tom Paine's phrase) and forgetting the dying bird; or, in the words of another critic, behaved like the cat after the family has removed. Boswell struggled with drink and his memories to produce an immortal memorial to a man and his times. The square-cut coats and heavy wigs were giving way to the smoother line of the cutaway and natural hair, tied with a black ribbon.

There was an ebb, therefore, as well as a new flow. In many respects the society of the last quarter of the eighteenth century was to be more rigid and defensive than the society of a hundred years before it. The way ahead, extraordinary as it was to be, was unclear, whereas under William III and Marlborough the opportunities had been manifest. That Britain was more powerful than it had ever been was plain to the men of the seventies, even in defeat. As Horace Walpole was to write of Chatham on his death—'under him we attained not only our highest elevation but the most solid authority in Europe.' Yet this in itself was an aspiring remark, from a man growing old who was conscious of the road that had been travelled and the comparatively modest starting point. It does not yet strike the note of conscious, lasting superiority which is characteristic of the next century. For that it is necessary to refer to the conscious development of the middle and the working classes. Both these expressions, significantly enough, emerge into print in the early years of the nineteenth century —and within a year of each other. Robert Owen coined 'working class' in 1813; Leigh Hunt produced 'middle class' in 1812.

The confidence of the eighteenth century in England was not widely diffused. It was selective and individual. For the urban poor the struggle to survive was enough, and for the rural worker the limitations were still so narrow that one can almost understand Arthur Young's calculation contrasting the cost of keeping a man with that of keeping a horse. To rise it was necessary to be remarkable, and to hold a position to which one was born it was necessary to sustain the style that society thought appropriate. The dynamism of the society arose almost entirely from the former group—from Charles Montagu and Isaac Newton, Pope, Mansfield and Warburton, Chatham, Johnson, Gainsborough and Cook. Early Victorian society cannot hold a candle to their self-help.

If eighteenth-century society seems cold, selfish, calculating, and cruel—and one thinks of the slave trade, the hideous succession of executions, the savagery of naval and military discipline—it also contained the first clumsy evolution towards a greater measure of humanity. Johnson's lines about the seedy poor man's doctor, Levet, could not belong to any earlier century:*

Yet still he fills affection's eye,
Obscurely wise, and coarsely kind;
Nor, letter'd arrogance, deny
Thy praise to merit unrefin'd.

In misery's darkest cavern's known,
His useful care was ever nigh,
Where hopeless anguish pour'd his groan,
And lonely want retir'd to die.

When it is added that Levet lived with Johnson 'as a sort of *necessary man* or surgeon to the wretched household he kept in Bolt Court; where blind Mrs Williams, dropsical Mrs Desmoulines, Black Francis and his white wife's bastard, with a wretched Mrs White, and a thing he called Poll, shared his bounty and increased his dirt', it is possible to grasp both the revolting conditions of late eighteenth-century London and beginnings of human sympathy which it contained.

Nor was it only in the beginnings of a new attitude to human suffering that the eighteenth century can claim to lay the foundations of a profound change of approach. The legal position of women was the same by the end of the century as it had been at the beginning, and the relationship between the sexes was still governed by the concepts of property vested in the man and protection for the woman. Between typical married couples there was a tenderness and a practicality which is in many ways attractive, and the attitude to what was improper was blunt and conventional rather than emotional and shockable. The Taunton justices, confronted with a woman who in the

* 'On the Death of Mr Robert Levet, a Practiser in Physick'.

disguise of a man had gone through a series of 'marriages', refused to be deterred by difficulties about the charge or concern about the prisoner's psychology, and determined that 'he or she, the prisoner at the bar, is an uncommon and notorious cheat, and the Court do sentence her or him, whichever he or she may be, to be imprisoned six months.'

Despite the unchanging legal position, the social position of women was quietly changing. Mrs Montagu, the blue-stocking hostess, and her friend Mrs Delany, may have been snobs, but they stood on their own ground, not only as social figures, but as a social influence.* Through Mary Delany Fanny Burney found her way forward, and in *Evelina* produced a novel which was far superior to any produced by Englishwomen before her. The leisure of upper-class women made them readers on a considerable scale, as their reading lists bear witness, and by the end of the century women, in spite of their lack of formal education, made up a large section of the reading public. The right of a daughter to a veto over a marriage proposed by her parents was becoming widely recognized as part of the conventions governing family life. There were now serious business women, such as Mrs Elizabeth Coade, who inherited the formula for the synthetic material coadestone, and marketed it with notable effects on the decoration of London buildings, as can be seen in Bedford Square today. Only two years separate the publication of Tom Paine's *Rights of Man* from Mary Wollstonecraft's *Vindication of the Rights of Women*.

Beyond 1776 a whole new range of social relationships opens up to a world in which progress, reform, and development come to have a meaning for millions. The eighteenth century brought Britain to that brink, while retaining in the minds of most people the idea of an unchanging world, in which most of the answers were known. The landscape ahead, as one descends the forward slope, is utterly different from the one that has been left behind in the ascent. By the last quarter of the century the very history on which the Whig account of the Revolution of 1688 and 'our present happy constitution' had been founded was being undermined. The documents published by Macpherson and Dalrymple about the reigns of William III and Anne showed the tarnish on the supposedly blameless patriots who had

* Elizabeth Montagu (1720–1800) established her literary salon in the 1750s and continued to exert literary and moral influence until the end of the century. Mary Delany (1700–88) had been a protégée of Swift, and was courted as a girl by John Wesley. Anna Seward (1747–1809) is now better remembered for her literary friendships, notably with Dr Johnson, than for her six volumes of collected prose and verse.

brought about the change of dynasty, and the real motives which had brought William to England. Even Horace Walpole, thorough-going Whig though he was, accepted Williams' expedition as a move in international politics rather than a vindication of British liberty. But the Revolution had worked. It had opened the road from privilege to pluralism, given birth to a transatlantic continental power and provided the commercial base for the first industrial empire.

Appendix 1   The Population

Spurious accuracy is to be avoided in historical demography. There are no census figures for England and Wales until 1801, or for America until 1790. Scotland was the subject of a single well-organized census by private enterprise in 1755. Figures for population in the eighteenth century must therefore be estimates. Until a great deal more work has been done on local records, we are still mainly dependent for English estimates on the work of Gregory King, and on the work of two historical demographers of the early years of this century, J. Brownlee, 'The History of the Birth and Death Rates in England and Wales', *Public Health*, vol. 24 (1916); G. T. Griffith, *Population Problems of the Age of Malthus* (Cambridge, 1926). Their work has been extensively reviewed and discussed, notably by D. V. Glass and E. D. C. Eversley in *Population in History*. A useful summary of the subject is provided by M. W. Flinn, *British Population Growth, 1700–1800* (Macmillan, 1970).

The estimates of Brownlee and Griffith for the population of England and Wales, though arrived at by different methods, are consistent with one another in their pattern—that is to say they both show comparative stagnation during the first forty years of the century, with the upturn in the fifth decade. The estimate of Griffith is, however, higher than Brownlee's—by about 12·5 per cent at the beginning of the century and almost 17·5 per cent by 1770.

Table 1 uses King's figures (as corrected by Glass) for 1690, and the estimates of Talbot Griffith (which may be on the high side) for the remainder of the column for England and Wales. The figures for Scotland are based on the census of 1755 (see J. G. Kyd, 'Scottish Population Statistics', 3rd series, vol. 44, *Proceedings of the Scottish Historical Society* (1952)), those for Ireland on the (very unreliable) estimates assembled by Talbot Griffith (*op. cit.*, p. 45), and those for North America on Potter's estimates in Glass and Eversley (*op. cit.*, pp. 644f.). The result, while certainly inaccurate, gives a general conspectus of the size and rate of growth of population in the British lands during the

186

eighteenth century and, what is historically more significant, the changing differences between the four components.

Table 1

Total population of the British lands 1690–1780 (in millions)

	England and Wales	Scotland	Ireland	North American Colonies*	Total
1690	5·20	0·75†	1·0†	0·20†	7·15
1700	5·80	0·82	1·5†	0·28	8·40
1710	6·01	0·90	2·0	0·36	9·27
1720	6·05	0·98	2·2	0·47	9·70
1730	6·01	1·06	2·2	0·66	9·93
1740	6·01	1·12	2·3	0·89	10·32
1750	6·25	1·21	2·4	1·21	11·07
1760	6·66	1·29	2·5	1·61	12·06
1770	7·12	1·37	2·6	2·21	13·30
1780	7·60†	1·45	2·8	[2·78]	14·63

* Excluding the West Indian Islands; white population only included.
† Figures estimated very approximately for this table.

Gregory King produced an estimate of age distribution, and was the first demographer to do so.

Table 2

Distribution by age and sex 1695 (in thousands)

Age in years	Male	Female	Total
Under 1	90	80	170
Under 5	415	405	820
Under 10	764	756	1,520
Under 16	1,122	1,118	2,240
Over 16	1,578	1,682	3,260
Total	2,700	2,800	5,500
Over 21	1,300	1,400	2,700
Over 25	1,150	1,250	2,400
Over 60	270	330	600

By interpolation Table 2 can be used to estimate that about 38 per cent of the population was under the age of 15, and that about 16 per cent was over 50. Only about 10 per cent was over 60.

Finally, can anything substantial be said about population densities and the size of towns?

For London, Gregory King's estimate for 1695 was 527,000. It is probably too low. In *London Life in the Eighteenth Century*, p. 329, M. Dorothy George gives figures of 674,350 for 1700 and 676,250 for 1750 'based on the baptisms in the parish registers', but the method of calculation is unclear. By 1801 London was found to contain 900,000 inhabitants, and it is unlikely that it contained fewer than 750,000 by 1776. It is probable that Mrs George's figure for 1700 is too high.

Webster's Scottish census of 1755 gives the following spot figures for the main towns in Scotland. Their 1970 populations are given in brackets.

Edinburgh	31,122	(466,464)
Glasgow	23,546	(945,034)
Dundee	12,477	(182,340)
Aberdeen	10,785	(181,386)
Inverness	9,730	(31,914)
Perth	9,019	(41,409)

From the same source, and from Kyd (*op. cit*, p. xviii) it is possible to calculate the following information for Scottish population densities per square mile:

	1755	1951
Highland	31	47
Central*	110	900
Southern	36	61

For Scottish counties the following figures, from the same source, are instructive. The figures are for 1755, with 1961 populations in brackets:

Sutherland	20,744	(13,243)
Ross & Cromarty	48,084	(57,388)
Inverness	59,563	(82,264)
Argyll	66,286	(60,226)
Perthshire	120,116	(124,441)
Orkney	23,381	(18,531)
Shetland	15,210	(17,537)
Renfrew	26,645	(342,938)

* Ayr, Dumbarton, Lanark, Renfrew, Clackmannan, Stirling, Lothians, Fife, and Dundee.

Finally there is some information on the population densities of English counties in the work of E. C. K. Gonner, 'The Population of England in the Eighteenth Century', *Journal of the Royal Statistical Society*, vol. 76 (1913):

	Population per square mile		
	1700	*1750*	*1801*
Lancashire	127	179	253
Yorks, West Riding	91	122	212
Worcestershire	141	139	189
Cheshire	92	105	174
Staffordshire	111	133	210
Warwickshire	112	152	236
Average	112	138	212

Appendix 2 The Development of the National Debt, 1715–83

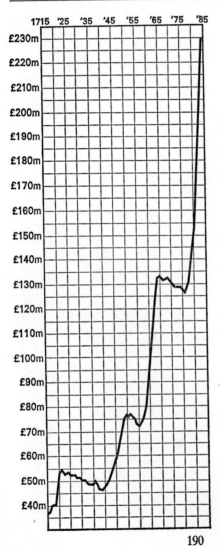

1. Each upturn marks a war —The War of William and Anne; the War of the Austrian Succession; the Seven Years' War; and the War of American Independence.

2. Each subsequent step marks the effort, on the return of peace, to check or reduce the debt. Note the solitary success of this policy during Walpole's period of power (1721–1742).

3. Each war was more expensive than the previous one.

4. The total debt (i.e. borrowing by government capitalized in the hands of private individuals) multiplied sevenfold in seventy years.

(Reproduced, with permission, from *English Historical Documents 1714–83*, vol. 10, eds Horn and Ransome, Eyre Methuen Ltd, 1957.)

Appendix 3   The Movement of
Wheat Prices, 1715–83

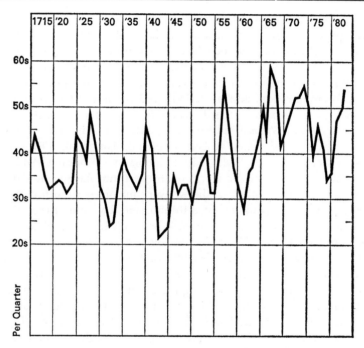

(Reproduced, with permission, from *English Farming Past and Present*, Prothero, Longman.)

1. Bread was the basic diet of the great majority, and its price is probably the best guide to the cost of living during this period.
2. The general picture is one of long-term stability of price lasting over several generations, with sharp, short-term variations related to the success or otherwise of harvests. The peaks, therefore, have some coincidence with periods of distress and consequent unrest.
3. From about 1760 onwards there is a gentle, but noticeable upward trend perhaps associated with increasing urbanization.

Further Reading

Anything whatever written during a period—diaries, letters, memoirs, newspapers, poetry, fiction, history, philosophy, science, directories —is material for that period's history. To 'read in the period' is the best way of coming to understand it. Memoirs and letters are especially fruitful for the eighteenth century, in which there was time for their careful composition, and no serious student should fail to look at least into the *Memoirs* of Lord Hervey (shortened version, Romney Sedgwick (ed.), William Kimber, 1952), letters of Lady Mary Wortley Montagu (*Selected Letters*, Robert Halsband, Longman, 1970), and Boswell's *Journals* (F. A. Pottle (ed.), Heinemann, various dates). I have not, however, tried to list works of this sort, nor have I entered on the vast field of biography. Almost every major eighteenth-century figure has several books devoted to him, and few even of the minor characters have not at least one each. Boswell's *Life of Samuel Johnson* is, of course, the greatest biography of its own age, and one of the greatest of any—there are innumerable editions. Among modern biographies J. H. Plumb's two volume work *Sir Robert Walpole* (Cresset Press, 1956 and 1960) is outstanding as giving the flavour of an age as well as of the man. Much biographical information about both the great and the obscure will be found in the five volumes of *The History of Parliament* covering the period 1715–1790 (*The Commons 1715–1754*, Romney Sedgwick (ed.), HMSO, 1970; *The Commons 1754–1790*, Sir Lewis Namier and John Brooke (eds.), HMSO, 1964), which provide the nearest thing to a *Who's Who* for the eighteenth-century governing class as will ever be achieved. These volumes also tell all that needs to be known about the organization and work of Parliament, the pattern of constituencies, and the grouping of political factions.

Most of the works so far mentioned have appeared since the standard bibliography of the period was compiled (S. Pargellis and D. J. Medley, *Bibliography of British History. The Eighteenth Century. 1714–1789*, Oxford, 1951). This work is nevertheless still invaluable for its listing of source material and older secondary works, few of which therefore

192

occur in the list which follows here. Selections of documents, from which the student can get the full wording of the most important texts and the general flavour of eighteenth-century documentation are also available. Probably the most useful are those in the series *English Historical Documents* under the general editorship of David C. Douglas and published by Eyre & Spottiswoode. The relevant volumes for this period are VIII (1660–1714) edited by Andrew Browning; IX (American to 1776) edited by Merrill Jensen; and X (1714–1783) edited by D. B. Horn and Mary Ransome. These volumes also contain extremely good and comprehensive lists of office-holders, maps, and genealogical trees.

The list which follows is mainly a selection of modern secondary works, together with a few well-established older ones.

Ashley, Maurice, *The Glorious Revolution of 1688* (Hodder & Stoughton, 1966).

Ashton, T. S., *An Economic History of England: The Eighteenth Century* (Home University Library and Barnes & Noble, 1955).

Ashton, T. S., *Economic Fluctuations in England, 1700–1800* (Oxford, 1959).

Baxter, S., *Development of the English Treasury, 1660–1702* (Longmans, 1957).

Baynes, John, *The Jacobite Rising of 1715* (Cassell, 1970).

Beattie, John M., *The English Court in the Reign of George I* (Cambridge, 1967).

Bebb, E. D., *Nonconformity and Social and Economic Life, 1660–1800* (Epworth Press, 1935 and Kelley, 1970).

Briggs, Asa, *How They Lived, 1700–1815* (Blackwell, 1969).

Brooke, John, *The Chatham Administration* (Macmillan and Verry, 1956).

Carswell, John, *The Old Cause (Whiggism)* (Cresset Press, 1954).

Carswell, John, *The South Sea Bubble* (Cresset Press, 1960).

Carswell, John, *The Descent on England (The Revolution of 1688)* (Cresset Press and John Day, 1969).

Chambers, J. D., *Nottinghamshire in the Eighteenth Century* (P. S. King and Kelley, 1932).

Clark, Dora Mae, *The Rise of the British Treasury* (Yale, 1960 and David & Charles, 1969).

Clark, G. N., *The Later Stuarts*, 2nd ed. (Oxford, 1955).

Court, W. H. B., *The Rise of Midland Industries, 1600–1838* (Oxford, 1938).

Dickson, P. G. M., *The Financial Revolution in England 1688–1756* (Macmillan and St Martin's Press, 1967).

Donoughue, Bernard, *British Politics and the American Revolution: the Path to War, 1773–5* (Macmillan, 1964).

Edwards, Maldwyn, *John Wesley and the Eighteenth Century* (Epworth Press, 1955).

Ellis, Aytoun, *The Penny Universities. A History of the Coffee Houses* (Secker & Warburg and Gale, 1956).

Feiling, Sir Keith, *A History of the Tory Party, 1640–1715* (Oxford, 1924).

George, M. Dorothy, *London Life in the Eighteenth Century* (Kegan Paul, 1930 and Putnam, 1965).

Glass, D. V., and Eversley, D. E. C., *Population in History* (Edward Arnold and Aldine, 1965).

Graham, Henry Grey, *The Social Life of Scotland in the Eighteenth Century* (A. & C. Black, 1901).

Graham, I. C. G., *Colonists from Scotland* (American Historical Association, 1956).

Holmes, Geoffrey, *Britain after the Glorious Revolution, 1689–1714* (Macmillan and St Martin's Press, 1969).

Hughes, E., *North Country Life in the Eighteenth Century*, 4 vols. (University of Durham Press and Oxford, 1952–65).

Kemp, Betty, *King and Commons, 1660–1832* (Macmillan and St Martin's Press, 1957).

Laprade, W. T., *Public Opinion and Politics in Eighteenth Century England to the Fall of Walpole* (Greenwood, 1971).

MacLachlan, H., *English Education under the Test Acts. The History of Nonconformist Academies, 1662–1820* (Manchester University Press, 1931).

Marshall, Dorothy, *English People in the Eighteenth Century* (Longmans and Humanities Press, 1956).

Marshall, Dorothy, *Eighteenth Century England* (Longmans and McKay, 1962).

Mathias, P., *The Brewing Industry in England, 1700–1830* (Cambridge University Press, 1959).

Maxwell, Constantia, *Dublin under the Georges* (Faber & Faber, 1956).

Mingay, G. E., *English Landed Society in the Eighteenth Century* (Routledge & Kegan Paul and University of Toronto Press, 1963).

Namier, Sir Lewis B., *The Structure of Politics at the Accession of George III*, 2nd ed. (Macmillan and St Martin's Press, 1957).

Namier, Sir Lewis B., *England in the Age of the American Revolution*, 2nd ed. (Macmillan and St Martin's Press, 1961).

Nef, J. U., *The Rise of the British Coal Industry* (Cass, 1966).

Ogg, D., *England in the Reigns of James II and William III* (Oxford, 1955).

Owen, John B., *The Rise of the Pelhams* (Macmillan and Barnes & Noble, 1957).

Parreaux, André, *La Société Anglaise de 1760 à 1810* (Presses Universitaires de France, 1966).

Perry, Thomas W., *Public Opinion, Propaganda and Politics in Eighteenth Century England* (Oxford and Harvard, 1962).

Petrie, Sir Charles, *The Jacobite Movement*, 3rd ed. (Eyre & Spottiswoode, 1958 and Dufour, 1960).

Plumb, J. H., *England in the Eighteenth Century* (Penguin, 1950).

Plumb, J. H., *The Growth of Political Stability in England* (Macmillan, 1967).

Rudé, George, *Wilkes and Liberty* (Oxford, 1962).

Speck, W. A., *Tory and Whig, 1701–1715* (Macmillan and St Martin's Press, 1970).

Summerson, Sir John, *Georgian London* (Penguin, 1962 and Praeger, 1970).

Sutherland, L. S., *The East India Company in Eighteenth Century Politics* (Oxford, 1952).

Sykes, Norman, *Church and State in England in the Eighteenth Century* (Oxford, 1934).

Trevelyan, G. M., *England under Queen Anne*, 4 vols (Longmans, 1930–4 and Humanities Press, 1948).

Turberville, A. S., *English Men and Manners in the Eighteenth Century* (Oxford, 1926).

Turberville, A. S., *The House of Lords in the Eighteenth Century* (Oxford and Greenwood, 1927).

Turberville, A. S., *Johnson's England* (Oxford, 1933).

Veitch, G. S., *The Genesis of Parliamentary Reform* (Constable and Archon, 1965).

Walcott, Robert, *English Politics in the Early Eighteenth Century* (Oxford, 1956).

Ward, W. R., *Georgian Oxford* (Oxford, 1958).

Watson, J. S., *England in the Reign of George III* (Oxford, 1960).

Wearmouth, R. F., *Methodism and the Common People in the Eighteenth Century* (Epworth Press, 1945).

Willan, T. S., *River Navigation in England, 1600–1750* (Manchester University Press and Kelley, 1936).

Willan, T. S., *The English Coasting Trade, 1600–1750* (Manchester University Press and Kelley, 1938).

Willey, Basil, *The Eighteenth Century Background* (Chatto & Windus, 1940 and Columbia University Press, 1941).

Williams, Basil, *The Whig Supremacy, 1714–1760*, 2nd ed. (Oxford, 1962).

Williams, E. N., *The Eighteenth Century Constitution, 1688–1715* (Cambridge, 1960).

Williamson, J. A., *Cook and the Opening of the Pacific* (Hodder & Stoughton, 1946).

Wilson, Charles H., *Anglo-Dutch Commerce and Finance in the Eighteenth Century* (Cambridge, 1941).

Wilson, Charles H., *England's Apprenticeship, 1603–1763* (Cambridge and St Martin's Press, 1965).

Index

202 Index

73137